W9-BMT-102

*Drama, Stage and
Audience*

By the same author

THE ELEMENTS OF DRAMA
THE DARK COMEDY
THE DRAMATIC EXPERIENCE
SHAKESPEARE'S STAGECRAFT
CHEKHOV IN PERFORMANCE
THE CHALLENGE OF THE THEATRE
(*Dickenson*)

Drama, Stage and Audience

J. L. STYAN

Andrew Mellon Professor of English
University of Pittsburgh

CAMBRIDGE UNIVERSITY PRESS

Published by the Syndics of the Cambridge University Press
Bentley House, 200 Euston Road, London NW1 2DB
American Branch: 32 East 57th Street, New York, N.Y. 10022

© Cambridge University Press 1975

Library of Congress Catalogue Card Number: 74-76948

ISBNs
0 521 20504 2 hard covers
0 521 09869 6 paperback

First published 1975

Photoset in Malta by St Paul's Press Ltd
Printed in the United States of America

Contents

Prefatory note

Drama, Stage and Audience is another attempt to embrace the most embracing of all art forms. It tries to shine the light on the sources of true theatrical excitement, what it is that creates a moment of life on the stage, what it is that generates energy in living theatre.

My first choice of a title was, indeed, *Dramatic Perception*, since, of course, any power in a play derives from the activity of perception in its audience. The book is a reminder that drama is not made of words alone, but of sights and sounds, stillness and motion, noise and silence, relationships and responses. Yet: these relationships and responses are not those between characters, rather those between actor and audience. Drama study insists, therefore, that we think of a particular social situation, a here-and-now — or (imperious demand!) a there-and-then recreated in the imagination to be a here-and-now. It should come as no surprise that most of the discussion turns on the work of the man whose dramatic stimuli are the richest: Shakespeare.

The script on the page is not the drama any more than a clod of earth is a field of corn: it is essential constantly to return to this. The words of *Hamlet* are merely signals for communication, in which (heresy, still, to some) the unspoken can be as important as the spoken, in which the nighted colour of the Prince's costume can be as urgent as the stroke of a poetic image. Thus, the criticism of drama must imply a study of stimulus and reaction, but this is a social study concerned with all the vagaries of human social behaviour.

As a genre, drama can never be on a par with the story or the poem. Thus Northrop Frye's 'simple' basis of generic distinctions in literature, which he finds in 'the radical of presentation,' suggesting that the genre is marked as dramatic when words are acted in front of a spectator (*Anatomy of Criticism*, pp. 246–7), assumes in the theatre the primacy of language. That this is radical is obviously untrue to any playgoer. When the spectator sees words acted, it is immediately apparent that something beyond the words, the primacy of the occasion, is paramount.

What that occasion is, whether the presence of the actor and what he does, the constitution of the audience, the nature of the play-house, or the role of the theatre in its society, it is our duty to find out before criticism can begin.

Some passages in this book have been taken or adapted from articles previously published in the following periodicals: *College English Association Critic, Comparative Drama, Costerus Essays in English and American Language and Literature, Educational Theatre Journal, Genre, Michigan Quarterly Review, Modern Language Quarterly, Speech and Drama.* I wish in addition to acknowledge by name some of my former students who contributed to the ideas which shaped this book: Gorman Beauchamp, Patricia Cornett, B. G. Cross, Elliott Denniston, Peter Ferran, Daniel Melcher, Barbra Morris, Michael Neuman, Bruce Sajdak, Douglas Sprigg.

J.L.S.

I

Communication in drama

It is self-evident that a play must communicate or it is not a play at all. We must concur with Peter Brook's fundamental tenet that 'the choices [a dramatist] makes and the values he observes are only powerful in proportion to what they create in the language of the theatre' (*The Empty Space*, p. 35). It may not 'work' if it is a bad play as such (*The Cenci, The Family Reunion, Camino Real, Tiny Alice*) or if it is a non-play (*Prometheus Unbound, The Shadowy Waters, The Dynasts*). With such intractable material we are not concerned. Kenneth Burke has said, 'Drama is dissolved by the turn from dramatic *act* to lyric *state*' (*A Grammar of Motives*, p. 441): and even this is generous because the *status* may never have been first an *actus*. But in some circumstances a play of little apparent value (*Titus Andronicus, The Rivals, The Colleen Bawn, Charley's Aunt*) can work well, and therefore is worth special attention. For we do not ask that a play communicate for ever; we do ask that a play communicate in its own time, through its own medium, for its own community. The task with plays great or trivial is to examine the line of communication, the transmission of signals between stage and audience and back again, the stimulus and the reaction, on the occasion. The first night of *Twelfth Night* in the Hall of the Middle Temple in 1602 should be no more interesting than its second night in, say, Tokyo.

Dramatic criticism, like any other, finds it hard not to be a generalizing activity, whereas the live theatre experience is always particular; criticism is docile or reflective or dead, whereas perception in the theatre is wild and immediate and alive: and that, of course, is when a play is actually communicating. Moreover, matching theory and practice is a very chancy business. On the one hand, a fine theory can be meaningless in the theatre – the time-honoured joke is 'When did you last have a catharsis?' On the other hand, something can work in the theatre which no theory can explain – like the provokingly unreal sound of the breaking string in realism's own *Cherry Orchard*.

I

At least, an hypothesis in dramatic theory, unlike one in literary theory, can usually be tested. The ultimate question, *Does it work?*, can be asked. The signs on the printed page are signals for something to happen in the theatre, and we can check that it does with our own senses and perceptions, and sometimes with those of others.

Of what the eye sees truly supports the words heard, for a simple example, something of good compounded theatre may result. Thus, as literary criticism knows, Shakespeare has Lear increasingly use the language of animals, but he does this as he is increasingly encouraged to look and sound like an animal himself. Though he thinks himself a philosopher, on 'Off, off, you lendings!' we see him tear off his royal robes to look like Poor Tom, who has minutely described himself as a beast. When the King regains his mind and soul in the presence of Cordelia, he is wearing 'fresh garments' and the animals cease snarling, but only until we hear that terrifying half-animal 'Howl, howl, howl!' as he enters with the dead girl, mad again with anguish. All this we *perceive*: in the theatre, where the eye can reinforce the ear to compel attention to what Shakespeare seems to have determined must be inescapable. The theatre is the testing ground for the validity of words and images.

However, the proof of effective working in the theatre is endlessly complicated by the nature of dramatic experience. A play's meaning is not wholly what its author thinks it means, and Tyrone Guthrie believed that 'if the objective meaning of a work of art were known, there would be no point in its existence. It exists merely to suggest many ways in which an undefined truth may be approached' (*A Life in the Theatre*, p. 124). The image of meaning which the stage transmits and which a spectator may hope to receive is the product of what Kenneth Boulding would call 'a universe of discourse' (*The Image*, p. 132), a process of sharing messages and experiences. If a king or a beggar is a stable image within a community, the idea of a king or a beggar will be shared in the theatre. However, what happens *to* them may not be shared. For the drama must by definition be *doing* something, and although an abstract king and beggar may be stable images in print, the interaction of Shakespeare's king and beggar may be anything but predictable. An audience must contribute by responding to the stimulus if it is to enjoy its theatre, but the kind and degree of that contribution is never slavish. If it is rich and worthwhile, it is also alive and independent.

Nothing would happen unless the conditions for such experience were there. The miracle of theatre is that a community, an audience, has agreed to let drama happen. In the make-believe of a theatrical situation, the impossible, even the irrational, is feasible and free to take place by common consent. As Marshall McLuhan would have it, the medium takes charge. Those who go to a play are secretly seeking the experience called 'theatre'. So it is that the medium can have more force and importance for the individual or his society than what is perceptibly fed into it. It follows too, that the drama's medium calls for as much consideration as its content: we must know the theatre at least as well as we know the play.

As it happens, McLuhan has nothing to say about the drama, but he does leave us with two catchwords, 'hot' and 'cool'. A cool medium, he argues, is one in which the audience is encouraged to participate: perversely, he names television as his prime example of a 'low intensity' medium which must involve its audience. A hot medium is one of such 'high definition' that the audience is denied the chance to participate: curiously again, he names the cinema as the medium which requires the least effort of completion. Clearly, these notions are wholly relative. Bad television can be quite passive in its effect, and good cinema can be immensely active. What then of the theatre? To pursue McLuhan's terminology, no doubt the theatrical medium is icy cold, since participation is essential for its existence. However, it must immediately occur to the reader that a proscenium-arch play must be more hot than cold, and an open-stage play, in which the spectator has no choice but to be intimately engaged more cold than hot. Or more subtly, a tragedy in which the feelings are more highly defined is likely to be less cold than a comedy which usually manipulates its audience more obliquely. Or again, a soliloquy addressed as it should be directly to its audience may well be hotter than the low intensity action which surrounds it.

Drama calls for a virtually unlimited range of such responses once its conventions are working freely, and it is for criticism to examine closely how a play blows hot and cold. McLuhan does not consider the theatre as a medium, for all it is the most ancient of the arts, and the must durable. Yet long after typographic man is supposed to have been thinking by linear reasoning, that of words spaced syntactically upon a printed page, the theatre persists in communicating by a simultaneity of sensory impressions. Now as then, it demands that its audience perceive its configuration, its *Gestalt*, of impressions. In its long history, the theatre has been at one time or another to a greater or lesser degree verbal in its methods and emphasis, but it has always excited its audiences by the immediacy of its stimuli. Imaginative immediacy is characteristic of the medium, and again and again down the ages the theatre has shown that the medium is the message.

The theatre reasserts that essentially primitive response to space and movement, colour and sound, the elements which literate man finds so alarming and perilous. For the spectator in the theatre scarcely reasons the relationship between king and beggar before he senses it in voice, posture, costume and the physical bond between them. He scans the picture as if he were many cameras with many lenses. Both in the conception and in the communication of drama, the picture must always anticipate the words, and by generalized impressions the spectator is powerfully prepared for the specific and incisive focus of the words. The study of the drama is the study of how the stage compels its audience to be involved in its actual processes. The spectator interprets and so contributes to and finally becomes the play, whose image is all and only in his mind.

It is this high degree of involvement which makes theatre at its best so appealing: yet not by encouraging such a kind of licence that the result is riot. The stage, with its mesh of strong sensory details, can exercise a superb control over the spectator, and flex it as the occasion demands. There are times when some of the dullest things in the world – husband talking to wife, Hjalmar Ekdal to Gina, or mother to child, Ranevskaya to Anya – can rivet attention, simply by allowing the audience to feed into a commonplace human relationship its own elementary knowledge of life. There are other times when word and deed can overwhelm by sheer inflammatory theatre, and leave the audience room only for passive assimilation. We are back with McLuhan's hot and cold: except that within the infinite elasticity of the theatre medium we must admit the fundamental and serviceable interdependence of these contrary elements. *Romeo and Juliet* opens with an impersonal and indeed metaphysical statement in formal sonnet form, which is then sharply brushed aside as the streets of Verona graphically illustrate the prologue's message.

Even at the level of clothes and paint and noise, the theatre bombards its audience with a hundred simultaneous capsules of information, anything capable of reaching the mind and imagination through the eye or the ear. The critic, equipped with literary apparatus, the linear logic of cause and effect, cannot cope with such an assault. Yet dramatic simultaneity, the synaesthesia of the senses and perceptions,

4

is the object of study: for from it come the concepts by which the experience is to be judged, and by no other way.

McLuhan's guidelines and warnings (in *Understanding Media*, pp. 32–3), loaded as they seem to be with his freewheeling generalities, are nevertheless pertinent here. The effect of the form is not necessarily related to its content, nor does the effect occur at the level of 'opinion'; but the form *will* alter patterns of perception. Radio drama can immediately transport the listener into its special world of fantasy; music in drama can enlarge the perceptions by its extraordinary power of generalizing; the stylizing of high theatre can implant a unique degree of aesthetic detachment between actor and spectator to lead the audience to the apprehension of reality. 'Each form of transport not only carries, but translates and transforms, the sender, the receiver, and the message. The use of any kind of medium or extension of man alters the patterns of interdependence among people, as it alters the ratios among our senses' (p. 91). McLuhan's central assertion here is our springboard to an understanding of the particular things that happen in a play.

Aristotelian and linear thinking about drama, which seems to disentangle elements like plot, character and spectacle, theme and style, invites a degree of failure: this kind of information not only belongs to a world outside the theatre, but must remain at such a level of abstraction and fragmentation that it cannot account for what happens to an audience. Bernard Beckerman has described this as studying a play by 'striation': 'The habit of mind that chooses to treat a play as a collection of strands inhibits an appreciation of it as a sequence of total experiences. . .As a scene unfolds, it is impossible to know what is "plot" and what is "character"' (*Dynamics of Drama*, p. 36). A play's affective elements escape, the actualities which determine the moment-by-moment response. All theories of tragedy evaporate when Macbeth trips over the carpet or when Hamlet wears pink.

The critic must continually remind himself how complex an event is the play, how subtle the weaving that makes up the happening. Drama has its own discipline, one which is not an extension of that of literature. While it borrows from a dozen other arts, it owes allegiance to none. At its centre is the theatre experience, which is capable of analysis, recreation and judgment of its methods and purposes like those of any other art. The task is complicated, however, by the need to give attention to four distinct focal points in its composition: the writer's background and conditions of work as they affect the *conception* of the play, the book of the play – the arrangement of *words* he must substitute for his conception, the *performance* of the play with particular actors in a particular playhouse, and – most fickle of all – the *audience* to whom it is addressed.

Each of these constituents calls for close examination, leading the student perhaps into verbal, linguistic and gestic studies, an appreciation of allied crafts and arts like music and design, and into history and social philosophy, but always with reference to the central notion of a creative, living theatre. The discipline of identifying himself with author, director, actor or spectator, as preliminary to the critical evaluation of intentions and results, is the complete drama student's first and essential acquisition.

A play, in sum, is an historical event, and the focus of attention is the experience of that play in a particular time. The true student of drama will find a bad play to be as exciting as a good one, that in its time the failure of Goldsmith's *The Good-Natur'd Man* is as engrossing as the success of *She Stoops to Conquer*. For such a student, the doldrums of dramatic history are as worthy of his interest as the great periods of so-called flowering, and Victorian domestic melodrama clamors for attention as much as Shaw's attack on it. The implication is that, in a social and historical context, the audience – any audience – is as important as the playwright, however great.

If a play is a set of living, shifting relationships in a human, social situation, these relationships are painfully difficult to represent without some kind of inadequately diagrammatic suggestion laid out in three dimensions. The patterns which follow are an attempt to build up such a diagram in leaps of two dimensions at a time.

The irreducible theatre event is contained in these three elements:

SCRIPT————¹————ACTOR————²————AUDIENCE

The playwright is setting down his play on paper works perforce by a code of words. The text is a coded pattern of signals to the actor, and the resulting performance is a further coded pattern of signals to the spectator. Any study of a play is impossible without an initial decoding of all signals, and the skill of decoding constitutes the introductory training of the student. It may seem that the primary evidence of the play resides in the most stable element in the line of transmission, in the script itself. But the script is not the play. The meaning of this evidence is deceptive since it is only to be found by constant reference to the interstices in the diagram, which represent the truly mercurial relationships:

1→ (a) the script's anticipation of the behaviour of the actor
1← (b) the interpretation of the signals in the script by the actor
1-2(c) the quality and accuracy of the signals transmitted in performance
2← (d) their reception or rejection in whatever degree by an audience
2→(e) the actor's response to the reception of his signals
1-2(f) the flexibility or otherwise of the script under the pressure of performance

In fine analysis, it is clearly as important to know what is being returned by the spectator to the actor, and by the actor to the script, as to know the intentions of the script in the first place. Arguably, intentions are of no consequence whatsoever.

These elements are irreducible because they constitute the three living links in the chain. If they are examined individually, certain organs of vital function are found in each. Peter Brook has observed that words in a play are 'an end product which begins as an impulse. This process occurs inside the dramatist; it is repeated inside the actor' (*The Empty Space*, p. 12). For some actors a script will be alive insofar as it offers particular opportunities for recreation: a viable characterization, in whatever mode, may be of first importance; or a particular kind of speech, perhaps helpful in tonal or gestic qualities; or clear signals for a dominant style or spirit in the playing. The student also, like the actor, will look into the lines and ask, Is this speech or is it song? He will wish to determine the mood and atmosphere of the whole. What order of life, natural or supranatural, is to be represented? What order of experience, comic or tragic or of any sort between, do the words try to establish? A script will answer most of such questions, and if it is alive it can be seized and invigorated by actor and spectator. If it is only partly alive, this also is important.

It is equally valid to determine the equipment of the actor in order to know the quality of visual and aural signals he could or should convey to an audience in performance. What result if Hamlet were old or Coriolanus a weakling? Even in the absence of histrionic possibility, sensory judgment can remain: as when one hears a child read Shakespeare's vividly textured lines or when a scene is presented in a classroom without a true stage/auditorium relationship, or even when a reader sits in his chair to read the text in silence. It is a poor play-reader who cannot gain some sense of what is required of the actor in mime, gesture, facial expression, kind of movement and characteristic style between dance and stillness, the decorum of the part. We can strain to recognize in the darkness of the text the signals of costume, its cut and colour, period and idiosyncrasy, with or without mask or make-up. We can to a degree imagine the appropriate human voice as an instrument for tone and attitude, even the manner of its delivery, realistic and introverted or explicit and projected.

It is not so easy outside the theatre, as Granville-Barker long ago pointed out, to see and hear in imagination two or more players working together. The life in a single character is determined by the better script to a good degree, although those early readers who thought of Lady Macbeth as in the spirit of a fourth witch must have been surprised by Mrs Siddons's tenderness: the spectrum of a great part can be proved only in performance. It is for the actor, finally, to crystallize the nature of the intended impersonation by revealing the measure of individuality or impersonality most apt for the representation. But in a busy scene only the stage can point and particularize the relationship of one character to another, or one to two or more, in their infinite permutations of age and sex, status social and moral, mood sad and joyful.

Discrete speculations about the audience are not easy, but are essential. At what time and place did it assemble? What of its size?— a mass audience made up of ones and twos for radio or television, or of tens of thousands for the ancient Greek theatre? What was the occasion of its assembly?—holy or profane, coming together at regular or irregular intervals? Its cultural assumptions, its social and political background: these must be known. Should we reckon with notions of the mass psychology of emotion, or of laughter; or distinguish between the response of women and men; or contrast that of the younger with that of the older generation? What are an audience's communal needs and wishes, and its mood at the given time? Synge's *Playboy* would be a different creature ten years later. Shakespeare required that Gloucester be tied to a chair for his blinding, in order to return the playhouse to the bear-pit, with the old earl pinioned and bound fast, 'tied to th' stake', with Cornwall and Regan yapping their repetitions, 'Wherefore to Dover?', like two dogs before they tear his flesh with 'boarish fangs' and send him off like an animal to 'smell his way to Dover'. What if a modern audience instinctively substitutes the image of the third degree for this *Gestalt* of Elizabethan bear-baiting?

Once these lively partners are identified, then some of the work of synthesis may begin. It may be necessary to ask to what extent the actor was aware of the condition of his audience, or whether the script was appropriate to the occasion. Did the characterization confirm the spectator's attitudes, or divide him against himself by some structural dialectic? Did the performance engage his mind or his feelings? Or both by calculated interaction? Did the signals of the script or the actor turn the mood in the auditorium towards a position romantic or realistic, comfortable or disturbing? Was the key-note spiritual or perhaps cynical? Was the final impact emotive and persuasive, or intellectual and reflective? All questions are proper which examine the inescapable ties between one partner and another in playmaking. And they all deal in practices, not systems.

It is natural for the critic to wonder where along the chain is the point of creation. Is it in the conception of the script and its pre-judged effect? Is it in the moment of recreated meaning on a particular stage? Is it in the image of the play relived by the fusing of its elements in the mind of the spectator undergoing the event? Doubtless the writer should take first honours, but it is also true that a great play can provoke the finest performance and the most brilliant response. The apt analogy is that of film-making, where the creative explosion may occur in the scenario, or behind the camera, or in the cutting-room, or when the viewer makes a connection of his own. So, too, a play may cohere creatively by the choice of a verbal stroke in the script, or a compelling inflection of voice on the stage, or a sharp recognition by the audience. We may assume that Shakespeare intended to balance the positive sexuality of Lady Macduff with the negative sexuality of Lady Macbeth, but it is for the two players to strike the contrast and for the spectator to perceive the force of the relationship. The script separates to join them, like Theseus and Oberon, or Falstaff and King Henry IV, but only the interdependence of the parties to the play sparks the vision behind the experience.

The simplest ingredients of the play as an event are, however, complicated by other people and other factors. Behind the script there is an author; behind the actor there may be a promoter, a producer or

9

a director; behind the audience lies a whole society. New relationships are involved, and the map of the play expands.

2.

SCRIPT————————ACTOR————————AUDIENCE

AUTHOR————————PRODUCER————————SOCIETY

Whatever the 'new criticism' may say, a knowledge of each artist behind the artifact elucidates his creative contribution. The author's conditions of working, his status in society as a professional and as a person, the pressures upon him of implicit or explicit censorship by government or society, or the *Zeitgeist* encouragement of his artistic freedom, may not affect the experience of the theatre event, but it would be frivolous to deny that they penetrate to the core of the event itself. Some of these circumstances are self-imposed by his conformity or non-conformity as an artist; and knowledge of his personal philosophy, or religious or political position, or his stance for the occasion, must be of keen interest. If familiarity with every passing caprice of Bernard Shaw's mind has proved a distraction to the dramatic critic, what would we not give to glimpse a corner of Shakespeare's? Intention itself is to be scrutinized in its minute particulars.

There are few periods in the history of drama when it is unnecessary for the student to recognize the presence of a producer of some kind. A controlling influence upon performance has usually been identifiable – a priest, a master of a guild, a leading player, a theatre manager, an actor-manager, an impresario, a financier. But what degree of control? What was his purpose? What freedom did he assume? Who granted it him – the author, the text, the company, the audience? Was his the choice of play, the casting, the angle of vision, the emphasis of characterization or blocking, the tempo and spirit of the whole? What did the notion of loyalty to the text signify in his time? Not even the most ardent purist denies that the director's duty in the business of communication today is equally to author and to audience; but the balance is delicately subjective. The 'futurist' productions of *A Midsummer Night's Dream* by Granville-Barker with his stylized golden fairies (1914) and by Brook with his magic circus (1970) – both shockingly untraditional – were outstandingly true to the original because directed accurately at their contemporary audiences.

With the study of the society that a particular audience represented.

or failed to represent, the complexities of investigation assume formidable proportions. The social history which lies behind the play as a public event can offer unpredictable insights into the source of its vitality. Drama is an expression of community, feeling the pulse of an age or of a moment in time like no other art. A play is a social event or it is nothing. To acquire any sense of *The Birds* or *Richard II* or *Three Sisters* calls for excursions into changing Athens during the last cynical years of the Peloponnesian War, England precarious during the declining reign of Elizabeth I, Russia restless at the turn of the nineteenth century. 'Taste' itself determined that an eighteenth-century audience could paradoxically enjoy *The Country Wife* on Monday and admire Hugh Kelly's maudlin *False Delicacy* on Tuesday. One is inclined to resist Northrop Frye's conclusion (*Anatomy of Criticism*, p. 18) that the history of taste is no part of the structure of criticism.

In the synoptic view of drama study, again, it is every new set of relationships which insists upon attention. What is the author's regard for the actors who serve him? Scott writes in his Preface to *Halidon Hill* (1822), 'The drama (if it can be termed one) is, in no particular, either designed or calculated for the stage.' Scott was right, but the implied attitude of author to actor in this statement in part explains the abortive thing he fathered. It is a greater challenge to assess an author's 'tone', in I. A. Richards's sense, towards his public. Is it one of over-respect or disrespect, Eliot's or Genêt's? What role in society does the promoter see for his company and the theatre generally in terms of *this* play – educational, religious, commercial? How far was an audience attending a play by Yeats or Albee aware of a cultural occasion, selfconsciously affecting the response? Does not the mass audience have a parallel awareness of another kind of occasion when it flocks to the cinema as it did in the 1930's or switches on a popular television program?

The irresistible comparison is with genuine ritual. A mystery cycle was shaped, O. B. Hardison suggests in *Christian Rite and Christian Drama in the Middle Ages*, as an extension of the Easter celebration itself, having a beginning, a middle and an end in which the middle, the climax of the Crucifixion, determined the parts that preceded and succeeded it. Our medieval forebears were caught up in a pattern of response from *tristitia* to *gaudium*, exactly echoing the ritual sequence traced by the Mass which nourished them. On another level, a script altered to meet certain modern needs, as when Irving playing Shylock lopped off the fifth act of *The Merchant of Venice* or Mrs Siddons playing Lady Macbeth cut all after the sleep-walking scene, can teach sharp lessons about the social role of the stage. Each ingredient relates to each other, and in this endless variety is found the life of the drama, sometimes inspired, sometimes mundane.

The web of the play grows increasingly tangled at stage three (although stage three might well have been stage one, since inter-action is simultaneous). The diagram moves into another dimension, but again starts from the basic ingredients:

3.

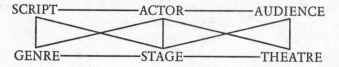

Behind the conception of the script lie the genre conventions which it adopted or refused; behind the actor's technical conventions of playing lie the demands of a particular playhouse, its shape and equip-ment, which condition, encourage and limit the performer's ways of signalling; behind the audience and its society are their conven-tional presumptions and the esteem in which the theatre is held.

It would be to harass the reader to argue here these divergent notions of 'convention'. It is worth remarking, however, that the term is meaningless until particularized. Conventions of accepted usage infiltrate every department of theatre: conventions of genre, form and style, of acting on a particular stage or of an audience's expecta-tions based on previous practice. We acknowledge that the conven-tional pressures on a script if a playwright decides to write an English tragedy in 1590 are different from those in 1690. What is the known expectation, the past experience, of the spectator? These questions raise such commonplace matters as those of character stereotypes, the use of verse or prose, and couplet or blank verse, the control or improvisation of the action, the dramatic unities, and many more. Was Molière pleased to offer an unchanging succession of mindless pantaloons, or was the genius of John Webster actually content to reproduce stereotypical Italianate villains and courtesans without occasionally surprising an audience he knew to be surfeited on male and female Machiavels? The vitality of a convention is in its joyous capacity for being inflected or subverted.

It is urgent to know what in terms of convention are the strengths and weaknesses of a large or small auditorium, and the effect of the stage shape, whether jutting aggressively into the house or coyly withdrawn into a room merely adjacent to the audience. For much of the author's and the actor's choice of speech, gesture and movement is decided by the witchery concealed in the relation of acting area to auditorium. What properties were possible, manageable or meaningful for dramatic statements of realism or symbolism? What emphasis did play or actor place on costume, décor, colour, light? Were these representational or non-representational? What use was made of music, sounds and effects? (It is all too easy to read that 'music plays' without making any effort to recognize gay from sober, quiet from loud, Wagner from Debussy, a galliard from a pavane. Nor is it often acknowledged that music had a part to play in drama the world over until the late nineteenth century.) All these seemingly lesser elements of communication in practice constitute the stuff of perception, powerful in that they guide the eye and ear to meaning and value. This will be a major concern in chapter 2.

How would such merely physical elements affect the sense of location, or the treatment of time, chronological or theatrical, in the narrative of the play? Did the auditorium encourage ritual or illusion? Was the experience of a play in a certain playhouse participatory or passive? We should entertain some doubt about the imaginary siting of the ideal 'fourth wall' the naturalistic movement boasted in the proscenium-arch theatre: if Ibsen contrived to draw his audience through the arch, this is hardly true of the objective didacticism of Shaw, whose methods of comic equipoise require the spectator to keep his distance. However, there is a case to be made that the shape of the stage determined absolutely an audience's illusory or non-illusory experience of theatre. Yet what other qualities were brought to the experience if the play were performed in a public street, a church or a private room?

Only an inexhaustible reader will wish to scrutinize the inexhaustible number of other links between the nine interrelated elements identified in the play event. In practice, the student probes that part of the matrix which seems to hold the secret of the play's nature and success. While it is fascinating to know that the heroines of early Victorian domestic drama always wore white through thick and thin and several costume changes, the enquiring mind will look towards the attitudes of the early nineteenth-century audience to answer the essential questions which surround the phenomenal popularity of plays like *The Drunkard* on both sides of the Atlantic. Perhaps the widening of the Restoration coterie audience explains the provincial excursions of a *Recruiting Officer*, but only the continuing intimacy of the late Restoration playhouse accounts for the way Farquhar's play is made to operate. Nevertheless, a further dimension must be added. The serious student will wish to contemplate the fourth dimension, time. We have emphasized that a play is a sensitive historical barometer, and, like any other artifact, one which is no accident. Every play and its performance falls into a recognizable time zone of human activity, as this next extension of the pattern may suggest.

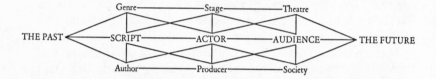

Perhaps it is understandable that, in reviewing contemporary plays, the newspaper critics seem more at home debating the future than examining the present; they assume a prophetic role. As for the researcher, he will always wish to know where the conventions of the script, the acting and the audience came from, and often where they went to, and why. For a convention is never fixed, but is constantly changing. Each new play, indeed each new performance, alters in however slight a degree, the matrix of conventions, and thus the form of the genre and its impact. Shakespeare added humour, even charm, to the received villainy of Richard Crookback, induced realism into the received faithlessness of Cressida, and in each case created the genre anew, putting it to the living test. This is again the story of tradition and the individual talent, as they nourish the organism of the theatre experience.

This book offers to scan a little of the fabric of the drama. But theory is of no account without practice and demonstration. So here a respite with, first, a particular pedestrian and familiar short example of play script to suggest an initial direction in which dramatic analysis could go. It exemplifies stage one of the process above.

The first scene of *Macbeth* has twelve lines. They may be so familiar that in reading the eye skips over the scene to arrive at the apparent action, the meeting of Duncan with the 'bleeding captain' of the Folio. In performance, whether played for a ghastly humour as in former years or for the realism of Joseph Papp's and lately Polanski's scavengers of the battlefield, the impact of this opening is inescapable and compulsive: Shakespeare intended it to be so. As a man of the theatre, he ensures that the passage is richly textured. However, *Macbeth* the play begins with noise and light:

> *Thunder and lightning. Enter three Witches.*
>
> 1 WITCH: When shall we three meet again?
> In thunder, lightning, or in rain?
>
> 2 WITCH: When the hurly-burly's done,
> When the battle's lost, and won.
>
> 3 WITCH: That will be ere the set of sun.
>
> 1 WITCH: Where the place?
>
> 2 WITCH: Upon the heath.
>
> 3 WITCH: There to meet with Macbeth.
>
> 1 WITCH: I come, Graymalkin.
>
> ALL: Paddock calls anon:
> Fair is foul, and foul is fair,
> Hover through the fog and filthy air.
>
> *Exeunt.*

Philology, first, has little of help in all this pudder. It would recognize 'Graymalkin' as the First Witch's grey cat, 'Paddock' as a word of Scots origin for a frog or toad, and that both refer to the pets and familiar spirits popularly associated with witchcraft. Evocative names indeed, but with a tenth of their meaning out of the context of the stage.

Still with an eye on the text, a prosodic interest would draw attention to the rhyming couplets and their strongly metrical four-beat lines. But as soon as rhyme and rhythm have been remarked, the first theatrical signals have been heard, and these immediately call for demonstration. The aural signals are so powerful, so unlike ordinary speech, that read aloud they prompt pressing sensations of ritualistic intoning. Add to this that the couplets are first passed as question and answer from one player to another, until the lines, but not the rhymes, are broken, and the sounds insist upon gesture and activity. They set in motion a circular, accelerating dance movement, one in which each line is delivered at a new pitch as the dancer arrives at a place nearest the centre of the auditorium. The later breaking of the lines suggests the quickening of pace and increasing urgency of tone, until speech and song in unison slow the movement and fade the sound for the exit. The script has already left the page, words have become voices and voices gestures. The verse is dramatic, carrying more meaning if read aloud, more still if the body is moving.

Such rendering of the lines to elicit their quality and sense demands a stage, but cannot proceed unless the speakers and dancers supply a physical human image: the players impersonate witches. This impersonation today seems to raise a number of peripheral queries about our modern assumptions concerning the supernatural, and what must be done to create an equivalent effect upon the sceptical, making the Weird Women more shadowy, more illusory, or even omitting them in their persons altogether; more on this later. To understand the first performance, reference to Reginald Scot's *Discovery of Witchcraft* (1584) suggests that Elizabethan witches were 'commonly old, lame, blear-eyed, pale, foul, and full of wrinkles . . . in whose drowsy minds the Devil hath gotten a fine seat . . . They are lean and deformed, showing melancholy in their faces, to the horror of all that see them.' Such a contemporary document is bristling with clues for costume, gesture and miming, although only Shakespeare's lines exactly determine the spirit of Macbeth's witches. External evidence is supplemented by internal evidence on appearance, movement and speech, in the way Shakespeare seems always instinctively to supply: Banquo says they have beards (I.iii.46 in the *New Cambridge Shakespeare*), but then the players were men; they or their arms seem to 'hover' (I.i.12); alliterative effects in their speech (th . . . s . . . f) reflect a certain hissing and lisping in their voices. All to help the actors.

Once the actors are on the stage performing 'in character', the physical claims of the Elizabethan platform, with other playhouse features, define their style and effect. The dance might have spread over the 1,000 square feet of the platform, growing from the huddling conspiracy of the opening lines to the more impersonal address to the audience at large of their conclusions. The pattern is one of a widening, involving, embracing attack on the spectator. The vision of the unearthly they embody will doubtless be enhanced by the Globe's effects-man with his thunder-stones and flashing mirrors, and doubtless their entrance and exit through the central trap in the floor of the platform will conventionally signify their abode as hell or purgatory. The image conspicuously establishes that, in the medieval tradition, supernatural powers are to have a hand in the affairs of this world. Inspection of the evidence has moved through the first two focal points of the first diagram, touching on the most immediate signals between script and actor.

Judgment begins with an assessment of the specific response of the audience. It may seem perverse that a human drama should be introduced by witchcraft: it is very intentionally so. Did the playwright assume that his audience believed in witches, and so must a modern audience also believe, in order to experience the play? It is known that many of Shakespeare's contemporaries did not so believe, and it would be a wise guess that Shakespeare was seeking some effect other than that of a mere *representation* of the supernatural. It is more reasonable to assume that he simply anticipated that the Devil's business itself was real enough to his audience, and that *in conditions of theatre* the symbolism of his intoned and stylized lines would prompt imaginative belief and the play could proceed. This is as true now as it was then. If the trick works for the embodiment of Banquo's ghost in act III, it works for the Witches from the beginning. A practical man of the theatre would not risk disaster in an opening scene: Shakespeare reckoned upon a positive and controllable response to a striking initial effect.

It is the spirit of this perverse prologue which speaks to Elizabethan moral attitudes, and it is this which sets up incipient tensions that are, for a secular drama, curiously religious in implication. The Witches raise questions about the free agency of man (in spite of Bradley's non-theatrical deliberations to the contrary in his *Shakespearean Tragedy*, pp. 340–9). When as a trio they speak like demoniacal conspirators, their function is of course for the play itself, their unearthly presence from the beginning governing in unknown ways the actions of its characters. More importantly, by the increasing insistence of their lines, they stimulate fearful presuppositions in their audience.

Above all, by beginning his play with such pointedly ominous riddles as the Witches speak, Shakespeare casts the audience in the role of conspirators plotting with the forces of the supernatural at the outset.

The quality of the dramaturgy is now felt. The scene is of unusual brevity: shorter than a presenter's prologue, it is a mere subliminal glimpse of a theme. Yet it is a more graphic enactment of a design than any formal prologue could manage. It remains abstract and elusive, yet it is direct and unavoidable. The Witches' strange chant and macabre dance prepare a sharp response to a play which deals in partly controlled, partly uncontrollable, evil. On a surface level, the scene offers expository information about the time, the place and the occasion, the weather, the mood and the atmosphere of battle –

'lost, and won', since victories must also be defeats, defeats victories, for one or other of the combatants. Notably, in this context of war the Witches name Macbeth, the name heard for the first time like a bell as the word hits the rhyme with a reverberating echo: Macbeth will be the centre of attention, ours and theirs, although only they know of the 'meeting', which to him will seem chance.

With 'fair is foul, and foul is fair', the scene makes glancing reference to the evil lurking beneath good appearances, a devilish paradox echoed later by Macbeth's own sense of 'so foul and fair a day', a musical motif here initiated. Supported as it is by the conventional symbolism of the storm, it provokes the strongest idea of upsetting the natural order. It offers equally urgent presentiments of moral desolation to follow ('Hover through the fog and filthy air'), and these will later be pursued by the specific thoughts and actions of the protagonist ('Hell is murky'). To catch all this on the threshold of consciousness, we do not have to debate whether these characters were intended to be figures of fate, or merely the 'weird sisters' of the Holinshed source: their theatrical impact is sensory and it is primary. Ambiguous evil flutters, grimaces, and spits in the face of the spectator.

Nor in the theatre, in any case, is there time to reflect whether the Witches are real or unreal. The narrative action of the play has begun before their last sighing, moaning notes have ceased. The play passes rapidly from the abstract to the concrete: as they vanish through their trap, the captain has staggered his thirty feet down to the centre of the house, a loser and a winner both, in victory spilling his life's blood. The suggestion of blood through the play is touched off by this most fierce of visual stage devices, linked with the 'foul' and the 'filth' on a more immediate plane than even that of the opening scene. Shakespeare illustrates his illustration, and the wounded soldier, more than a mere messenger, is the Witches' first example. That is to start another story. The topping of one dramatic impression by another in their planned sequence as the play pushes on in its pre-ordained tempo checks and directs the contributing imagination of the spectator, whose pleasurable task is to synthesize all the signals in transit. The designed complexity is defined and evaluated by the effectiveness and emphasis of every element, the music and dance of the lines, the forceful presence of the actors, all the visual, aural and verbal ingredients, as they are transmitted and received by human agents in performance.

It is more difficult to proceed constructively past the obvious and central stages of dramatic communication. In the history of dramatic criticism there have been notorious insensibilities, failures of understanding and distractions from the main business. Today, critics are skilled in the analysis of texts, and discussion of the actor and his audience is not unknown, but there remain gaping omissions in the interstices of our diagram, the relationships within the play event which constitute its organic life. In spite of the mountain of material that has been written, Shakespearian criticism is the poorest: his theatre is too strange, too good for us. Yet in other periods also, peculiar forces working on the theatre event have been neglected. Drama is always an immediate experience, but criticism too often circles around without seeing the when, where and how of the actuality.

Place any of the medieval mystery cycles in the matrix, and it reveals its own sources of energy, elements which seem to demand immediate explanation. Scholarship has given its attention to the relationship between the script and the genre, seeking patterns from the past (and more often from the future, the false bright star of Elizabethan theatre leading the traveller astray) in order to explain the phenomenon of the present. This is a detective exercise of immense fascination, and it takes us nearer the heart of the medieval experience to establish the canonical and liturgical sources of the cycles. No question, it is right to try to recreate the spirit of the medieval church service felt in the plays.

Yet, arguably, a more immediate need is to examine the relationship between the non-professional actors and their kinsmen and friends in the streets and market-places. The mystery of the medieval drama lies hidden in its blending of impersonality and intimacy, brought about by the ritual performance of amateurs in narrow medieval cities of a transcendent subject, the story of the soul of man from the Creation to the Last Judgment. The mixture of direct histrionic appeal and personal religious admonition, delivered from mansion or pageant to the citizen spectators, calls for sensitive appraisal. The actor/audience relationship, were it known, would certainly tell us more about the working of the drama in medieval society than that relationship today would tell us about the modern theatre. Even if such an examination of the teasingly comic, homely and savage elements in the divine pattern, together with more formalistic study, leaves us with only an approximation of the medieval experience, it might lead us to a better understanding of the ethos of the playhouse experience of Elizabethan times. The kind of non-illusory participation peculiar to the playgoer seeing Macbeth at the Globe was closer to the middle ages than to the twentieth century.

Again, it is necessary to look to the periphery of the play to find its heart. This actor/audience relationship, together with the vanishing Elizabethan conventions, help explain the more enigmatic scenes in Shakespeare. In *Measure for Measure*, Pompey's prison scene, IV.iii, must seem secondary at this distance, but because of the brilliant thrust of its theatricality it was doubtless central in its time. How little we understand the workings of a subplot. This scene opens with the Clown and all the aggressive expansion of the action that this implies. Pompey the pimp, in his clown's address and caper to the audience, leaps and points at one or another of us wickedly: 'I am as well acquainted here, as I was in our house of profession!' Through the outrageous licence of the company's clown, every spectator is reminded that he too is a sinner of the flesh, in prison and awaiting execution, that death and judgment are inevitable. Claudio's agonized apprehension of his end is made more immediately ours, but by the obliquity of its comic presentation the notion is still palatable.

The entrance of the terrible figure of Abhorson the executioner (evocative name, mixed of 'abhor' and 'son of a whore'), wearing his black cowl and carrying his gruesome axe, is the very image of retribution, sensual death and the mortality of man. His formally earnest and professional speech and manner stress the serious side of the scene's vision. It is, however, the Clown in his motley who now is appointed his assistant executioner – Shakespeare's unerring touch – and he offers the alternative view of death, death the jester, the grinning ape. Symbolically they take up positions on opposite sides, the grim chopping block perhaps between them as the most urgent emblem on the stage. The medieval dance of death is grotesquely visualized, the grin in the skull dramatized.

When Barnardine, the confirmed criminal and murderer, makes his sottish entrance, the image widens again. We see him as poor Claudio's extreme counterpart, but laughably drunk and ridiculously, clownishly casual in the face of death. His presence blasphemously belittles the idea of humunculus confronting his Maker. Indeed, the figure of the Duke, hooded darkly as a friar, mysteriously representing both state and church, makes the fourth entrance and remains impersonally upstage overseeing the whole scene. It is as if he had descended to impose the law of man and God upon the blockish Barnardine and pathetic Claudio, and, too, on the spectators trapped by the Clown's convention, as if he has come to determine and hasten the mortal inevitability for all. Here is a theatrically pointed scene directed at its contemporary audience in every comic and sinister particular. To recreate it imaginatively, it must be examined for its links between past and present, and between stage and audience. The function of *Measure for Measure* as an event relied on such connections.

To our shame, the neglect continues of the real achievement in the slippery comedy of the Restoration. It is surely the conclusive example of the social role of the theatre. But the comic world of Wycherley and Etherege is as difficult for the literary student to grasp as that of the *Commedia dell'arte*: its language signals are hardly verbal before they are histrionic, tonal and gestic. At no time in the history of the drama had so fraternal a coterie entertainment existed at that of the Restoration immediately after 1660. The reason for the phenomenon lies in the unique conditions of its writing and playing. The comedy of the Restoration was conceived to serve the smallest public theatre with the smallest audience; in social rank this audience was of the highest and the narrowest, whereas in social rank the actor was among the lowest. What lines does a court wit write for a prostitute playing a great lady in the physical conditions of intimate cabaret? The Restoration playwright deals instinctively in the concealed audience address and the implicit asides (not necessarily the plot asides assigned in the scripts) designed to be heard at close quarters and redoubled in meaning by the inflection of a voice and the flick of a fan.

Margery Pinchwife's opening line in *The Country Wife*, 'Pray, sister, where are the best fields and woods to walk in, in London?' was very different from the original, one suspects, when delivered by Miss Joan Plowright at the Royal Court in 1957. The teasing of the line by the popular, petite, pert Mistress Boutel at the Theatre Royal, Drury Lane, in 1675 was no doubt of another order of drama. Its surface meaning implies the thinking of a country girl unused to the town, but when from the stage the pretty blonde Elizabeth Boutel flirted on the words with, probably, the Earl of Rochester, the 'wink' in the line made it electrifying. The early comedies of the Restoration point to a quite exceptional solidarity in the house by which the excessive conventionality of the entertainment could remain congenial while monstrous versions of the truth could be told. To fathom it we must not only search out their quality of superb style, but also deeply understand the spirited homogeneity enjoyed by author, actor and audience. Only then should we dare to join in the game of evaluation which has be-devilled Restoration dramatic criticism for 250 years.

All is confusion in the commentary on the drama of the modern age, chiefly because its critics seek their answer in genre theory, looking for the egg and not the chicken. From Ibsen to the Absurdists, it has been in vain to identify the infinite mixture of conventions at the command of the modern playwright. Was *The Wild Duck* a tragedy? – if so, its hero was missing. Was *The Cherry Orchard* a farce? – its author claimed that its ingredients belonged to *vaudeville*. In *Six Characters* was Pirandello writing a play of unrealistic illusion or of nonillusory realism? Was *The Glass Menagerie* naturalistic or expressionistic? – it depends whether you look at the picture or the frame. In America, *Death of a Salesman* was the great twentieth-century tragedy; in Europe, it was the final *drame satirique* on materialism. Critics trip over their Aristotelian feet when they try to circumscribe such plays by form, characterization or tone. Each is mixed: the form a meaningless 'tragicomedy'; the central characters are 'anti-heroes', the tone ambiguous. Only recent theories deriving from Brecht's shrewd thinking on distancing an audience have offered some new insight. By the trick of switching convention, the link between stage and audience retains an elasticity which in part explains what is happening. The impulse is to return the theatre to its earlier modes, expanding its possibilities by anti-illusory tactics; and a later chapter will return to the problems of perception in such theatre.

The student begins again with more objectivity in his judgment, since to pronounce a verdict on the aesthetic distancing of a character, an action, a line or a style is impossible without turning to a performance and the response to it. Next year's critic will sit looking at the audience as well as at the stage. 'I'm in mourning for my life', says Masha by way of introducing the world of *The Seagull*, and at the same time she prepares to take a pinch of snuff. Measure the response to that kind of detail by convention or genre if you can. Or as Gogo in *Waiting for Godot* prepares to hang himself for positively the last time, his baggy trousers fall about his ankles and the laughter from the gallery is the ridicule of the Gods, heard once before when Lear's Gloucester tried to jump from Dover Cliff and fell flat on his face

on the stage. Gogo's genre is that of the *Commedia,* his acting convention that of a circus clown, his verbal patterns that of the music hall,
but the effect in the Théâtre Babylone in 1952 was that of an intense
and thought-provoking drama which was quickly snatched up by the
fashionable existentialists to pin to their banner. Beckett has suffered
from this facile mishandling ever since.

In the twentieth century, it is the freedom with which new experiences can be made up of old conventions that insists that the critic
constantly examine the relationships between script, stage and audience. Upon these depend the degree and quality of comic alienation
possible and necessary, the tension in the live theatre that determines
the true value of the modern play.

The aim is an objective scholarship for drama, one which moves
from the centre outwards. A correct analysis is a complete analysis,
although this is not necessarily to admit pluralism in dramatic criticism as the solution to the art of the theatre merely because it is complex. In the chaos of modern studies drama bows under a multi-
plicity of approaches which with today's professionalism can pro-
foundly mislead. One thinks of the psychological approach, which
would treat a character as a life or a play as a case history; or the
myth-makers who would find the ritualism of the dramatic experience
(which surely exists) in the plotting of the action and the telling of the
story, and not in the presuppositions of the spectators where ritual
must start and finish. Quasi-philosophical and moral approaches to
drama are the most susceptible to abuse, being the most subjective.
But the play-world, as Charles Lamb once unsuccessfully argued, is
essentially amoral, and can no more be challenged for its bad teaching
than it is answerable to the vagaries of the imagination. Must the
spectator morally love or hate Macbeth or Othello to experience their
plays?

A purely social judgment on the drama is also likely to be faulty.
That historical criticism which works over the drama as a 'reflection
of the times' must be wary lest the times are inaccurately reproduced
upon the stage and diffused by the medium: in the creative activity
between artist and audience it is in the nature of the theatre to encourage distortion. It is still a commonplace to hear Ulysses cited as
Shakespeare's mouthpiece in *Troilus and Cressida* and the speech on
degree as the authentic Elizabethan view of government, this in spite
of overwhelming evidence in the play that Ulysses is the consummate
politician. It is a mere convenience to label Middleton's city

comedies as 'realistic', when they are simply dealing in intrigue in London and not in Genoa or Malta. The equisitely controlled stylization in the plays of Oscar Wilde can only with Procrustean stretching and chopping be regarded as a mirror image the *fin de siècle* audience of Victorian England. No play is a photograph, and at any time the gap of actuality between stage and audience must be sensitively measured by instruments appropriate to the medium before historical deductions can be drawn.

A complete analysis of a play examines its experience in a live, social context. If we concede that a play is a thousand interacting details of human communication, it is for us first to see, hear and receive these. That is difficulty enough.

The inference from example after example is that in the theatre experience it is not so much the elements of drama on the stage or the perceptions of the audience which are important, as the relationships between them. In the mesh of every successful performance, the signals from the script to the actor, and from the actor to the spectator and back again, complete a dramatic circuit of which the audience is an indispensable part. Drama needs an audience to throw the switch: no audience, no circuit; no circuit, no play. It is a short step to the next critical syllogism: bad drama, no current; and no current, therefore, no genuinely dramatic experience. The critic starts by measuring the current.

Indeed, to assess the force of any circumstantial element in a play, the test is always of the live circuit. Thus, music: scene v in *Mother Courage* is enacted against a victory march played offstage with spirited fifes and drums, while on stage peasants are dying in pain. Any verbal comment by Brecht on the distinction between victors and victims is rendered unnecessary: the audience is left to make the ironic connection. Forty years before, *Three Sisters* similarly employed the gay sound of a departing regimental band fading into the distance as the sisters are left behind clinging to one another in their loss. The music is appropriately jaunty, as if Chekhov's men are marching away in quick time, a tune which makes theatrical meaning because it mocks the audience's own feeling of being abandoned.

Three hundred years before that, in *Romeo and Juliet*, the ballroom scene called for the music of something like a lively galliard, its tone set by the bawdy high spirits of old Capulet. The music here was also a carefully incongruous accompaniment, this time to Romeo's rhapsodical acknowledgment of Juliet's beauty, which in his eyes seemed to 'teach the torches to burn bright'. (Zeffirelli's saccharine love song, misinterpreting Shakespeare's intention, destroyed the discord intended to grip the audience.) But old Capulet's same jolly tune does double duty when against it, even more incongruously, is heard Tybalt's hymn of hate:

> Now by the stock and honour of my kin,
> To strike him dead I hold it not a sin.

The audience, its eyes at odds with its ears, sets Tybalt against Romeo, hate against love, a threat against a kiss (that most vivid symbolic gesture), and the spirit of the party music against everything. Triple counterpoint and multiple alienation-effect, making the familiar strange and yet more strange, work to compel the audience to make the essential connections.

To examine in this manner the dramatic use of music, or costumes, or properties, or whatever, is to make value judgments on the experience from which any 'meaning' in the play stems. But, like sex, it is unnatural to analyze it while having the experience. Spontaneity cannot be trapped, yet it is the animal life of the drama and must be acknowledged.

Richard Southern insists that the essence of drama is felt in its reciprocal power: 'The essence of theatre does not lie in what is performed. It does not lie even in the way it is performed. The essence of theatre lies in the impression made on the audience by the manner in which you perform. Theatre is essentially a reactive art' (*The Seven Ages of the Theatre*, p. 26). A reactive art, unfortunately, defies measurement, the *rapprochement* of a social event remains subjective. Yet it is nonetheless real for that. It is important to know why an apple was thrown at Mrs Siddons playing Volumnia in 1806. It is essential to know what a Jacobean audience expected when a play including the character of Cleopatra or Helen of Troy was announced. Did Congreve's audience at Lincoln Inn Fields see the character Millamant, or did they see the charming Ann Bracegirdle playing Millamant, an actress of whom Colley Cibber said, 'In all the chief parts she acted, the desirable was so predominant, that no judge could be cold enough to consider, from what other particular excellence she became delightful' (*An Apology for the Life of Mr Colley Cibber, Gentleman*, p. 98). Did the author anticipate their predilection? Sheridan did not delineate his Lady Teazle as 'the daughter of a plain country squire', the triumph of sophistication over artlessness, because his plot needed it (the school for scandal should never have admitted her), nor because of familiar echoes from Molière's *école* and Garrick's *County Girl*. The answer is to be found elsewhere – in the Theatre Royal, Drury Lane, in 1777.

Our concern is therefore for reaction and 'feedback', all the alchemical changes that occur during the reception of theatrical signals. 'Dramatism' is Kenneth Burke's significant coinage to embrace his discussion of cause and motivation over a wide field of human culture, because he wishes to regard language and thought 'primarily as modes of action'. He clarifies for us the notion that the *agent* or the *agency* in the *act* of dramatism usually requires further subdivision: 'an agent might have his act modified (hence partly motivated) by friends (co-agents) or enemies (counter-agents)' (*A Grammar of Motives*, p. xxi). The friends and enemies may be on the stage itself, but they will inevitably be in the audience too. We forget the enemy at our peril. The textual and stage stimuli, the signals, may be simple to detect (although it is surprising how few people in reading a play acquire this mandatory skill of detection), but if thought is also a mode of action, it is even more surprising that the response of those in the audience is rarely questioned. The analysis of audience must most of the time be a matter of speculation and mere opinion; but speculation and opinion are the marks of any extended aesthetic criticism.

A study of the passage of signals and responses in the theatre, like that of semantics, cybernetics, or any other system of communication, must be descriptive before it is prescriptive. The activity is alive and organic, constantly escaping our vigilance. Wittgenstein said that some things cannot be said, but only shown, and the good dramatist shows us his thought and feeling by embodying and impersonating it, not by analysing it. The best we can do, after assembling all the data for judgment, is to try to recognize the processes of process, the shape of an experience in the shaping, the image as it is imagined. How can we know the dancer from the dance?

Even if one believes that the quintessential reason for going to a play is to discover its 'meaning', it is beyond dispute that dramatic meaning cannot lie in words alone, but in voices and the tone of voices, in the pace of the speaking and the silences between; and not alone in this, but also in the gesture and expression of the actor, the physical distinctions between him and others, the statuary of tragedy

26

and the curlicues of comedy, stylistic suggestion beyond reckoning. There are so many variables simultaneously working to create meaning on the stage that it is impertinent to identify it in terms other than its own. The experience is the meaning.

The muted print on the page is shorn of all specificity, and the reading of a play should disclose the chasm between dramatic life and death. Drama, as no other art, uses man's capacity for piecing together vast and varied amounts of sense information with which to build patterns for thinking and acting, just as in life. The spectator is required to organize the information until it grows, Kenneth Boulding would say, into large and complex images. But in good drama it is organized growth. Boulding contrasts the unorganized growth of natural phenomena with the erection of a well-planned building: 'Crystals and cancers grow by accretion, a building grows "toward" a blueprint. There is an image in the mind and indeed on the plans of the builder which determines the collection of material and the whole growth of the object' (*The Image*, p. 34). A play is a growing organism, reborn at each performance, but it has a plan; and if the experience is the meaning, the meaning is in the growth and not the unrealized intention. The values we place upon Hamlet derive from our changing assessment of why and how he sits apart and wears black, speaks to us so often and so intimately, challenges our view of the others on the stage. As the spectator sees and hears, he recreates or destroys.

Drama deals therefore in a quality we may call 'emergent meaning,' as opposed to the inherent quality natural to a lyrical poem, that of Angus Fletcher's 'immanent meaning' (*Allegory: Theory of a Symbolic Mode*). A poem harbours and nurtures its sense within itself like a flower in bloom, it glories in its own being beyond the power of description, but unlike a flower it remains itself after it has been dissected. A play has no such independent life, and it flourishes and blossoms only in its growth. In performance we do not stop to ask whether Desdemona had time to commit adultery with Cassio because, at the time when the issue might be considered, the mind is thrashing like the Moor's. In performance we do not stop to ask whether Lear dies of grief or joy: like the King, we are overwhelmed by the play's last blow, the death of Cordelia, and no more capable of reasoning why we have been thrust back to the delirium of the storm scenes than Lear himself. Under such pressure, we accept that he died of both. Ostensibly, there is to be no easy resolution of the problem of suffering, which, as Yeats would say, is the question of tragedy; for to make a decision about justice is to arrest the image, which must continue to grow after the play is done. 'The cold winds blow across our hands, upon our faces, the thermometer falls' (Yeats, *Essays and Introductions*, p. 523).

The power and depth of the play's emergent meaning is directly related to its rhythm and form. In its own temporal and spatial dimensions, tempo and shape control the intensity with which an audience receives its image. 'Form' may have little to do with story or plot: a play does not exist primarily to tell a story, and its narrative function can be incidental or non-existent. Nineteenth-century concepts derived from a narrative theatre of realism, concepts such as exposition, crisis and resolution, are all open for reformulating as elements of drama that essentially attack, control and release an audience.

Thus the exposition of a play like Ibsen's *The Master Builder* seems in the study to 'narrate' Solness's domination of his workers Ragnar and Brovik, and of his women Kaia and Aline. In performance the impression is of a scene in dim light, of whispers of the past, one in which work tyrannizes over domestic happiness, telling us more of the nature than the history of Solness's professional and sexual success. Evolving in moods and personalities, the image is of a prison of the mind, and beneath his dark, virile exterior Solness's unease reflects a whole community in a state of fear and slavery. When youth comes knocking at the door, it is not in the expected image of young Ragnar or Kaia, nor of a strong young man contesting the master's authority; instead, the challenge to this formidable tyrant of the play's opening minutes comes from a pert young girl who can laugh at his ponderous bewilderment. Hilde Wangel, dressed for climbing and wearing the latest sailor suit, breezes into his presence bringing with her fresh sea and mountain air. Her challenge to middle-age is one of both youth and sex. This ironic superimposition of one impression upon another is managed within a controlling rhythm which sweeps the play into poetic drama as could no details of mere narrative.

To know and recognize its 'form' is one way to identify the pattern of vitality in a play. 'All artistic conventions are devices for creating forms that express some idea of vitality or emotion', writes Susanne Langer (*Feeling and Form*, p. 280). Form, which we think of too often as prescriptive, imposed from without, is surely descriptive. When in *A Midsummer Night's Dream* we see Shakespeare make use of Bottom and Flute to burlesque Pyramus and Thisbe, the dis-

tortion is a final twisted echo of the whole play's concern with undying love. If we did not previously question the antic reversals of
passion by the lovers, we do now. Act V is a formal coda which caps
one grotesque image with a stronger. The laughter of burlesque becomes the natural extension of our ridicule of those we were less
inclined to laugh at in the sober beginning of the play when Egeus
was dictating tragic conditions to his daughter; and when the lovers,
an on-stage audience, ridicule the clowns who parody their sentiments in the play-within-the-play, we, the offstage audience, see both
groups in satisfying perspective.

The transition from tragedy to comedy in *The Winter's Tale* is
usually attributed to the change in imagery, the passage of time
and the use of clowns and a bear. For another but different sample
of formal parallelism in Shakespearian comedy, we should sense how
the play moves gracefully into its new mood after its ominous start
when we see how the lady Paulina presents a far less submissive
Hermione and her husband Antigonus a far more hapless Leontes.
'What? canst not rule her?' cries the tyrant (II.iii), and by comic perspective again we see in a moment the natural inversion of jealousy
and servility. Leontes faced with a Paulina is quite at a loss, and the
shaping of the action at this critical point is not to distract us with a
second foundering marriage, but to float us from one mood to another, preparatory to the reversal. For this reversal must be conceived
by the audience before it happens to Leontes.

Form is not a pattern for conformity; it is created to satisfy the
organic needs of an audience in their response to the play. We
may wonder why so many Hollywood westerns and war films
mechanically reserve their fighting for the last reel, when Shakespeare
has demonstrated that a battle can serve as a brilliant exposition in
act I of *Cariolanus*, or make us feel a theme in progress in act IV of
Antony and Cleopatra. We may wonder why he chose to produce the
bodies of Goneril and Regan in the fifth act of *Lear*, when we have
thoughts only for the King and Cordelia: but Shakespeare knew that
the shape of his play would be complete only when his three sisters of
act I were together again, this time in death and with the father now
spurning those he cherished before. The playwright was catering for
our needs.

Susanne Langer writes pleasingly of 'vital' form which conveys
the illusion of growth and the appearance of life. Artistic communication takes note of our awareness also of 'latent' form, which gratifies

our sense of unity by an 'illusion of a visible future': Destiny is a name for it.

This wide awareness, which we owe to our peculiarly human talent of symbolic expression, is rooted, however, in the elementary rhythms which we share with all other organisms, and the Destiny which dramatic art creates bears the stamp of organic process – of predeterminate function, tendency, growth, and completion ... Literally, 'organic process' is a biological concept; 'life,' 'growth,' 'development,' 'decline,' 'death' – all these are strictly biological terms. They are applicable only to organisms.

(Feeling and Form, pp. 311–12).

What is right for a theatre audience is necessary for the organic life of the play, whether the larger shaping of *Hamlet* to its inevitable contest with Claudius, or the little detail of a man popping a caramel into his mouth to comfort himself, like Gaev in *The Cherry Orchard*. Both are the substance of form: the test of dramatic communication is whether it kindles an audience, makes the image grow, creates life.

2

Dramatic signals

A play works by the exhibition of details that are seen and heard. These are the vocabulary of drama, and an audience learns it by its constant perception. Occasionally the senses other than sight and hearing are evoked: Othello forsakes his role as priest to bend over the sleeping rose Desdemona, 'I'll smell thee on the tree. / Oh balmy breath', or persuades us of her death as he touches her, 'Cold, cold, my girl?', just as with Lear we seem to feel Cordelia's cheeks, 'Be your tears wet? yes, faith', and with the Messenger kiss Cleopatra's 'bluest veins' before she strikes him. But eyes and ears are properly the agents of perception in the theatre, whose stimuli to be effective must be specific.

At its peril does a play begin with ideas, abstractions, themes, intellection. It is for the audience to take from the play the impressions and images from which to construct its *concepts*: by this act of apparent discernment it enjoys the excitement of apparent discovery. A play is poetry, something made; it is drama, something done; and theatre, something *perceived*. Schopenhauer argued that a work of art must be perceptual before it could carry allegorical or any other value, and to be perceived the work must be particular. 'God preserve us from generalizations', was the watchword of Chekhov the writer. Do nothing in general, for 'generality is the enemy of art', urged Stanislavsky the actor. And Peter Brook, the most visionary director of our time, has concluded that 'through the concrete we recognize the abstract'. The refrain persists among all who practise the art of the theatre, and here is a sound guideline for its students.

It is true, as we saw, that Shakespeare prefaces *Romeo and Juliet* with a wholly abstract sonnet in the metaphysical manner:

> Two households both alike in dignity,
> (In fair Verona where we lay our scene)

From ancient grudge, break to new mutiny,
Where civil blood makes civil hands unclean:
From forth the fatal loins of these two foes,
A pair of star-crossed lovers, take their life
Whose misadventur'd piteous overthrows,
Doth with their death bury their parents' strife.

This formal statement rehearses all the themes of the play, the pressure of yesterday on today, the conflict of youth and age, the curse of history and the hope for the future, death set against love and rebirth. Why, after such a prologue, stay for the play? Because, however incisively worded, the ideas have no *perceptual* meaning for an audience. Shakespeare is solemnly ritualizing the action to come, but he is quick to follow the generalities with a fiercely attacking scene which repeats the message with blood and feud and sword-play: actuality follows hard upon the conceptual. In *Macbeth*, Lennox speaks low and in accents terrible of prophecies of 'dire combustion, and confus'd events', but only as a prelude to pandemonium in Inverness. Lear prays for 'poor naked wretches', but with what irony!—since this speech falls immediately before he sees the embodiment of all poverty, nakedness and wretchedness in the person of Edgar in his pretence as a Bedlam beggar: a monstrous variant of the technique, no doubt.

Susanne Langer summarizes: 'Art does not generalize and classify; art sets forth the individuality of forms which discourse, being essentially general, has to suppress' (*Feeling and Form*, p. 327). In drama this individuality must be received as sensory perception which contributes to an image of life.

If there is further proof needed for the modern theory of sensory perception which insists that the mind plays an active role, the theatre experience should supply it. Perception is more than a system of passively reporting information to the brain in order to be sorted, assembled and filed as for a news sheet: an unskilled camera takes a snapshot which only accidentally catches a significant moment. Perception in the theatre selects and orders its data from a mass of impressions both emphatic and fleeting; but activity of mind in the audience is essential to this process. Without the cooperative effort of choice and control by the spectator, in which he reconciles what is gathered from one scene with what is offered by another, or supports or refutes his memory by the observations he makes of word and deed in a context he understands, no assault on his senses would matter, however tremendous. Stimuli from the stage will most usually, of course, be initiated and given initial point by a writer's and director's hand, but the act of perception requires that the world of available information sponsored by the stage is explored like a new environment. Without this, there could be no creative invention to produce the synthesis of learning and recognition, and the excitement of waiting and suspense.

A play exposes its audience to an environment of significant stimuli as soon and as often as it can. A play about civil tyranny begins with the common citizens of Rome; a play about infernal regicide begins with witches. The initial vitality of *Julius Caesar* or *Macbeth* strikes us because we recognize and respond (though not necessarily with approval) to the machinations of witches or the fickle loyalties of the public. The world they inhabit takes on a reality, constructed by painstaking detail.

Such detail continues its work throughout the play, even at moments of great crisis when the fusion of many impressions seems to assert a generality. Why is Cleopatra's crown awry? In her great speech of suicide, 'Give me my robe, put on my crown', Shakespeare has his queen represent all the values of nobility in death while at the same time insisting that her immortality reposes in simple, mortal feelings. On her throne she is majestic, she is fire and air, giving her other elements to baser life, yet baser life lingers on. She thinks of her great Roman general, Antony, as a modest 'husband', and the stroke of death is reduced to 'a lover's pinch'; she prepares to die magnificently, but she suffers a twinge of common jealousy when Iras dies before her and could receive Antony's first kiss; nor in her most glorious moment can she forbear maliciously mentioning her delight at having outwitted Caesar; finally, at the very point of death, she hugs the asp to her breast as if it were her baby 'that sucks the nurse asleep' – the image of motherhood. Even then, and after Charmian's inspiriting finale, 'Now boast thee, death', Shakespeare completes this extraordinary tension between mortality and immortality by the superbly apt detail of the crown. The death scene began with a splendid transformation as she was robed and crowned by her women; it ends with Charmian's observation, 'Your crown's awry.' At her most sublime moment, Shakespeare's Cleopatra remains mortal, her love immortal and human, both.

So it is with the feather and button of King Lear, on which Shakespeare dares all. In his final giant agonies, the King becomes a man again as we strain to see the imperceptible feather stir on Cordelia's lips, he seems human as we reach with Kent to undo the diminutive button that suffocates him, humility in his 'Pray you'. Othello's obsessive role as sacrificial priest is strangely deflated as at the point of murdering his wife he must kiss her and kiss her again. Nor, as he tries to keep an even tenor in his voice at the moment of his greatest resolution, can he refrain from recalling the miserable handkerchief and naming his rival Cassio like a paranoiac. Not only is the girl who is to appear to be a ritual sacrifice within the Christian framework of the play to remain human and real, but so is her murderer. He loves her as he kills her, and as we observe the particulars of their behaviour, we perceive how the distinction between crime and sin is lost.

Stage signals can be subtle as well as violent, but what may seem sensational may work to subtle effect if perfectly integrated in context. The bear that originally chased old Antigonus off the scene in *The Winter's Tale* was a complicated bear indeed. It was, first, no mere verbal figment, no symbolic beast, but most likely the real thing, as Quiller-Couch deduced from the uniqueness of the stage direction and the presence of tame bears in *Mucedorus* and Jonson's *Oberon* (the New Cambridge *Winter's Tale*, pp. 156–7). Only the actuality of this bear could touch both horror and farce at the same time, and thus swiftly and without a word build a bridge between the tragedy of Hermione and the comedy of the Shepherds. By tricking the senses, a bear could make our laughter alarming and our alarm laughable. In contemporary drama, the stoning of the baby in Edward Bond's *Saved* and the unexpected shooting down of the elderly colonial officer at the end of Osborne's *West of Suez* fall equally as sensations which nevertheless gather into one fierce action the argument of their plays. The blinding of Gloucester, violent to the point of nausea though it is, exactly matches our sensation of the rape of Lear's mind.

The value of a stage signal is always determined by its dramatic context. The authority of one perception is proportionate to its consistency with others, and it will penetrate the imagination if it fits.

Even at the level of simple or supposedly simple sense perception we are increasingly discovering that the message which comes through the senses is itself mediated through a value system. We do not perceive our sense data raw; they are mediated through a highly learned process of interpretation and acceptance. (*The Image*, pp. 13–14)

Boulding writes of the nature of cognition, but a similar value system also exists within the play. It is set up by the audience as it seeks the thousand compromises between the conventions of the play and the realities of the life it knows. Certainly, for successful drama, the perceptions received from the stage cannot be independent of all value systems: they must always be bridging gaps, like Antigonus's bear, gaps within the play and between the stage and the audience. Random signals have no place in art.

To support this thought requires a review of all possible dramatic signals, from a shadow on a wall to a quaver in a voice. In act IV of *The Wild Duck*, the afternoon sun goes down as the truth of Gina's past comes out. In act II of *Major Barbara*, Barbara recognizes despair to 'a wedding chorus from one of Donizetti's operas' played by the brass band of the Salvation Army to which she has devoted her life. From the theatre's arsenal of signals, of course, those of the character, his speech and behaviour, are the most evident: we watch Sir Andrew Aguecheek listen to his challenge to Viola with all the vanity of authorship on his face (*Twelfth Night*, III.iv); we hear Kent slip from verse to prose as he adopts the role of servant to Lear (*King Lear*, I.iv). Yet in cold analysis many signals may elude us.

Spatial values in drama are of such a kind: the signals of movement and physical relationship. The Elizabethan playhouse was blessed with a vast three-dimensional stage, so that the representation of space, reinforced by extremes of convention, came easily. A soliloquy was a statement about solitude, and, like an aside to the audience, also a joining of hands. An actor's march of thirty or more feet into the centre of the theatre produced a visual sensation equivalent to a physical encounter with the spectator, much as painting or sculpture causes in the viewer visual associations which 'put us in mind of correlated tactile sensations' (Richard Wollheim, *Art and its Objects*, p. 69).

Troilus's first meeting with Cressida (III.ii) is ostensibly located in an amorous setting ('Walk here i' th' orchard'), but the lover's delayed and uncertain entrance, marked by Pandarus's mocking 'How now, how now?' in complicity half addressed to the audience, is of a more exalted order:

> I stalk about her door
> Like a strange soul upon the Stygian banks
> Staying for waftage.

With Pandarus's cynical eyes we are to follow his giddy step down-stage into limbo, as his thoughts fly to wallowing in 'the lily beds'. The same thirty feet has other meaning when Othello, smarting from his suspicions, orders Desdemona to his side in IV.ii:

> – Bid her come hither: go.
> – Pray you, chuck, come hither.
> – Let me see your eyes: look in my face.

The unhappy wife, still stunned from the Moor's blow in the previous scene, must tread the long journey in fear to the very last foot where he can grasp her and stare hard into her eyes. Space in these incidents is a gift to the player and a boon to the play.

If dramatic space can lend physical impact to a scene, noises off can lend it aural perspective. In *Julius Caesar*, I.ii, Brutus and Cassius initiate their conspiracy when alone on the large empty stage, but as if to suggest that the major action of the play is happening in their absence, Caesar's procession has left them in its wake and their secret words are twice carefully punctuated by a '*flourish and shout*' – the sounds of Caesar's celebration of the Lupercalia. The roar offstage neatly reminds them and us of the wider political situation, with Cassius's somewhat suspect help, prompting Brutus's unease at Caesar's power, pointing Cassius's description of him as a man 'now become a god'. In *Troilus and Cressida*, IV.iv, the lovers have their grief at parting interrupted by the impatient, thoughtless tones of Aeneas and Paris offstage:

> – My lord, is the lady ready?
> – Nay, my good lord –
> – Brother Troilus!

While Troilus explodes with the very speech which bewails 'injurious time', the moment of pain is made real by the martial voices with their implication of 'Make haste! – the war will not wait upon lovers'.

The range of signals is unlimited. If the notes which follow chiefly discuss perceptions in costume, properties and music, the excuse is that these are the neglected areas of literary/dramatic criticism. Any element of stage life can concentrate or dissipate energy within the play. In good playwriting, these three have the power to fuse the perceptions of the audience to an extraordinary degree.

Costume is more important to a play than many critics will allow. Its importance is borne out by the universal theatrical impulse towards assuming a character – what James Laver believes was the essentially dramatic gesture of 'dressing up to dance' evident in primitive role-playing and mimetic magic (*Costume in the Theatre*, pp. 15 ff.). It is also an indispensable element in the ritual of theatrical presentation at any time. We cannot ignore the close attention given to costume by the Greek actors in their impersonation of mythical figures, or the care with which the *Commedia dell'arte* characters were traditionally delineated by their dress, or what must seem the disproportionate amount of money lavished on the wardrobe of an Elizabethan acting company. The great playwrights often use this simple convention of costume with subtle discrimination to further their purposes.

We saw that in *The Master Builder* Hilde Wangel makes her entrance like a breadth of fresh air:

She is of medium height, lithe, of slim build. Slightly tanned by the sun. She wears walking clothes, with her skirt hitched up, a sailor's collar open at the neck, and a small sailor hat on her head. She has a rucksack on her back, a plaid in a strap, and a long alpenstock.

(trans. J. W. McFarlane)

In contrast with Kaia's careful office wear and Aline's mourning black, Hilde brings the vigour of youth with her into the stuffy home with its pinched minds that dark evening; and she brings with her, too, something of the sea and the mountains, with their freedom and light, yet at the same time the disorder and destruction of a demon, of the troll, perhaps a touch of evil. All this suggestion can work easily within the narrow bounds of naturalism. So, too, in *The Seagull*, Chekhov insists that his tired author Trigorin shall not be dressed as a matinee idol, but wear checked trousers and old shoes. These details are to contribute to our sense of the man, and, as the seducer of Nina, maintain a balance of sympathy towards him. He is to be not simply the famous writer attractive to women young and old, but also the rather passive man a little beyond caring, the rather shy man who no longer has much faith in his vocation as a writer, a man who chooses to display no confident public image. By those checked trousers and old shoes, Chekhov allows no facile, melodramatic judgment: costume is part of the Chekhovian experience.

The apparel oft proclaims the man. It is, however, in non-illusory drama, where costume can speak boldly as a truly theatrical convention, that we may expect to find its use overtly presentational, even emblematic. Such well-pointed signals need not be unsubtle: within the convention of the play they can be shaped for an immediate joke, or extended and elaborated into a whole structure of symbolism.

In Genêt's *The Balcony*, the fantasy bishop who opens the play is more magnificently dressed than any bishop would be:

The Bishop, in mitre and gilded cope is sitting in [a yellow armchair]. He is obviously larger than life. The role is played by an actor wearing tragedian's cothurni about twenty inches high. His shoulders, on which the cope lies, are inordinately broadened so that when the curtain rises he looks huge. (trans. Bernard Frechtman)

If we have been impressed by the character's overweening bearing, his grand words and his tyrannical treatment of his whore, within a few moments Genêt has him undressed, and there stands before us a little man shivering in his underwear, 'the normal size of an actor, of the most ordinary of actors', a gasman, no less. It is the beginning of a whole excursion into costume magic by which the pretensions of one social ritual after another is set up for mockery. In scene 12 of *Galileo*, Brecht reverses this process with an equal effect of irony by robing Pope Urban VIII on stage. Even to dress an unclothed character in papal majesty places appearance and reality in startling visual conflict. But the grandfather of these costume tricks is found in Sir John Vanbrugh's *The Relapse; or, Virtue in Danger* (1696) in the scene of Lord Foppington's toilet.

Foppington, the former Sir Novelty Fashion now elevated to the peerage, is shown as if emerging from his bedroom. Straight from sleep, he is of course in his nightgown and wearing a nightcap over his wigless, shaven pate. This is the Restoration fop without the adornment of his ostentatious dress, a fat man strutting across the stage in slippers or bare feet: a social joke in itself, and Vanbrugh devotes the next ten minutes to the absorbing business of transforming him back into fop, full-bottomed wig and all. But first the joke of the undressed fop is played for all it is worth with an exquisitely conceived address to the audience: one apt for the character, exploiting the sheer conventionality of the soliloquy, a perfect moment of incisive theatre. Alone on the stage, Foppington does not see himself as we see him, rather as he wishes to be: the newly created lord, splendidly arrayed and with everyone at his feet that night in the salon:

> Well, 'tis an unspeakable pleasure to be a man of
> quality — Strike me dumb — My Lord — Your lordship —
> My Lord Foppington —

He struts and pomps about the stage like a plucked turkey, receiving his imaginary underlings in all his imaginary finery, every pretension grotesquely revealed to his delighted audience by his nakedness. By the agency of costume, or absence of it, theatre plays a game by which we may measure nobility against its travesty.

In the unreal theatre of the Elizabethans, Shakespeare leaves us in no doubt when he wants a costume to contribute to his stage meaning. In *Twelfth Night*, the Malvolio action properly begins when Sir Toby and his crew are drunk and caterwauling in the night (II.iii). From that time the audience is made sharply aware of two key changes of costume to undercut the virtuous steward's initially decorous, traditionally puritanical appearance. Roused from his sleep by the singing, he is seen as a vision in nightgown and nightcap, so that his haughty lines and manner jar with his risible appearance:

My masters, are you mad? Or what are you? Have you no wit, manners, nor honesty, but to gabble like tinkers at this time of night?

He speaks, of course, as if he were still dressed formally, and so grants us a preparatory glimpse of his pretentions. Preparatory, because the full explosion of the costume joke is still to come. Malvolio is vain, and Shakespeare shows how much through dress. The ruse of Maria's letter is to have him show himself as a fop wearing yellow stockings cross-gartered and with a fixed smile on his unaccustomed face. The sober 'turkey-cock' is transformed in III.iv into a grinning ape of a lover, and in the most ridiculous love scene in drama the audience looks through the different eyes of the gleeful Maria and the melancholy Olivia as he advances frighteningly on his mistress. The lady gives a double-take as she sees him:

OLIVIA: How now, Malvolio?
MALVOLIO: Sweet lady, ho, ho!

The clumsy gallantry, the unpractised flirting, the mixture of self-confidence and stupidity in the costume deflates the romantic illusion in this play yet again.

If Malvolio must wear three costumes, so must Hamlet, Lear and Coriolanus too: such Elizabethan 'shifts' seem to be a practice with Shakespeare. In 'The World of *Hamlet*', Maynard Mack noticed the visual extension given to the Prince's three moods which structure the play. The 'inky cloak' of his opening scene (I.ii) emphasizes his mourning for his father and his melancholy; but the particular insight belonging to the perception is pointed in his lines to his mother:

> ... I have that within which passeth show;
> These but the trappings and the suits of woe.

The antic disposition is marked by the disarray described by Ophelia in II.i – 'his doublet all unbrac'd; / No hat upon his head'. But bearing in mind what 'passeth show', the audience delights in seeing him ironically with the special perspective granted to it, and not as the Court does. Yet a third image of costume is implied for v. i, that of the true Hamlet, the returning traveller, now composed to face his destiny. Such changes, in tragedy as in comedy, in part control the shape of our response.

The whole shape of the *Lear* experience is marked out by the simple sequence of his costumes. His initial strength is visible in the majesty of his robes, and he wears these through his confrontation with Goneril, then Regan, and on to the heath; when he makes his challenge to the Deity, he remains the tyrant and retains his divinity, his soul and his wits. Only at the crisis of the play does Lear try to liken himself to Poor Tom, and it is Edgar's planning his disguise which anticipates the King's new image:

> To take the basest, and most poorest shape
> That ever penury in contempt of man,
> Brought near to beast; my face I'll grime with filth,
> Blanket my loins, elf all my hairs in knots,
> And with presented nakedness out-face
> The winds, and persecutions of the sky.   (II.iii)

It is this 'unaccommodated man', madly acting and therefore acting more than madness, whom Lear sees as himself in III.iv ('Didst thou give all to thy daughters?'). At the bottom of his fortunes, he strips off the 'lendings' of his royalty. He joins Edgar in despair and madness, soon to appear crowned with 'all the idle weeds that grow' (from Cordelia's report in IV.iv), the visual extension of his insanity. His third costume belongs to the chosen moment of the scene of reconciliation with Cordelia (IV.vii), when 'fresh garments' match the music, daylight, human kindness and his new repose. The King's last costume here must be neither royal nor base: he is neither king nor beggar but simple Adam at last.

The progress of Coriolanus is also matched by his costumes. No borrowed robes are these: they reveal the mind and spirit of the man himself. Caius Marcius is at all times the soldier, but it is only in act I and early act II that he wears Roman uniform — it is significant that Shakespeare's great tragic soldier fights his only war at the beginning of the play. He is soon to 'put on the gown, stand naked' (II.ii), presenting himself in that maddening gown of humility, and it is in this that we see the striking contradiction in the two roles expected of the man, soldier and politician. When bright armour is replaced with the coarse cloth of 'humble weeds', posture and voice betray his lack of humility, and we see the impossibility of his satisfying patrician and plebeian both. Finally, in exile in Antium (IV.iv), he is shown 'in mean apparel, disguis'd, and muffled', the servant of his direst enemy. Uneasy among the alien colours of Aufidius and his Volscians, he is seen incongruously again, and we know him to be trapped at the last.

It is impossible to estimate the strength in its simplicity of a costume perception. Macbeth's Porter roused from his drunken sleep may be presumed to be dressing himself as he answers the knocking, adding point to the bantering reluctance which cuts across the tension of Duncan's murder. This business is itself in contrast with the brisk entrance of Macduff and Lennox fully dressed: in their appearance, speech and manner, they bring the daylight with them after the long, murky experience of the murder scene. These two remain in contrast with the equivocating Macbeth who greets them in his careful undress ('Get on your nightgown, lest occasion call us', II.ii). When the action surges forward upon Macduff's discovery of the King's death, alarum bell ringing, voices raised on and off the stage as the castle is roused ('strange screams of death'), the stage filling with shaken figures swirling in confusion, it is the unaccustomed vision of unbuttoned dress and flying gowns ('As from your graves rise up, and walk like sprites') that fixes the image of all hell let loose ('the earth was feverous, / And did shake').

In non-illusory drama, then, costume achieves symbolism with ease. The machiavellian Spaniards of Middleton's masque-like *A Game at Chess* (1624) – notably the Black King Philip IV and the Black Knight, the Count of Gondomar – and the villains of nine-teenth-century melodrama all appear in the devil's colour; Anouilh's pure Antigone stands all in white against the black evening dress of Creon. So in Shakespeare. Isabella the novice in *Measure for Measure* shows her innocence by her white habit, while Angelo attempts her seduction in legal black; interestingly, the Duke who so imper-sonally surveys his subjects' conduct chooses to disguise himself in the neutral grey habit of a friar (I.iii). In *Love's Labour's Lost*, it is not alone the lord Mercade's heavy news of the French king's death that at the end casts a mourning cloud over the irresponsible love-games of Navarre: reality swiftly returns in the décor of the scene itself when each lady dons a 'black gown', as Maria suggests (v.ii). The darker quality of the comedy in *All's Well That Ends Well* is foreshadowed from the start when the play opens with those in the palace of Rousillon '*all in black*', mourning the death of the Count.

In every case, Shakespeare intends an inescapable perception. Our estimate of an effect of costume must always be uncertain, but so powerful a signal cannot help but be vivid and pervasive. In puzzling out the playwright's complex intentions, costume is primary evidence, to be supported by the host of other signs which point to the play's experience.

Like costume, 'props' are not extraneous to the play, although in naturalistic drama, where everything on the stage must support the verisimilitude of life, symbolism borrowed from less realistic con-ventions can seem intrusive, as with Chekhov's somewhat embarras-sing seagull and Miss Julie's over-strident birdcage in Strindberg's play.

In nineteenth-century naturalistic drama, the stage may be cluttered with properties as fussily as in a Victorian room. Even so, the better dramatist ensures that even the smallest adjunct to the stage makes a functional contribution to dramatic meaning. At one extreme it may be Hedda Gabler's ominous pistols, at once the noble symbol of her family's military past, and the menace in her romantic illusions. At another it may be the little green eyeshade which masks Kaia Fosli's modesty in *The Master Builder*, until she reveals her sexual servitude to Solness by the slight gesture of removing it in his presence. In *Ghosts*, Mrs Alving's scandalous collection of free-thinking books sits prominently on her drawing-room table to signify her liberal persuasion and start the debate with Parson Manders. Or in *The Wild Duck*, Hjalmar Ekdal's piece of crusty bread turns to ridicule his account of his daughter's incipient blindness:

Happy and carefree, just like a little singing bird, there she goes fluttering into a life of eternal night. (*Overcome.*) Oh, it's quite heart-breaking for me, Gregers! (HEDVIG *enters carrying a tray with beer and glasses which she puts on the table.* HJALMAR *strokes her head.*) Thank you, Hedvig. (HEDVIG *puts her arms round his neck and whispers in his ear.*) No, no sandwiches just now. (*Looks across.*) Unless perhaps Gregers would like some? (GREGERS *declines.* HJALMAR *still sadly.*) Well, perhaps you might fetch a few, after all. If you've a crust, that would be all right. But mind you see there's plenty of butter on. (trans. J. W. McFarlane)

The quality of his despair, and our cynical view of him, are mercilessly measured out in slices of that same bread and butter.

The master of the seemingly insignificant property is Chekhov, and from *The Cherry Orchard* alone one could muster a lengthy list: Gaev's caramels, Ranevskaia's telegrams, Varya's keys, Anya's brooch, Firs's stick, Charlotta's dog, Dunyasha's powder-puff, and so on – every one a characteristically personal property through which the actor can reveal the character's mood of the moment and his place in the pattern. There is space here to mention only Yasha's cigar as an example of the comic potential in a small hand-property. This amusingly insolent manservant produces his cigar in the abortive love-scene at the beginning of the second act, intending to impress the servant-girl Dunyasha. Smoking a cigar is evidently an elegant gesture he picked up from associating with his betters in Paris, as is hinted when he lights up in response to the girl's pleasing prompt, 'What happiness, though, to visit foreign lands.' Yasha's cigar matches Dunyasha's own attempt to ape her mistress with the powder-puff, but in particular it subversively suggests that he would never think of marrying a girl of her class. It also carries a comic charge, since he is not so familiar with the ways of the upper classes as to know it to be boorish to smoke in the presence of the opposite sex. Indeed, it must appear that he puffs smoke in her face as she presses closer to him on the bench, even kisses her through the cloud. When on the approach of his mistress he brushes her aside, it is Dunyasha's delicious line which places him precisely: she coughs delicately like a lady and says, 'The cigar has made my head ache'. She at least knows how the gentry should behave, while the audience knows more than both of them. By repercussive comic detail, completely envisaged by its inventor, the cigar has exemplified Yasha's pretensions directly and exactly.

In Shakespeare, properties are few, but when one is introduced it will be both an extension of a character's mood as in realistic drama, and a strong, often symbolic, indication of theme. As a dramatic emblem Richard II's crown seems in IV.i to embody the statement of the play:

> Give me the crown. Here, cousin, seize the crown;
> Here cousin;
> On this side my hand, and on that side thine.

This business with the crown represents the action of abdication and usurpation, and Bolingbroke's hesitation, marked by the pause of the broken line, is highly appropriate. When Falstaff parodies the King in *I Henry IV*, II.iv, the audience is comically reminded of the violent source of Henry Bolingbroke's power by the articles the fat knight chooses for the charade: 'This chair shall be my state, this dagger my sceptre, and this cushion my crown.' In a theatre where every property carries meaning, thrones and crowns can be as easily come by as chairs and cushions, and a dagger makes an ironic sceptre indeed.

In the theatre, Richard Crookback woos the Lady Anne in electrifying circumstances, when the coffin bearing the body of King Henry VI is seen to grace the arena of his love-making (*Richard III*, I.ii). The coffin, single upon the empty stage, seems to symbolize not only the murder of Anne's father-in-law the King, whom Richard had killed in the Tower, but also that of her husband Prince Edward, whom he had stabbed to death at Tewkesbury. It is as if Shakespeare perversely sets up an insuperable physical barrier to the success of his courtship in order to render more outrageous his conquest of her honour. Anne finally takes his ring:

Look, how my ring encompasseth thy finger,
Even so thy breast encloseth my poor heart;
Wear both of them, for both of them are thine.

His voice has dropped, and the intimacy of his speech suggests that
he has closed upon her beside the coffin, until he draws her away
on 'leave these sad designs / To him that hath most cause to be a
mourner.' Here is one of the first among several daring transmutations of simple stage properties, until Shakespeare can turn
the whole theatre into a place of execution with a block and an
axe (*Measure for Measure*, IV.iii), transform Desdemona's bed into
an altar for Othello's sacrificial act (V.ii) or have a joint-stool suggest
a prisoner in the dock for Lear to arraign his daughters in a scene
of wild and incredible fancy (III.vi).

Measure for Measure also risks the ambiguously comic use of a
severed head in typically Jacobean style. In IV.iii, it is the Provost
who proposes mercifully enough that the pirate Ragozine's head be
sent to Angelo in place of Claudio's, but it is the omnipotent Duke
of Vienna who oversees the substitution, and by this grim joke has
us share his teasing of the fastidious but distraught Isabella and help
torture the sensualist Angelo. Hamlet's symbol of death is used even
more extravagantly. When he takes in his hand the skull the Grave-
digger throws up and talks of 'poor Yorick' (a stroke of familiar
genius that the death's-head should be a jester's, and M. C. Bradbrook's suggestion that Shakespeare had in mind the recent death of
Tarlton, chief clown to the Lord Chamberlain's Men, would be
especially relevant for the contemporary audience), *we* of course know
that the grave being dug is Ophelia's. But if in Yorick's skull we
see the fair Ophelia, in the Prince's imagination the grisly object
begins to mutate yet another way. 'Now get you to my lady's
chamber ... let her laugh at that': Hamlet has seen in it the image
of his mother and all womankind. Still the skull grows, and just as
Olivier's film had the shadow of Hamlet's own head seem to clothe
the grinning jaws in flesh, so he begins to see himself: 'To what
base uses we may return, Horatio.' One skull grins, but all young,
desirable life squats there. And shall we, with the clowns, laugh at
that? The initial impulse to laugh is confounded by the mixture of
our perceptions. Our eyes on the skull generalize against the specific
references of the sobering voice of Hamlet himself. So it is with
Macbeth's dagger, the real thing at his waist, but the dagger of the

45

mind burgeoning to the speaking imagination. The daggers which kill Duncan are magic before they touch him, as Hamlet is dead before he dies.

In the comedies Shakespeare introduces with care, and sparingly, a few of the simplest props. Some are implicit in the text, as when Toby, Fabian and Maria mimic the business of exorcizing the devil in Malvolio: 'Which way is he in the name of sanctity? (*Twelfth Night*, III.iv). Carrying crucifix, bell and censer, the conspirators mockingly defend themselves against the oblivious Steward. However, in this play it is probably Maria's forged letter to him, that 'obscure epistle of love', which springs to mind. Certainly that simple paper prompts from him more proof than the most delighted imagination could anticipate of that gentleman's inflated self-opinion. The letter also provides the actor with the rarest opportunity for tonal and gestic expression in his part: this is Shakespeare's typical gift of improvisational freedom for his collaborator, a gift which makes the letter scene (II.v) immediate and alive in every performance from that day to this. Yet this same paper lies in Malvolio's path for over fifty lines before he sees it. As he struts like 'a rare turkey-cock', eyes in air, stepping back and forth over that tormenting object, his 'demure travel of regard' all but discovers his bobbing and manoeuvring eavesdroppers before the letter itself. The director who recognizes Shakespeare's visual idiom here will have Toby, Andrew and Fabian come from hiding to replace the letter in Malvolio's path, and even, finally, put it into his hand: the more blind he seems, the more exquisite the comic action. Malvolio's whole ridiculous exhibition is in fact set up in conjunction with what that very letter will elicit from him, with redoubled laughter, when he does find it. It will also be in subtextual counterpoint with his love-scene with Olivia in person, and again with the scenes of his shriving and final comeuppance. In other words, the response of the audience to that wonderful letter has been gauged precisely for its impact on the whole play, for Shakespeare never exhausts one joke without fertilizing the next.

How many devotees of this comedy recall its other major property? Olivia is given a more subtle instrument to reveal a more subtle self-deceiver. This is the veil with which, according to Valentine's report in the first scene, she will hide her face for seven years: 'like a cloistress she will veiled walk'; perhaps also the 'cypress' or black lawn she refers to in III.i. It will cloister her, make a nun of her and religiously inhibit her sexuality. This is the holy object which

Viola will first see (along with, necessarily, all the veils of the attendant ladies of Olivia's court) when as Cesario she doubtfully pleads Orsino's cause (I.v). An audience may be forgiven for questioning the efficacy of this veil before Olivia throws it over her face, since the tell-tale insistence of her repeated questions about the new young man at the gate will already have betrayed her. Indeed, Shakespeare has neatly apprised us of the fact that we are now to witness the confrontation of two amateur actresses. However, Olivia's face is her fortune, as well she knows, and Viola as her rival cannot suppress for long her desire to see the enemy. So, already half spotted with the plague of love, Olivia draws 'the curtain' slowly, teasingly, knowingly, as her words suggest: 'Is't not well done?' This is no nunlike modesty, but the coquetry of a girl behaving quite naturally. From Viola we get a little of the male – and, as the mask slips, a little of the female – reaction: 'Excellently done, if God did all.' The property veil has done its work: what was a mask of mourning, sweetly pretentious, has before our very eyes become the adjunct of a flirt, the property in entirely feminine terms making the sly point that the lady has clearly changed her mind.

Music and song are no less integral to the play experience than the spoken word. It should come as no surprise to Wagnerians that all the great periods of popularly acclaimed drama made use of music – the Greek, the medieval religious cycles, the *Commedia* and the theatre of Molière, the Elizabethan, the Victorian and in this century that of the cinema; only the advent of realism in the theatre inhibited its continuing contribution. Richard Wagner's notion of opera as *Gesamtkunstwerk*, a union of music, drama, poetry and all the visual arts of the theatre functioning together without respite in the flow of the score, would seem to have some justification in history. But where the orchestra of his music-drama was to interpret the stage as commentator and enlarge it into something greater, it tended to usurp it. Each art moves towards its own fulfilment, and the discipline of drama must remain stage-centred.

Nevertheless, our sense of the complete communication of drama is limited if we do not acknowledge the force of instrumental and vocal music. One has only to switch off the sound during an 'action sequence' in a film to see what a poor thing is left. Music guides and extends an audience's feeling and imagination, and can be dramatically complex, sometimes working structurally, sometimes

47

assuming the function of an unseen character underscoring the meaning of a scene.

Oriental drama is universally musical, and in the West the Greek *tragoidia* and the Christian liturgies suggest that the ritual origins of our drama are also essentially musical. In his introduction to *The Wakefield Mystery Plays*, Martial Rose finds a musical pattern within the cycles equivalent to that of the Church:

> The liturgical roots of the mystery plays are clearly seen in the persistence of the identical church music at the various dramatic climaxes: God creates the world, and the angels sing the *Te Deum*; Gabriel hails Mary at the Annunciation; the *Gloria* is sung by the angel to the shepherds; the souls delivered from hell burst into a joyful *Salvator Mundi*; as Christ rises from the tomb the two angels sing *Christus Resurgens*. (p. 48)

An angel choir was always at hand, and medieval instruments could promptly create an harmonious heaven or a cacophonous hell as needed. Processions and entries are accompanied by instruments: when Herod in the *Ludus Coventriae* passes into hell-mouth he is received with a fanfare, whereas the ringing of bells marks the Nativity and the Resurrection.

Song may even outline the form and unity of a pageant play, and in *The Second Shepherds' Play* of the Wakefield Cycle, the contrast between the songs indicates how the shepherds pass from the misery of a northern winter to the wonder and joy that follows the descent of the Angel.

> 1 SHEP: ... By the rood, these nights are long!
>   Yet I would, ere we rode, one gave us a song.
> 2 SHEP: So I thought as I stood, to mirth us among.

The hardship of the wintry Yorkshire sheep country is established, and the pageant stage thereby localized. The medieval street audience would recognize in the complaints of the shepherds their own poverty and hunger, until the actors unexpectedly end the first movement of the play with a song to cheer themselves up:

> 1 SHEP: Let me sing the tenory.
> 2 SHEP: And I the treble so high.
> 3 SHEP: Then the mean falls to me.

The song also provides a transition in mood from the 'realism' of the play's beginning to the fun of the middle, but when the joke of Mak's sheep-stealing is over, as unexpectedly the Angel appears and sings *Gloria in excelsis* with these comforting words:

> Rise, herdmen hend, for now is he born
> That shall take from the fiend that Adam had lorn;
> That warlock to shend, this night is he born.
> God is made your friend now at this morn.

With the promise and the song in their ears, they start on their way to Bethlehem — a good step from Yorkshire! — trying to sing the Angel's hymn:

> Be merry and not sad — of mirth is our song!

When they make their final exit, they sing a carol at the tops of their voices:

> To sing are we bun:
> Let take on loft!

The singing shapes the meaning and feeling in the action as well as a Greek chorus, and the medieval citizen did not doubt that God's grand design for the Christian life included both the suffering and the reward: the play is a *divina commedia* in little.

It may seem improper to jump some 600 years to the far more complex drama of Bertolt Brecht, but it is instructive to find a sophisticated modern dramatist also freely employing song in order to unify his play and evoke the response he wants. Throughout *Mother Courage* Brecht uses ballads simultaneously as a choric and structural device and as an ironic means of distancing his audience. Brecht is also determining the total style of his play by the frank music hall manner of songs sung *at* the audience. The songs interrupt the action to make a point, yet have the immediacy of ballads. Brecht moreover asks his actor to sing or speak *against* the music in a way which will 'set the text forth', not merely accompany or heighten it. At the same time, the musicians are *seen* to be playing, separately lit. So in *The Caucasian Chalk Circle*, the Singer sings of Grusche's perils coldly and unemotionally as she mimes them on the stage. With tacks in the hammers in Paul Dessau's piano for *Mother Courage*, his discords, flat tones and choppy rhythms seem to make the music a speaking character in itself, urging its own comment, forcing a criticism.

'The Song of the Fishwife and the Soldier' in scene two of *Mother Courage* performs several functional tasks. On a divided stage it is sung first by the simpleton son Finnish Eilif in the Commander's tent, and then, for a clever effect of ironic echo, by Courage herself from the Commander's kitchen where she is working. Childishly proud of his new reputation as a soldier, Eilif sings the first verses while performing a barbaric sabre dance to the naive refrain, 'It's the life of a hero for me!' At the same time his words prophesy his own death:

> A gun will shoot, a knife will knife,
> You will drown if you fall in the sea.

The two aspects of the Thirty Years' War, those of military chauvinism and the futile sacrifice of human life, merge in the song. The audience is further alerted to the young man's stupidity by seeing Courage on the other side of the stage more and more furiously plucking a chicken, until she can contain her impatience no longer. Beating out the rhythm noisily with a spoon on a pan, she takes over the singing in a new key and in her raucous voice.

> And the fishwife old does what she's told:
> Down upon her knees drops she.
> When the smoke is gone, the air is cold:
> Your heroic deeds won't warm me!

> (trans. E. R. Bentley)

The mood of the scene has abruptly changed, the war dance stops, and Eilif recognizes with amazement the voice of his mother. He runs to embrace her with joy, but for his pains she boxes his ear: thus the audience interprets her attitude to his heroics. The scene ends in this flat anticlimax, denying the sentimentality of a family reunion. The dialectical message Brecht intends is contained in the change in tone of the song, and the contradictions in the two meanings of the singing, of the stage and of the war are resolved in Brechtian irony.

Shakespeare uses music and song in a comparable variety of ways. In *Othello*, IV.iii, for example, Desdemona's willow song is as functional as Eilif's song of the war. This popular contemporary ballad seems so casually introduced at the height of the play's tension, yet it is accurately timed to have us reflect upon the human values at the crisis of Othello's tragedy. This is the woman who is about to die, and the song sharply reminds us that the adulterous monster of the Moor's ugly imagination is still indeed the feminine creature we met earlier in the play, and the little details of her broken singing make her immediately familiar and realistic. Meanwhile, the willow is an emblem of unrequited love, and the words of the song itself tell of a poor Barbary whose case ominously corresponds with Desdemona's own. Thus the more sweetly she sings it, the more the audience is compelled to anticipate the scene of her death.

In the comedies especially, Shakespeare's songs are wholly functional, and it is often their conspicuous incongruity that makes the point. When Bottom's friends desert him in the moonlit wood (*A Midsummer Night's Dream*, III.i), the song he sings to restore his self-confidence – this is the only time in the play that it deserts him – must seem quite unlikely:

> The woosell cock, so black of hue,
> With orange-tawny bill,
> The throstle, with his note so true,
> The wren, with little quill.

As Shakespeare decided upon the lines to give his arch-fool wearing Puck's ass's-head, it was no doubt with his tongue in his cheek that he asked himself what could be more appropriate to a woodland scene than a pretty lyric about bird-songs. With his theatrical ear, however, Shakespeare also heard the coarse voice of his clown unmusically croaking the delicate words, his voice as unlike a bird-song as anything imaginable. The trick he is about to play on his audience, of course, is an exact extension of this aural joke, for also on the stage, we remember, is that most delicate of feminine immortals, the Queen of the Fairies asleep with Puck's love-juice in her eyes. Bottom's song will rouse her to a perfectly lyrical iambic pentameter, a song in itself:

> What angel wakes me from my flowery bed?

All this is in prelude to the most ill-matched love encounter in the play, that between Titania and her new changeling, the man who looks and sounds like an ass. It is possible humourlessly to conceptualize this scene with Jan Kott as the depiction of female animalism, or to place it in the pattern and spirit of the rest of the play as one more comic representation of amorous fatuity. Bottom's song is as ridiculous as Titania's mannered verse, and against such verbal nonsense so ill-assorted an alliance can reach the height of human incongruity.

In the comedies a song always coaxes the audience to an extended perception of character or situation. Orsino's sentimental song in *Twelfth Night*, II.iv, 'Come away, come away, death', is marked by Feste's gentle mockery of its excess by the plaintiveness of his rendering:

DUKE: There's for thy pains.

CLOWN: No pains, sir, I take pleasure in singing, sir.

If we doubted Orsino's self-love before, the melancholy self-indulgence of a song that belongs to

The spinsters and the knitters in the sun,
And the free maids that weave their thread with bones

must now set us right. With Andrew Aguecheek's song, II.iii, Shakespeare had no need to exercise himself with such hints, since Sir Andrew's actual presence as the Lady Olivia's most foolish lover speaks for him. Yet, in the mere reading, how many have not found the sweet sensuality of

O mistress mine, where are you roaming?

as 'mellifluous' as Andrew declares it to be? On the stage the foolish knight who could not accost Maria when invited, and the traditional demand of the song to seize the moment,

Then come kiss me, sweet and twenty:
Youth's a stuff will not endure,

are in ludicrous counterpoint. As Andrew swoons to hear his love-song, the vacant expression on his face and the stoup of wine in his hand will marvellously reflect upon Orsino's parallel stupor in the next scene.

Instrumental music is also regularly used by Shakespeare for dramatic pointing. In every instance it seems as if he is experimenting with a musical effect in order to call upon his audience's perceptiveness. In *Troilus and Cressida*, they are sarcastic trumpets which urge the reluctant warriors to do battle in their unending war. In *King Lear*, V.iii, three trumpets sound for Edmund's formal challenge to the world to dare question his title, until we unexpectedly hear Edgar's trumpet in answer afar off like those in Beethoven's *Fidelio*, the effect of which is strangely inspiriting 'when our suspense is keenest', as Granville-Barker noted. In *The Winter's Tale*, V.iii, the mock-magic of Paulina's comedy priestess is delightfully enhanced by the music which punctuates the clipped phrases with which she wakes the 'dead' Hermione. The more awesome the sound, the better the jest, since the audience guesses more than Leontes that the statue lives by a pre-arranged miracle to test his repentance, and so assumes Paulina's careful mysticism to enjoy the role of magician itself.

In the exceptional case of *Coriolanus*, music even suggests a framework for the play's ironic development. Caius Martius's glory after the battle of Corioles is received with an excessive amount of noise — the repeated flourishes of cornets, trumpets and drums — in spite of his own disclaimer and warning:

> May these same instruments, which you profane,
> Never sound more: when drums and trumpets shall
> I' th' field prove flatterers, let courts and cities be
> Made all of false-fac'd soothing. (I.x)

Their martial sounds grow increasingly questionable, and the audience is fully intended to hear the implicit criticism, for a moment or two later flourishes are heard again, and Volumnia his mother unwittingly proclaims,

> These are the ushers of Martius:
> Before him he carries noise;
> And behind him, he leaves tears. (II.i)

Soon this same man will be a traitor in exile. When the news arrives that Volumnia has persuaded him to return to Rome, again Shakespeare exploits music for its irony:

> Why, hark you!
> (*Trumpets, hautboys, drums beat, all together*)
> The trumpets, sackbuts, psalteries, and fifes,
> Tabors, and cymbals, and the shouting Romans,
> Make the sun dance. Hark you! (V.iv)

Jubilation continues to the end of the scene ('*music still*'), and Volumnia ('our patroness, the life of Rome') and the Roman ladies make their last appearance to full orchestra, the sound barely dying away as Aufidius is heard making plans with his conspirators in Corioles for the treacherous slaying of Coriolanus. The play offers a unique example of music as mockery, underscoring the fatal implications of the action. This play ends appropriately with '*a dead march sounded*'.

It is evident from such instances that dramatic perception has little to do with formal literacy. Words in the theatre are heard and not read, which may explain why the Elizabethan theatre flourished in an age when the majority were illiterate: sops for the groundlings are an academic myth. Marshall McLuhan takes a typically extreme position and even denies his 'literate man' the power to integrate his perceptions, arguing that he undergoes a separation of his imaginative, emotional and sensory life. Had words truly this power of limitation, we might mistrust literacy indeed; nevertheless, the integration of the perceptions is what the theatre habitually demands, and for a theatregoer in the throes, a purely verbal apprehension is not enough. McLuhan offers this:

Literate people think of cause and effect as sequential, as if one thing pushed another along by physical force. Nonliterate people register very little interest in this kind of 'efficient' cause and effect, but are fascinated by hidden forms that produce magical results. Inner, rather than outer, causes interest the nonliterate and nonvisual cultures. And that is why the literate West sees the rest of the world as caught in the seamless web of superstition. (*Understanding Media*, p. 251)

This generalization about nonliterate people may well apply to the imaginative fusion of impressions which occurs in the theatre. The drama of logical cause and effect, character and motivation, with which Ibsen is associated, is atypical of what the theatre has traditionally done. The plays of the Greeks, of Shakespeare, of the *Commedia* and Molière were plays of hidden forms, magical results and inner causes, and were thoroughly caught in the seamless web of superstition. Today, with a renewed impulse towards 'poetry of the theatre', the theatre of the absurd, the theatre of cruelty and other manifestations, the stage is assuming its accustomed, illogical role.

McLuhan also believes that consciousness is not a verbal process, not analytic like language, but an inclusive *Gestalt*. 'Consciousness is regarded as the mark of a rational being, yet there is nothing lineal or sequential about the total field of awareness that exists in any moment of consciousness' (p. 87). The psychology of perception tells us that we respond equally to words, images and imageless thoughts, but that perception is only *completed* when 'meaning' results from the activity of memory and judgment working upon the mosaic of sensations and assumptions. *Gestalt* theories assume that the *organization* of the whole perceptual field is more important than the sensations themselves. Such special stimuli as shape and movement, which assist the making of a configuration, become central, and psychology believes that a *Gestalt* is more than the sum of its parts – like a poetic metaphor whose ingredients fuse to create a *tertium aliquid*. The forces existing within the perceptual field assume power which, like poetry, can acquire the properties of a magic beyond mechanics.

In this century we turn to visionaries like Edward Gordon Craig, Antonin Artaud and Peter Brook for the precepts of dramatic theory. Craig in his *Second Dialogue* (1910) believed that theatre must be made out of three elements: *action*, by which he meant 'gesture and dancing, the prose and poetry of action'; *scene*, by which he meant 'all which comes before the eye, such as the lighting, costume, as well as the scenery'; and *voice*, by which he meant 'the spoken word or the word which is sung, in contradiction to the word which is read'. Of these three, he insisted that 'one is no more important than the other, no more than one colour is more important to a painter than another, or one note more important than another to a musician'.

With the publication in 1938 of Artaud's *Le Théâtre et son double*, the same strain of thinking was heard again. In discussing the Oriental theatre, Artaud arrived at a concept of theatre which he suggested was 'prior to language', a state of theatre which could choose what it needed from music, gestures, movements and words, a 'pure theatrical language' which he defined as the 'language of the *mise en scène*'. He also believed that the fusing of the elements of dance, song and pantomime created a sensation of richness and spirituality: 'The most commanding interpenetrations join sight to sound, intellect to sensibility, the gesture of a character to the evocation of a plant's movement across the scream of an instrument' (trans. M. C. Richards, p. 55). The Occidental theatre, he thought, needed to take lessons from the Balinese in 'everything that makes theatre, everything that exists in the air of the stage, which is measured and circumscribed by that air and has a density in space — movements, shapes, colours, vibrations, attitudes, screams'.

In 1968, Peter Brook urges the argument a step further. He identifies the world of good drama and theatre as an artistic extension of living. The theatre can be divorced from life, because it is so different; but the demands of the medium, the unique concentration of the art, involve everyone in immediate aesthetic choices of immense variety, although all directed to one end:

In the theatre there is no such separation [between art and living]: at every instant the practical question is an artistic one: the most incoherent, uncouth player is as much involved in matters of pitch and pace, intonation and rhythm, position, distance, colour and shape as the most sophisticated. In rehearsal, the height of the chair, the texture of the costume, the brightness of the light, the quality of emotion, matter all the time: the aesthetics are practical. (*The Empty Space*, p. 89)

Drama for the audience too is living under pressure, consciousness heightened as by drugs, perception directed as by the sentence of time.

To return. Dramatic perception involves a capacity beyond literacy, a sensitivity to the kind of amalgam of the arts natural to the theatre. It has its reference points simultaneously in life and on the stage, and acts through all the arts just as their incipient elements persist in everyday life.

This may shock those who believe that when the thematic imagery of poetry appears in drama it is of the highest importance for an understanding of the play. The impact of imagery studies on the understanding of Shakespeare has been out of all proportion to the function of imagery in the theatre. Sometimes, indeed, imagery may lead us astray unless we first recognize its theatrical context. For an obvious example, we remember how Romeo greets Juliet at Capulet's ball with that remarkable sonnet,

> If I profane with my unworthiest hand,
> This holy shrine, the gentle sin is this. (I.v)

The imagery of saints and pilgrims falls within the literary mode of courtly love, but it is an error to accept it on this level. On the stage the eye belies the idealism of the words, since the same words describe a pattern of gesture and behaviour that scarcely fits either saint or pilgrim: in the acting the sonnet seems more like a series of cues for a flirtation. Not only does Romeo take Juliet by the hand and lead her out of the dance, but he kisses it and then her lips, and these not once but twice. Juliet, for her part, is no shy virgin, and on

> Saints do not move, though grant for prayers' sake

she actually takes the initiative while denying her power to initiate: in all this her wit is quite equal to Romeo's. The whole rhythm of gesture in the piece, while exactly planned for performance, also makes a mockery of the Petrarchan convention, eyes contradicting ears.

Shakespeare is obviously not unaware of the force of verbal imagery. The essential step is to assess its stage contribution by testing it against corroborative dramatic elements surrounding it. When Gloucester asserts that he is 'tied to th' stake' (*King Lear*, III.vii), the verbal concept matches what the eye sees. Verbal and visual are mutually dependent, reinforcing each other. When the pervasive imagery of animals in *Lear* ceases during his reconciliation with Cordelia, the picture of happy prisoners is extended imaginatively with

> We two will sing like birds i' th' cage, (v.iii)

and the imagery here shapes the experience itself, changing the tenor of the action.

In *Othello*, the emerging imagery of hell and the devil carefully traces the condition of the Moor's mind, and at the same time it guides the actor in his behaviour and objectively shapes the play. Proof of the significance the playwright attached to the word 'devil' must be sought in the physical theatre, and it is found in that ugly incident in which Desdemona is struck (IV.i). As Iago stands in silence, with the audience watching his handiwork take its effect, the wife in her innocence is still pleading with Lodovico for the reinstatement of Cassio, the very name a knife in Othello's side. Her thrice repeated, increasingly querulous 'My Lord?' is finally felt as a gesture of affection, almost a declaration of her unquestioning love: 'Why, sweet Othello?' But upon this, the Moor turns and strikes her: 'Devil!' The blow and the word are one, equally shocking. The immediate climax of the scene's physical action brings in its train the long-drawn climax of Satanic thinking: Othello now speaks in Iago's idiom and at the same time embodies his spirit. The blow and the word show us the hero mad, possessed of the Devil, like a puppet doing the work of the still, silent Iago. The action itself is thus thematic, as our eyes and ears insist. As for our response, this is redoubled beyond reason by the device of an on-stage audience. For the assault upon *us* is made through the Venetian senator Lodovico. The degradation of the Moor and his wife is done by public exhibition and is seen through public eyes as a new height of horror. We are given insight into the minds of the two principals while simultaneously we see the whole issue in perspective, see it through the sane, misunderstanding eyes of a stranger. Eyes, ears, mind, two minds, three: the point is exquisitely felt.

Dramatic effects are thus effects of a multifarious medium, not alone of the 'content' of the play. The medium is a hybrid of the most delicate pedigree, transforming the simple verbal meaning of the text, generating new energy through our senses, recreating experience irresistibly.

For a last familiar instance, this time from comedy, the reiterated verbal references to madness in *Twelfth Night* are amazingly integrated into the action. While Olivia is displaying her crazy infatuation with another girl in the person of Cesario, Shakespeare confronts her with an even more bizarre *amour* in Malvolio:

> Go call him hither. I am as mad as he,
> If sad and merry madness equal be. (III.iv)

In the Folio, the Steward makes his entrance two lines before this, so that as we hear Olivia's lines we see those yellow stockings and cross-garters, the smile stretching his pained face as he simpers down to her. The moment is indeed one of 'very midsummer madness', and shortly Toby and his gang will come to exorcise the devil possessing Malvolio. This madness persists and rises to a pitch, until the twin Sebastian is brought back into the action in order that his new, sane eyes shall show how delirious the world of Illyria has grown. When Andrew, confident from his earlier engagement with Cesario, attacks Sebastian in mistake (IV.i), only the audience knows the whole truth: the joke is on everyone, and even Feste finds that 'nothing that is so, is so'. To Andrew's surprise, Sebastian retaliates with normal but unexpected vigour, and in a daze unwittingly speaks for the audience: 'Are all the people mad?' Olivia also mistakes Sebastian for Cesario, and in caressing tones ('Be not offended, dear Cesario') offers her enticing invitation to a complete stranger. By this contrivance, the audience sees the stage actually enact the self-delusion of love, and again Sebastian speaks for the play as a whole:

> What relish is in this? How runs the stream?
> Or am I mad, or else this is a dream.

Happily for Olivia, he again obeys his normal instincts and responds readily to her overtures. Again we see a comic presentation of love as something helplessly irrational: what a mad, mad world, my masters! The verbal notion of lunacy seems a proper echo to the stage picture, for like Sebastian the audience in the theatre may briefly experience the madness itself.

In good theatre words support the eye, eye reinforces ear. The spectator gives attention, gains conviction, is ready to contribute. An involved audience stores up a suppressed energy, the process of involving an audience being a way of generating strength. The particulars of the stage mix in unknown ways to energize the audience, extend its perceptions, make it hyper-conscious, brilliantly aware.

In the communication of the theatre, there are two kinds of energy, that created by (i) a fusion of impressions and (ii) an opposition of impressions, a fission which precedes the final fusion. The first, the mutual illumination and expansion of perceptions, is the most common. At the crisis of *Oedipus Rex*, the Messenger from the palace speaks at length, and in the most vivid terms, of the blinding of the King: it is a speech to gorge us.

> He struck at his eyes – not once, but many times;
> And the blood spattered his beard,
> Bursting from his ruined sockets like red hail.
>
> (trans. D. Fitts and R. Fitzgerald)

The picture is painted as luridly as possible in preparation for the announcement of the Messenger,

> Look, the doors are opening; in a moment
> You will see a thing that would crush a heart of stone.

We strain to see, and are shocked by the blood-stained mask that Oedipus now wears. The Chorus with its cry and song of horror teaches us how to respond, until the King himself takes up the tune: 'God! God!' Impression builds upon impression for the crisis of the play, together working upon the audience in a manner befitting a transporting religious ritual, fusing idea and sensation, uniting play and audience.

In Shakespeare's *The Winter's Tale*, III.ii, Hermione stands trial and is condemned before her lord, her plight made more painful by the oracle's assertion of her innocence which follows, the almost immediate announcement of her son's death, and finally her fainting. A due excess, no doubt, for the turning point of the play.

In Shaw's *Man and Superman*, Jack Tanner, sensing his danger, tells Ann Whitefield aggressively: 'The boa constrictor doesn't mind the opinions of the stag one little bit once she has got her coils round it.' To this she responds with a laugh and shamelessly throws her feather boa round his neck. He retreats, scandalized, whereupon for the boa she substitutes her arms: 'I suppose what you really meant by the boa constrictor was this'. The image, the property, the gesture – together they explode in a delightful overstatement in which his weakness and her strength are suddenly manifest.

Nevertheless, the fusion of impressions verbal and visual, their accumulation and overloading, is the most subject to abuse, and without the relief of irony may even set up resistance in the auditorium. It is liable to the kind of excess associated with such limited genres as heroic tragedy, melodrama, sentimental comedy, the theatre of cruelty and others. Only farce can take the strain of unwarranted extravagance on the stage – the preposterous is what makes it farce. Tragic drama is more than an over-charged emotional experience : it is a thinking one too. There is more comedy in *Romeo and Juliet* than in the best of Ben Jonson, because Shakespeare was concerned to undercut the sentimental simplicity of his source. His tragic heroes after Romeo have their virtues and vices of character uniquely mixed in order to produce a response richer, more objective and yet more involving. On the other hand, the best comedies of Shakespeare and Molière all introduce a disturbing thread of paradox and irony, a sobering note that inhibits our freedom to laugh. In his criticism of Shakespeare in 1777, Maurice Morgann began to probe in this direction when he found that the 'principles of this disagreement are really in human nature'.

At the root of our fullest involvement, therefore, is a deliberate disjunction of impressions, often what we see working against what we hear, or vice versa; often what we feel working against what we think. Lear has no sooner invoked his poor naked wretches than we see Poor Tom; but no sooner do we see Poor Tom than we recall that this is Edgar the impostor in an outrageous impersonation. The contradiction produces what Marshall McLuhan in discussing mixed media called 'hybrid energy' (*Understanding Media*, p. 57), the fission leading to the unpredictable results of newly released energy. Here follow some simple examples of aural/visual interaction in Shakespeare, the playwright who above all had the gift of being able to

> amaze indeed
> The very faculties of eyes and ears.   (*Hamlet*, II.ii)

In *A Midsummer Night's Dream*, fancy and dream are theme, structure and technique. The image is of love confounding reason by the puckish acceleration with which lovers chop and change partners, and the charming young people of the play, all equally deserving of a happy outcome, must be ridiculed to keep a moonlit festival. Is there a psychological, or even a physical, difference between one and another of the men or the girls? Indeed, after act I, an audience quickly forgets who was courting whom. At the start, Hermia is described as 'fair' and 'gentle', but so is Helena. In anger, however, Lysander calls Hermia an 'Ethiope' and then a 'dwarf' – adding 'minimus', 'bead' and 'acorn' for good measure – and Helena calls her a 'puppet' (III.ii). Hermia, angry in her turn, calls Helena 'tall' and a 'painted maypole'. Complexion and height are clearly irrelevant to their passions, for we otherwise learn that the girls 'grew together/Like to a double cherry'. Between the men also there is nothing to choose: 'Demetrius is a worthy gentlemen' – 'So is Lysander' (I.i). Chaucer's Palamon and Arcite may have been a source for some of this, but not to the extent that the differences between them would destroy the visual symmetry of Shakespeare's quartet of lovers. The point of the quarrelling is, surely, that they are essentially alike. Not that they are Plautine twins, but that the personal abuse is merely grasping at reasons, which are the more ridiculous if the differences are imperceptible. The huge joke is one of fission, so that Puck's idea, 'Jack shall have Jill', is borne out, no matter who, and what we see belies what they say.

> But all the story of the night told over,
> And all their minds transfigur'd so together,
> More witnesseth than fancy's images,
> And grows to something of great constancy;
> But howsoever, strange, and admirable.   (V.i)

Where the dramatist is a master of his craft, we discover a most pertinent interrelation between what the eye sees and what the ear hears: the eye generalizes what the precision of language particularizes. When in act II we watch Macbeth's pantomime as he contemplates the murder of Duncan, or relives it before his wife, or dissembles before Macduff, there is not a detail of it we do not have in our mind's eye, although we do not see the deed itself. As we listen to Hamlet's blasphemous contemplation of suicide, 'To be or not to be' (III.i), the cause and the context of his speech are visible as he speaks, with Claudius and Polonius shuffling behind their arras and Ophelia piously at her orisons. Words and spectacle are interdependent, Claudius's presence casting a political light, Ophelia's a religious one, on the speech.

What is Shakespeare's particular purpose in that lively scene of civil unrest, the familiar opening to *Romeo and Juliet*? He is simply taking the first of the verbal concepts of the sonnet-prologue, which states the purpose of the play in tidy metaphysical verse, and proving his point on our senses. The scene is a documentary demonstration of how people 'break to new mutiny', how wars erupt; it is an exercise in escalation. Sampson and Gregory make an entrance through the Capulet door and begin the slow, tense, if jocular, exposition as they swagger downstage. Tension increases and the jokes become sinister when two rivals are seen to enter through the Montague door, and the entrance of their betters promptly encourages the servants to take up arms. Interestingly, the stage direction of the First Quarto has the cue for Benvolio's entrance before that of Tybalt, even though Gregory first spies the approach of Tybalt his master. This is surely in order that an unbelieving Tybalt shall come upon Benvolio trying to stop the fighting: 'What, drawn and talk of peace?' Now with three duels on the stage, 'three or four Citizens' may join the mêlée. The intervals between entrances grow shorter as the pace quickens and the status of the combatants rises. An officer of the law arrives on the scene, only to make matters worse: 'Clubs, bills and partisans, strike, beat them down, / Down with the Capulets, down with the Montagues'. Old Capulet from his bed ('in his gown and his wife') cuts an incongruous figure as his lady cries after him, 'A crutch, a crutch, why call you for a sword?' But he has seen old Montague, and that is enough. The stage is filled with figures and the fighting has been seen to accelerate.

Now the 'neutral' eye, as McLuhan has it, open, associative, generalizing, synthesizing, shows us the broad image of young and old, high-born and low, the earnest and the ludicrous, all at war. With some difficulty the Prince from the balcony (the most obvious place from which to control the busy stage and be seen by the audience) calls them — and us — to attention. Thus with the change of pace, of tone and of verse the 'hyper-aesthetic' ear receives the ritual statement of the law. The ear ignores the panting figures and the smeared blood of the wounded, for the moment excludes all but the Prince, and Shakespeare returns to words to point his scene:

> If ever you disturb out streets again,
> Your lives will pay the forfeit of the peace.

The formal declaration is coloured by what the eye has seen, and the action leaps on. The inclusive, scanning eye complements the exclusive, focusing ear, a balanced arrangement for a complete, sensory impact.

So Shakespeare weaves his sensory web with our responses. At moments of great intensity and crisis, he pulls out all the stops to elicit our most incisive and defined response: eye and ear interact and we are captive, participating, enthralled.

Shakespeare gains such facility in superimposing the verbal and visual in cooperation or contradiction, that such a scene as that of Othello's eavesdropping (IV.i) inhibits any final analysis of the spectator's response. From the moment of Iago's direction to the Moor,

> Stand you awhile apart,
> Confine yourself but in a patient list,

the audience is made ready to witness two simultaneous actions, that of Cassio thinking of Bianca against that of Othello thinking of Desdemona, both engineered by Iago's double-talk. (In the unreal convention of the Elizabethan stage, there is no question of Othello's hiding, as so often on the proscenium stage; he remains visible.) Now with a certain inexplicable, vicarious pleasure, we play Iago's malevolent part for him:

> Now will I question Cassio of Bianca,
> A housewife that by selling her desires
> Buys herself bread and cloth.

As in his manner throughout the play, he draws an embarrassed audience into his scheme with his hissing lines.

As he shall smile, Othello shall go mad.

Othello now sees Cassio as his wife's lover for the first time, as Iago did once before when Desdemona landed on Cyprus, and, with Iago's coaching, we see how Cassio's every word and gesture can be misconstrued. The harmless 'Alas, poor caitiff' and 'Alas, poor rogue' are terrible to hear, accompanied as they are by Cassio's light laughter, for we interpret it all through Othello's appalled eyes as he sees his assumed rival laughing. We watch their two performances, Iago between them carefully throwing a line or two over his shoulder to Othello, beckoning his victim closer. Othello tenses when Cassio relaxes as he mimes his encounter with Bianca:

I was the other day talking on the sea-bank with certain Venetians, and thither comes the bauble, by this hand she falls me thus about my neck.

Cassio and Iago are two soldiers together: Cassio's arm 'thus' about Iago's neck, he seems to demonstrate to the unseen witness how Desdemona seduced him, and the eavesdropper gets his 'ocular proof' in a way that leaves him not a shred of dignity. But Shakespeare has not finished the torment. Iago, for whom everything is going well, receives a shock: Bianca herself unexpectedly comes in search of Cassio. She could spoil the whole scheme. Indeed, she is not at all the fawning courtesan of Cassio's pantomime: it was all a man's idle talk. When she flings something in Cassio's face with an oath, it is the devil's own luck for Iago that it is the very handkerchief Othello gave his wife:

There, give it your hobbyhorse, wheresoever you had it, I'll take out no work on't.

Iago hurries Bianca and Cassio away before his fortune turns, and Othello is spared his torture.

When Iago has his three pawns together, Othello is furnished with the demonstration he wants, and we with the experience of the misconstruction he makes. The pert behaviour of the real whore with her familiar manner and her painted face supplies Othello's picture of Desdemona, although we know the two women are poles apart. Bianca's appearance shows us the falseness of Iago's tongue and the error of Othello's brain. In Pirandellian fashion, Shakespeare progressively offers us several discordant images of Desdemona – the one we knew, the one Othello imagines, the one ridiculously enacted by

Bianca. In a moment the true Desdemona will return to measure the monstrousness of the mistake. It is commonly assumed that audiences can respond to only one effect at a time. 'Where the eye has too much to see the ear cannot listen', writes a leading director. But when the eye has something pertinent to see, especially a visual ambiguity, the ear hears with a sharply directed attention.

The notion of hybrid energy is simply that of putting two and two together, an activity thrust upon an audience in the theatre by the collision and blending of a play's many component parts – the totality which Artaud found in the dance and song of the Balinese theatre. Any art must engage its audience, and a play draws upon the peculiar powers of any or all of the arts to work its effects, verbal and lyrical, visual and kinetic, often juxtaposing what would otherwise seem inimical. The created energy is an activity of the imagination, and the two-and-two may add up to more than four, a mystery which Coleridge long ago recognized. The mystery is also that of what Kant called the productive imagination, creating art which has the nature of a living organism.

The *Gestalt* school of psychology would seem to support the romantic philosophers. The organism of the play's image in the mind of the audience is not of haphazard growth, nor are the elements of the stage like wild and uninhibited children, but they are carefully nurtured and trained to come when they are called and only acceptable when they have proved that they belong in the orderly mind. In the theatre we experience an isomorphic response to all that is going on, reproducing the life of the play by admitting only those perceptions which have passed our test. We do not allow Ophelia to show signs of pregnancy merely because of the circumstantial evidence of her association with Hamlet: the imagination draws upon the world of the play before that of real life, and refuses to destroy the established pattern of the characters' integrity. Or again: rather than reject the Witches in *Macbeth* and the Immortals in *A Midsummer Night's Dream* out of common disbelief, we allow them to sweep us into the metaphysical regions of a murderer's mind or lovers' fantasy.

The workings of stage *Gestalten* confirm earlier assertions that the text is only a plan for drama, and is equivalent at best to the scenario of a film or the choreography of a ballet, never the film or the dance itself. The familiar example is the exact union of the verbal and physical images of the degradation of Richard II before Flint Castle (III.iii). Beleaguered by Bolingbroke and his followers below on the 'base court' of the platform, the King is played on to the castle walls (the balcony) with the sounds of the 'brazen trumpet' and, from Bolingbroke's own lips, the regal strains of

> See, see, King Richard doth himself appear,
> As doth the blushing discontented sun.

When Richard takes up the dirge,

> Down, down, I come, like glistering Phaeton,

he ritualizes his abasement further by the reiterations of 'base court, where kings grow base' and 'down, court! down, king!' and leaves his high place to join his enemies on stage level. His descent matches the picture of Phaeton hurled from his chariot, and the total image of the sun king's downfall prefigures the abdication of the chronicles and the fall of a tragedy prince in a simple sculptural and musical design.

An astonishing dramatic *Gestalt* of impressions is created, as Glynne Wickham has recently reminded us in *Shakespeare's Dramatic Heritage* (pp. 214–24), by the scene of the discovery of Duncan's murder in *Macbeth*, II.iii. Wickham is chiefly concerned to trace how an Elizabethan audience would associate the entrance of Macduff with the harrowing of hell of the mystery cycles. Among his other tasks of providing for a passage of time and inducing laughter, Macbeth's Porter must present himself as 'porter of hell gate', so that Macduff's knocking on the stage door becomes the knocking on hell-gate, Inverness castle becomes hell, Macbeth the devil himself, and Macduff's performance a secular version of the harrowing of hell. But for all its mastery, the scene follows the common Shakespearian pattern of a demonstrated concept. The Porter's amusing contemporary examples of equivocation in a farmer, a Jesuit and a tailor, so casually jumbled together, are the clever comic prelude to Macbeth's own equivocation when Macduff and Lennox briskly bring in the day after the murky night. Macbeth's halting greeting, his hesitation before the door which conceals his treachery, his ambiguous answers,

> LENNOX: Goes the King hence today?
> MACBETH: He does: he did appoint so,

66

are a stage extension of the Porter's meaning. While the responses of the intruders are normal, reflecting those of the spectator, Macbeth, tense though he may be, wears his mask like the master of evil himself.

After the exit of Macduff to seek the King in his chamber, an exit which simultaneously adds to the suspense, Lennox magnifies the image of catastrophe with his tale of 'lamentings heard i' th' air' and 'dire combustion and confus'd events'. This provides the second, more pointed, prelude. Shakespeare supplies the cue for noise and pace,

> O horror, horror, horror,
> Tongue nor heart cannot conceive nor name thee,

and all hell seems indeed to break loose. The cacophony of a medieval hell scene is heard again upon the call for alarum bells — hell's bells, no less — and from the cries of startled figures running in confusion across the stage in a variety of undress. Macduff talks of seeing 'the great Doom's image', an explicit reference to the Last Judgment, and Lady Macbeth with her hair down is daringly given lines which recall the dead roused to meet their Maker:

> What's the business?
> That such a hideous trumpet calls to parley
> The sleepers of the house? speak, speak.

The sequence of rapid entrances which follows focuses on the cool, Satanic Macbeth himself with the blood of the grooms on his hands and steeped in the colours of his trade. In so animated a scene Shakespeare typically expands his concept by calling on all the elements of his medium.

The fullness of a fine dramatic imagination is revealed by the experience of performance, and through the varied stuff of the theatre a spectator can grasp at a greater man's image of the world. In his introduction to the *Marat/Sade* (1965), Brook argues that Shakespeare gives us more, moment for moment, for our money; free verse on an open stage 'enabled him to cut the inessential detail and the irrelevant realistic action: in their place he could cram sounds and ideas, thoughts and images which make each instant into a stunning mobile'. None of this could happen unless the stage satisfied those requirements of genre and style unique to each play, and to this matter we now turn.

3
Genre and style

Probably the most elusive and most neglected, but also the most essential, element of a play is its style. Style is the *sine qua non* of successful communication in the theatre, and therefore of the drama's affective meaning. Comic style is especially the source of numerous literary misunderstandings, but any style can be deceptive and treacherous. What if an audience feels for Orsino and laughs at Viola? laughs at Gloucester and feels for Edmund? – any of these is possible, and each response is determined absolutely by the manner of performance.

Who might not think from Olivia's generous reference to Malvolio's treatment in *Twelfth Night*, 'He hath been most notoriously abused', that this is not Shakespeare's cue for the playing of the Steward's part? But no actor has ever managed to play him for tragedy, not even Irving. Even when Charles Lamb wished upon him tragic overtones in his account of Robert Bensley's performance in his essay 'On Some of the Old Actors' – 'I confess that I never saw the catastrophe of this character, while Bensley played it, without a kind of tragic interest' – Elia was following his fancy and not the performance, as Sylvan Barnet has proved. The truth is that nothing in the style of Malvolio's turkeycock playing or its context permits this response, unless it is one engendered deviously outside the theatre. The image on the stage of what is properly a caricature of Puritanism acting the great lover should be enough to forestall any extra-theatrical judgment. Whoever had feelings about a caricature?

We may think of plays like *II Henry IV* and *Measure for Measure* as touching the real, but we should be on our guard for scenes which name characters like Doll Tearsheet, Mistress Quickly, Jane Nightwork, Mistress Overdone and Kate Keepdown. And how did Susan Grindstone and Nell get into the Verona of *Romeo and Juliet*? And how did Touchstone meet Jane Smile?

There is no true value judgment that can be appropriately made

68

about a play before it is rendered in the style it calls for. Not only is style the basis of meaning, as any regular literary criticism of verse or prose would insist, but in drama content and style are inseparably related by what we may call 'the audience equation'. Every play's style, in kind of speech and movement or degree of thought and feeling, is measured from the norm of the intended audience's actual behaviour, an extension of real life. The stage is always a mirror of the audience, although only an impossibly magnifying or reducing lens would enable the spectator to see in it his exact image. The difference between the reality of the audience and the unreality of the stage is the 'aesthetic distance' which sanctions the conventional signals and percepts of the performance. It is this that is the essential source of the play's style.

This is not to say that the play's style may not also be affected by the physical circumstances of performance: the giant arena of the Greeks both dictated and matched the stature of their tragic drama. But which came first, the tragic scale or the tragic concept? The ritualistic Aeschylean drama would not perhaps have emerged as we have it without its mighty auditorium, nor without its religious profundity, both working together.

At another extreme, the grotesque distortions in the dramatic images of Beckett or Ionesco are due to the unlovely content of their plays, replete with shocking concepts which would be unacceptable if played in any naturalistic manner. The style of *Endgame* or *Le Roi se meurt* necessarily widens the gap between the actuality and its image to enable the stage to communicate. Whether consciously or unconsciously, the playwright adopts his style much as a convention, to enable meaning to be transmitted, perceived, accepted and experienced, prior to judgment.

The tragic genre and style have received the most attention over the years, even though it is probably true that tragedy is the simplest dramatic kind to understand and perform. It need not take up much space in this study: today it is no longer heretical to suggest that tragedy is a lost genre. It has been occasionally embarrassing that grandiose conventions misappropriated from the ancient Greek theatre produced the fustian of later tragedy. When the ritual and religious sharing of the tragic experience ceased—quite early, probably before Euripides — then formal tragedy, as a dramatic composition dealing with a fateful theme, one in which a noble person breaks a divine moral law and brings about his downfall, could not long

69

survive. Croce warned that Shakespearian tragedy was a misnomer, for every play of his was different in tone and style. The truth may be that every age catches its own quasi-tragic mood, until the genre itself is indistinguishably blurred with the style the age practises.

Tragedy after the Greeks often borders on sentimentality and melodrama because of its magnification of feeling, but when its creatures endure to the limits of belief, it can truly enlarge its image of man in the imagination, and so show those who normally think small what greatness human kind is capable of. 'Nature makes use of the instrument of human fantasy to pursue her work of creation on a higher level', said Pirandello. None of this need have anything directly to do with individual human psychology. Nor need one say anything of happy or unhappy endings, of noble heroes, nor of the requirements of an inevitable future identified as fate or destiny: these belong to those themes which are prompted by the religious occasion of the play. Yet this urge towards magnification is the source of the tragic style, for it must lift itself into the realms of myth and legend which finally refuse to be measured by actual experience. In Susanne Langer's words, 'Tragic drama is so designed that the pro- tagonist grows mentally, emotionally, or morally, by the demand of the action, which he himself initiated, to the complete exhaustion of his powers, the limit of his possible development' (*Feeling and Form*, p. 357). The style which makes this exhaustion possible to accept is also exhaustive in special ways, and is immediately recognizable for its scale. Speech and gesture are immoderate, costume and mask preposterous. Giant figures challenge their gods, kill their brothers, their mothers and fathers, their offspring, even marry their mothers and put out their own eyes. Nothing more in this direction is imagin- able.

Only a revival of ritual would bring similar fantasies alive again for an audience. Spectators must anticipate the excesses of tragedy and wish them revealed in known ways; knowing them once, they will know them again. Today the study of Greek tragic style is there- fore chiefly a social study. Its enlarging elements of song and dance and gargantuan mime matched the homogeneity of the crowd within the Greek amphitheatres seating their tens of thousands. The colossal themes of the plays needed the help of a multiple chorus playing in the centre of the audience, teaching it how to think and feel, con- stantly reassessing the situation to the point where the choric songs *were* the play and the action of the masked players merely illustrations.

In *The Iceman, the Arsonist, and the Troubled Agent* (1973), Robert Heilman has refused to acknowledge the obituaries posted to commemorate the death of tragedy. Friedrich Dürrenmatt, for example, believes that we may not expect a return to the tragic impulse associated with the great age of Greek drama. The tragic figure is one who must display personal power, Dürrenmatt argues, and power today resides in something impersonal, automatic and essentially inhuman. By extension, man is too small and insignificant to have tragic stature in modern drama: in our time he is fit only to be a clown.

Heilman insists, however, that the tragic sense persists tenaciously, and it exists in modern drama as an unmistakable tendency. In trying to recognize the tragic accent in a variety of modern plays, he happily finds it necessary to redefine the loose concept of melodrama. This by-product of his study is immensely valuable in itself. As it is used in contemporary dramatic criticism, the term 'melodramatic' implies a form radically different from its mixed theatrical origins in early Victorian times, and is now no longer the harlot among the genres. Heilman's contribution is to lend her a little more respectability.

With his general lack of vigour and direction, modern man may be small, and smallness hardly meets Aristotelian criteria for high tragedy; moreover, the sense of being small encourages self-pity, which works against tragedy and promotes its uneasy counterpart, melodrama, a drama of pathos centred on sick characters. But Heilman refuses to allow the facile thinking that would always place the melodramatic below the tragic in the hierarchy of dramatic virtues: they are contiguous in that both offer different perspectives on the catastrophe that follows from human evil. This seems so much more helpful in squaring theory and practice than an automatic reversion to ancient standards.

Big men feel the imperatives that make for great drama, but insofar as they remain men, human passion divides them. De Montherlant believed that it is in man's nature to be attracted by opposites: 'It is his destiny always to be moving between polarities, between sensuality and chastity, for instance, between reason and unreason, between courage and cowardice. The central fact of human existence is inconsistency, an inconsistency that must be embraced, if one is to know the truth of life.' Tragedy and melodrama explore the region between animality and sublimity, and so discover our glorious and inglorious limitations. This schizophrenia is the source of hubris, the spirit of I-can-get-away-with-it; it is also the source of self-knowledge in our

71

representative on the stage, and therefore the source of engrossing drama.

It is disarming of Robert Heilman to treat tragedy as a neutral generic term and apply it to good plays and bad: he believes that tragic self-knowledge can emerge as either something mechanical or a triumph of insight. Conscience can be exhibited polemically, pointing to the evil in others and generating a drama of the I-told-you-so variety, or it can teach by evaluating the self, appalling as this process may be. If it proposes a narrower character for judgment, the audience is more likely to dissociate itself from him; but the greater the character, the more we feel his touch, his kinship, and we yield to him, overwhelmed. The former treatment leans towards melodrama, the latter towards tragedy; but there is an occasion for both.

The conflicts that make for the solemn in drama express themselves differently in tragedy and melodrama. The tensions that engage an audience are perceived in melodrama as between people set against each other, whereas in tragedy the fight is all within. While the stresses of melodrama can unite an audience against a common enemy and a common evil, those of tragedy can be more painful because they are difficult or impossible to resolve. You can throw rotten eggs at the villain of melodrama, a gesture impossible in tragedy, whose villain hides inside your own head. One passage of Heilman's argument invites quotation at length:

In tragedy, dividedness is inner; in melodrama, it is outer. In tragedy, one potentiality in man is pitted against another; in melodrama, man is pitted against another man, or against certain other men, or a social group or order, or a condition, or even against events and phenomena. In melodrama, one attacks or is attacked; it is always a kind of war. One may be fighting against injustice or for survival. In tragedy, good and evil are a private matter, whatever their public repercussions; in melodrama, they are a public matter, though they may have private repercussions. In tragedy, two alternative but incompatible goods may struggle for the soul; in melodrama, they struggle in society or in the world. But in melodrama we tend to conceive of the struggle as between good and evil; we convert the other man's good, which we do not embrace, into an evil so that we may have the vigor to contend against it. (p. 46)

Macbeth is a bad man who must be resisted, but he is also a deeply troubled man torn by conflicting compulsions which an audience can understand intimately. Thus the impulses of melodrama can coexist with those of tragedy.

The usefulness of these distinctions can be seen. The characters of Tennessee Williams tend to destroy themselves and would become the simple disasters of inadequate personality, lacking tragic stature because too pathetic. When he internalizes the drama of Blanche of *A Streetcar Named Desire*, Williams sounds a note of tragic self-recognition of immense appeal, although this is not at all intended to make the play a tragedy. By contrast, Willy Loman of Arthur Miller's *Death of a Salesman* remains a victim of his own inadequacy and obsolescence, and his story remains essentially pathetic; it also enforces that strong sense of community disorder which touches tragedy another way, although still without making the play a tragedy. In spite of these sober elements, the large infusion of the darkly satirical in both plays suggests that this quality suits their true intention. It is in the nature of criticism, as well as of drama, to wish to make orderly patterns of human experience. The joys of criticism, such as they are, turn upon the desire to abstract abstractions from what is particular and concrete, and nowhere is this crime against artistic endeavour so blatant as in the theoretical discussions that surround tragedy and the tragic.

Dissension begins with the other genres, most of them lightly labelled 'comedy'. For it is a silly accident of critical history that most plays which are not tragedy are taken to be some form of comedy. The rightful opposite to tragedy is not comedy, but farce, which may explain why tragedy and farce touch each other at so many points. Tragedy sets its picture of life at one extreme, farce at the other: both deal in excess. Tragedy creates a man who can sustain more than ordinary men, and places him in a situation which demands more of him than ordinary life would; the distortion and magnification are such as to cause wonder almost to the point of disbelief. The diminishing action of farce, which also demands more of its people than ordinary life would, results from having characters who are too small to cope with odds as overwhelming as those which faced Oedipus or Hamlet, and it too causes wonder to the point of disbelief.

If the genre at the other extreme from tragedy is farce, the *style* at the other extreme is naturalism. Naturalism may almost be thought of as a genre itself, since in the drive to make what is fictitious seem real, all moods tend to have the same stamp, and there is little distinction between tragedy and comedy in plays like *The Wild Duck*, *The Cherry Orchard* or *The Glass Menagerie*. The literal imitation of life on the stage seems to break the first rule of the theatre, that the spectator must use his imagination. We remember Dr Johnson's sagacity: 'It will be asked how the drama moves, if it is not credited. It is credited with all the credit due to a drama.' The naturalistic movement in the theatre of the West sought to close the aesthetic distance between the stage and the audience. It went as far as playwright and players dare go without a loss of dramatic form and direction, and without obscuring the perceptual signals of the stage.

Happily, the details and signals of naturalism are those that are perceptible to the average observer in real life. If Hjalmar Ekdal of *The Wild Duck* supports a shabby gentility in his clothing, or Tesman in *Hedda Gabler* lacks dignity in his joy at getting his slippers back, the spectator need draw upon no convention of theatre to understand the point. The naturalistic playwright would seem to have an easy task, needing to worry himself little about style.

This, of course, is untrue. The number of good naturalistic plays since *The Cherry Orchard* of 1904 is few. The style of naturalism acquires stature, purpose and universality not only in the accumulation of a thousand visual and aural details, but essentially in their careful choice and arrangement for perceptual meaning. Hjalmar's shabbiness is set against his dream of fame as an inventor; Tesman and his slippers are juxtaposed with Hedda and her personal ambition. Naturalistic detail is of no consequence unless it stands the only test: does it work to build a bigger statement than its trivial surface seems to permit? What Brook calls 'the flash of quick and changing impressions' – the subtly arranged hints of meaning which fall into place because they are conceived as inherent, rooted in character, situation or milieu – 'keeps the dart of the imagination at play'. The spectator rebuilds the conception. In the work of Chekhov especially, the 'series of impressions is equally a series of alienations: each rupture is a subtle provocation and a call to thought' (*The Empty Space*, p. 72). The well-wrought naturalistic style is both a method and an end: it must seem real and at the same time be purposeful. The genre therefore is fraught with the contradictions which arise from having to do two things simultaneously.

The contradition between means and end effects every department of realistic theatre. For the author, the necessity of seeing life at close quarters and reporting it in minute detail, individualized for a closely observed society and a psychological depth in each character, demands from him extraordinary industry. Yet these same demands are dangerously limiting too, for they deny the stage its traditional quality of generalized and universal reference. So we find that the lesser naturalists are narrow and short-lived, and that the greater soon resort to methods of symbolism: in order to widen their statement they employ extraneous allusion, or an imposed pattern of action or arrangement of characters. Occasionally the use in a fine play of an obtrusive property, like Chekhov's tiresome seagull, is actually self-defeating. Dialogue which is intended to seem colloquial and casual can at the same time strain for a subtextual significance and direction; when naturalistic speech seeks universal reference by manipulating language, perhaps the appropriate term for this quality should not be 'subtext' but 'supertext'. The flirtation of Strindberg's Miss Julie with her father's valet is thick with implied assertions about all men and all women, until a cheeky irreverence between mistress and servant on Midsummer's Eve in blown up to be an ubiquitous war between class and sex. Nevertheless, the basic requirement of naturalism, that it should tell the truth about people, can result in engaging an audience in the finest way: for truth, we know, is always dialectical, and true naturalism insists upon the spectator's objectivity.

For the actor playing naturalistic drama in the picture-frame we should feel a certain unease. He lost the direct contact with his audience that existed for 500 years before; he was set apart in a magic box and in another world, divided from the spectator by a wall of darkness; he lost his use of vocal range because in frontal acting all distance is equalized to that of the furthest spectator. All these factors turned the Victorian actor's advance in status into a retreat in range of skills. Yet there was compensation, for the genre demanded a psychological depth in character-playing, a three-dimensional quality of other-sidedness and personality development, an awareness of the imaginary past and a planting of roots in a particular community, and, above all, ensemble playing.

These new skills attracted and held the audience, not merely by the swing toward identification of spectator with character, but also by the need to understand the comprehensive human ambivalence in each character's every word and gesture, the ambivalence of not being entirely good or bad, heroic or villainous. Lopakhin crushes Mme Ranevsky by suggesting she should sell her cherry orchard, yet does so only out of his compassion for her. Gaev seems to make a fool of himself by making a self-defensively ironic speech to a bookcase, and yet every word he says obliquely reflects his heartfelt feeling toward his home, his past life and the traditional culture the orchard stands for.

Illusion of reality in complex characterization can transmit dramatic meaning of a truly moral kind, forcing the spectator to hesitate before condemning: we suspend judgment on the idea of mercy-killing by Mrs Alving, or on the 'murderess' and suicide Hedda Gabler, or the seducer Trigorin, or the prostitute Blanche Dubois, and in each case the arrest of response measures the essential quality of energy in the play. The best of the naturalists secured a degree of conviction in feeling and belief, and with that conviction came a new objectivity of response to the ambiguities of verisimilitude. Chekhov persuaded his audience to pass through the arch to identify with his muddled families by tricks of realism, only to thrust them back gently to sanity by his comic tricks of undercutting.

Yet at the same time the exclusion of the audience from the peep-show denied it the ritual involvement belonging to the theatre until the nineteenth century. The religious or social ritual changed to a consciously societal posture, Shaw's temple of fashion. It is interesting to speculate how the audience for Victorian melodrama sought to compensate for its loss. The heavy villain would challenge the house with his threats, working out of the frame until he received the mighty roar of condemnation he sought, and at that both actor and spectator would be content that rapport had been established so that applause could follow. Hissing and applause are not really in opposition here, although this kind of participation is a poor substitute for the shared experience of a dramatic ritual, since the laughter which could also follow the hissing betrayed its superficiality.

In his autobiography *A Life in the Theatre*, Tyrone Guthrie declared that the theatre was more interesting 'not the nearer it approached "reality", but the farther it retreated into its own sort of artifice' (p. 180). The bulk of the world's drama falls neither into the microscopic, photographic ways of naturalism, nor into the ritual manner of high tragedy. Most kinds of play combine some signs of human life to make the stage relevant to the world of the audience, with some degree of stylizing to set free the theatrical imagination.

This is one reason why all manner of dramatic modes have been lumped into the loose dramatic genre called 'comedy'. The category

is so wide as to make nonsense of theory. It embraces plays as far
apart in manner and purpose as the *Lysistrata*, characterized by an
Aristophanic madness and the broad playing due to its first conditions
of performance, and *The Way of the World*, exquisite with Congreve's
fine detail of intonation and gesture. It embraces the uncertain mood
of *Troilus and Cressida* and the quasi-tragedy of *The Wild Duck.* The
disintegration of a comic style is to be observed between Wycherley
and Sheridan, yet *The Country Wife* and *The School for Scandal*, the
one cynical and the other essentially sentimental, are both perfect
'comedies' of their kind.

In our schools and colleges the most ignored form of dramatic communication is that of farce, which could be considered 'pure' comedy.
At least, the term describes the mode of derision that lies at the heart
of comedy. The reason for our failure to meet the challenge of farce
is not far to seek: not only is the farcical element difficult to perform, but it also eludes analysis.

The nineteenth-century critic Francisque Sarcey knew from practice that 'All farces congeal when they are transferred from the stage
to a cold description of them', and the farceur Marcel Achard in his
introduction to Feydeau's *Théâtre Complet* echoed him when he said
that trying to write about farce was 'somewhat like being in the
position of the clockmaker who has to dismantle the carillon on
the Strasbourg cathedral' (translated M. D. Dirks). Both are echoing
an old complaint, first heard from Colley Cibber in his *Apology*:

Why the tragedian warms us into joy, or admiration, or sets our eyes on
flow with pity, we can easily explain to another's apprehension: but it
may sometimes puzzle the gravest spectator to account for that familiar
violence of laughter, that shall seize him, at some particular strokes of a
true comedian. How then shall describe what a better judge might not
be able to express? The rules to please the fancy cannot so easily be laid
down, as those that ought to govern the judgment.   (chapter v)

Cibber seems to argue that the 'decency' or decorum of style which is
observed in tragedy makes it manageable, compared with the 'almost
unlimited liberties' by which farce may 'play and wanton with nature',
As so often, Dr Johnson sums the matter up: 'Nothing is more hopeless than a scheme of merriment.'

Farce does not elude analysis in terms of its mechanical plot and
characterization, which are generally implausible anyway and arguably of least importance to its effect. The style of farce, or more

precisely its degree of stylizing, is inseparable from its working, and it is this key element which is hardest to recognize in reading and all but impossible to describe. The usual critical tools do not help, and our ignorance of its true mechanism – the way it energizes an audience – may be the reason why we undervalue it. In spite of its sorry critical history, we have still to explain why farce is the most ancient and perennial form of drama, and one which the playgoer would least gladly part with.

Both the problem and the solution lie in the degree of unreality an audience permits its stage. This is not a matter of sophistication, for we find that farce flourished as well in the primitive village drama of eleventh-century Korea or the street theatres of ancient Rome, as in the bedroom romps of the Aldwych of the 1930's or the Whitehall of the 1950's. It seems that the wilder the vision of the play, the wider must be the aesthetic distance created by its style of writing and presentation. How else to explain the abiding elements of violence in the *lazzi* and improvisation of the *Commedia dell'arte*? How else to explain the grim mode of such outstanding farceurs as Samuel Beckett and Eugène Ionesco? The degree of unreality is not the measure of value in comedy any more than it is in tragedy; but it is a guide to style, and thereby traces our imaginative level of apprehension and participation.

The value lies in the liberation of the spirit that the unreality permits. To submit a simple example: caricature is a form of stylization of human character which releases and stimulates free laughter. If it undermines seriousness, there is no limit to what may be accomplished once the process has begun. This episode from *Twelfth Night*, I.iii is perfectly shaped for its joke, but it assumes its full force as comedy only when it is perceived as part of an extended pattern signalled by laughter.

SIR ANDREW: Bless you, fair shrew.

MARIA: And you too, sir.

SIR TOBY: Accost, Sir Andrew, accost.

SIR ANDREW: What's that?

SIR TOBY: My niece's chambermaid.

SIR ANDREW: Good Mistress Accost, I desire better acquaintance.

MARIA: My name is Mary, sir.

SIR ANDREW: Good Mistress Mary Accost.

SIR TOBY: You mistake, knight: accost is front her, board her, woo her, assail her.

Genre and style

Laughter comes easily with Toby urging Andrew on to the point of exasperation, Maria the bland receptacle of each advance, and Andrew each time paying his addresses more apologetically, but each time falling more deeply into error. Sir Andrew has just been announced as a new wooer for the hand of the lady Olivia and 'as tall a man as any's in Illyria'. However, upon this early acquaintance he shows himself a poor figure of a lover, and Toby's lesson on how to court a lady reflects upon another self-proclaimed Lothario, the Duke Orsino. The farcical laughter here encourages the perception that Andrew's halting inadequacy is no worse than the Duke's courtly resort to music and sweet beds of flowers. The play deals out a whole series of unsatisfactory lovers, Orsino, Andrew, Cesario and Malvolio, each a travesty of, and 'funnier' than, the last. But of course they all reflect each other.

The impulse behind comedy is often towards burlesque, and the same kind of farcical parody is evident when Viola as Cesario mouths words to Olivia in III.i:

Most excellent and accomplished lady, the heavens rain odours on you.

Is this nonsense what a girl thinks a fine lover should say? But Viola does not wish to succeed in losing to another woman the man she loves. In some part her mask as Cesario is slipping. Sir Andrew Aguecheek, however, finds Viola's words just what he needs to furnish him as the accomplished wooer:

ANDREW: That youth's a rare courtier; rain odours, well.
VIOLA: My matter hath no voice, Lady, but to your own most pregnant and vouchsafed ear.
ANDREW: Odours, pregnant, and vouchsafed: I'll get 'em all three all ready.
OLIVIA: Let the garden door be shut, and leave me to my hearing.

Unluckily, first Viola, then Olivia, turn a cold shoulder on poor Andrew just as he is about to make use of his new technique of courtship. (It is interesting to note that the Folio does not have him exit here, and from III.ii we learn that Andrew seems to have watched the rest of the scene, implying that we are to see Olivia's humiliating chase of Cesario through Andrew's astonished but mistaken eyes.) At any rate, Andrew's simple admiration for Viola's bogus language guides us to the truth about her deception. Even then, the greater joke is on Olivia, for these same amorous terms serve well enough to woo an infatuated lady who is ready to accept at face value any pretty words from the one she loves; and the joke is redoubled when we remember this to be another woman.

Viola as Cesario is playing a game of love as falsely as may be, and this in turn prepares us for the most grotesque love scene of all — that between Olivia and Malvolio. As in *A Midsummer Night's Dream* and *As You Like It*, Shakespeare practises his irresistible stratagem of mixing his wildly different kinds of lover, Titania with Bottom, Rosalind/Ganymede with Phebe: fairy with clown, realistic girl with literary stereotype. His romantic comedies leap from the lyrical to the farcical, from one style, one level of comic apprehension to another — all to illuminate the world of true and false feeling which is the subject of these comedies.

Perhaps we should cease to take as our norm for comedy the subtle moments of witty interplay in Shakespeare. A quicker way to the truth of comic style is found in the humbler theatre of the *Commedia dell'arte*, whose 200 years of roaring life teach all the lessons about stage communication. If Aristotle guides us towards the elements of tragedy, the *Commedia* guides us towards those of essential comedy. Its forms embrace the work of the Elizabethan clowns and the puppet figures of Samuel Beckett, the caricatures of Jonson's *Volpone* and those of the films of Chaplin or Jacques Tati. We might heed the advice of Evert Sprinchorn in his introduction to Giacomo Oreglia's book *The Commedia dell'Arte*: 'Think of the Marx Brothers; add their customary accomplice, the buxom dowager Margaret Dumont; and you have before you a good modern equivalent of a small Commedia troupe. Wherever they found themselves, at the races, at the circus, at the opera, they remained the same' (p. xi). This kind of constellation of characters represents within the tradition of comedy something permanent and universal.

It is to court failure for a 'straight' actor carefully trained in character interpretation to try to apply his skills to a brilliantly flexible line like this of Lear's Fool:

May not an ass know when the cart draws the horse? Whoop, jug, I love thee.

When Touchstone is confronted by a lusty Audrey, his line implies a whole performance, a *burla*, in which Touchstone's intelligence meets its match in the amorous physical capers of a hoyden:

> We shall find time, Audrey; patience, gentle Audrey!

Such lines are cues for clowns. They are written in the spirit of improvisation, and take on their full force and meaning only when treated elastically and played whole-heartedly to the audience.

In the search for the frame of style within which comedy works, the *Commedia* found and perfected those elements which kept its troupes alive for a longer time than any other in theatre history. The improvisational element is one: the source of the actor's greatest contribution in any drama. By this is not meant a freedom to invent haphazardly, but it can include building upon the written word. The actor works within an implicit discipline granted by a known audience. Upon improvisation depends a play's immediacy, the audience's sense of 'now' that distinguishes the live theatre from its mechanical substitutes. For the audience, improvisation supplies the necessary quality of freshness and spontaneity which insists upon its concentration in its experience of the play, constantly anticipating, constantly surprised. Even in such details as whether the husband will appear at the door at an inopportune moment, or whether a cigarette lighter will work when it is struck, the skill of the actor lies in making the obvious unexpected. For the actor, the quality of improvisation in performance 'keeps the mind continually upon the stretch', as Chuzzlewit's Mrs Todgers would say. He reacts at once to the spectator, to his fellow actor and to the situation like a ball ricochetting across a snooker table, where all the balls assume new patterns when one is on the move. For the actor, comic business and dialogue are not a matter of memory but of imagination. So the comedy grows anew each night, and relevantly, for each new audience.

This applies equally to a closely-written comedy like *The School for Scandal*. In all essentials, the spirit of occasion is no different. When Lady Teazle is concealed behind Joseph Surface's screen, Sheridan supplies a line to compel her husband Sir Peter to advance upon her hiding-place:

> and you can even make your screen a source of knowledge – hung, I perceive, with maps.

The spectator is petrified, sharing the moment intensely with Joseph and Lady Teazle, yet able to enjoy their discomfort. The terrible moment of suspense implies the question, will Sir Peter walk round

the screen to examine its other side before Joseph can drag him away?
He saves the situation to our mixed disappointment and relief, but
in that moment improvisational theatre is at work, Peter deliberately
bumbling on, his spyglass closer to the edge of the screen, Joseph on
his toes, mouth agape, fighting for words: both are playing their
audience for all they are worth. Had they been Pantalone and Harlequin, no doubt Pantalone would have dodged behind the screen
to discover his Franceschina, who would immediately have had
to react by running to the front, and a typical chase would have
ensued around the screen. Perhaps: for the predictable must also be
unexpected.

The other energizing element of the *Commedia* is its use of the
mask, and here again the effects are so fundamental as to be almost
mystically beyond analysis. The mask, or what this implies of the
essential impersonation in all acting, is basic in some degree to all
drama, but in classical comedy it is the indispensable key to its
successful working. The clown dons his mask or his make-up as
automatically as he adopts the style of the comedy; indeed, the mask
of character is one mark of the play's style. Behind his mask the actor
hides his normal personality in order to assume the new one in the
spirit of the play. The mask releases his powers as an actor, and at the
same time it releases the audience from their earth-bound reality,
enabling the mirroring of drama to take place. The mask enlarges
performance, directing by its visual statement the activity of the
whole body, and in turn the responsive body, growing bolder, enlarges the mask. Paradoxically, the mask both fixes character and
allows it to burgeon in the imagination. It grants immediate recognition to the character and the instant freedom of role-playing for the
actor and role-sharing by the spectator.

When occasionally the modern dramatist has ventured into modest
experiments with actual masks (in Pirandello's *Six Characters in
Search of an Author*, 1921, O'Neill's *The Great God Brown*, 1926,
Anouilh's *Thieves' Carnival*, 1938, Brecht's *The Caucasian Chalk
Circle*, 1948, Genêt's *The Blacks*, 1958, and Arden's *The Happy
Haven*, 1960), in every case the paradox of simultaneous distancing
and involvement has electrified the theatre. The mask is a most
powerful catalyst, even today, and it returns style to the theatre as
soon as it appears.

The farther drama leans towards farce or tragedy, the more the actor

assumes the 'mask'. It lends impersonality to the experience, frees the
spectator from the need to sympathize, frees him to laugh, all without the tiresome restrictions of everyday life. A play needs only a
germ of probability to begin, but once begun it can soar with the
madness of hysteria or race faster than nightmare. Since at the
extreme the movements of either tragedy or farce border on dance
and its tones on song, the language of colloquial prose dialogue can
barely satisfy the needs of its stage. Yet, either in tragedy or in farce,
the actor immersed in its spirit stands outside his role while seeming
to believe utterly in its reality: both are the drama of the straight face,
while flamboyance is reflected in every department of the play –
garish costume, extravagant décor, improbable make-up.

Only in farce, however, are we at a loss when we look for purposes, or demand some moral evaluation of its final cause. Almost all
style, how can farce serve a moral end? Amoral in itself, how can
we pass any judgment upon it but the meaningless one of amorality?
When it reduces all of life, any aspect of man or society, to a thing
of no dignity, how can we admit that its posture of indifference is
valid and valuable in itself? We have this kind of difficulty with
much of Aristophanes, Molière and Feydeau.

Yet love and marriage, social forms and other familiar matters
are immediately visible in a new way through farce. Its clockwork
mechanism by its very consistency disarms us. In its spirit of violence
and riot, no doubt we should recognize that hidden depths of the
mind are being revealed. For it is aggressive theatre in that we laugh
heartily at the formidable dilemmas in which others find themselves.
We exhibit a cruelty as we would never dare do in life, and we yearn
for the breaking of rigid social rules as only those who observe them
can.

In *The Magistrate* (1885), Pinero's straight-laced judge Mr Posket
is faced with every embarrassment, including the final horror of
seeing his wife standing before him in his own dock. In *The School-
mistress* (1886), the headmistress of a most respectable establish-
ment for young ladies must secretly go on the stage to support her
rake of a husband. Hopelessly trapped in an unbelievable bedroom
scandal, company director M. Victor-Emmanuel Chaudebuse of
Feydeau's *La Puce à l'oreille* (1910) presents the image of respectability itself riding for a fall at a precipitous rate. In Ben Travers' *A
Cuckoo in the Nest* (1925), if once you make the mistake of pretending to be the husband of someone else's wife, fate must inexorably

lead you to her bed. Farce may be amoral, but at least, as Eric Bentley argues in his essay 'The Psychology of Farce', it must presuppose accepted social and moral standards if its humour is to emerge.

Thing follows upon thing in farce with the same fatal inevitability found in tragedy, and the structural likeness between tragedy and farce has frequently been remarked. Kenneth Tynan's programme for the British National Theatre production of the Feydeau play (with the English title *A Flea in Her Ear*, 1966) helpfully collected some clever *mots*. Archard observed how 'the events are linked together with the precision of a well-oiled machine', and Jean Cocteau, from whom the image of *la machine infernale* derives, talked of its 'mysterious inner mechanism'. In *Ape and Essence*, Aldous Huxley also saw the relationship as an essential one, believing that 'Tragedy is the farce that involves our sympathies; farce, the tragedy that happens to outsiders'. Marcel Achard sums up this thinking:

Feydeau's plays have the consecutiveness, the force, and the violence of tragedies. They have the same ineluctable fatality. In tragedy, one is stifled with horror. In Feydeau, one is suffocated with laughter. We are occasionally given some respite by the heroes of Shakespeare and Racine, when they melodiously bemoan their fate in beautiful poetry. But Feydeau's heroes haven't got time to complain.

(Introduction to Feydeau, *Théâtre complet*, trans. M. D. Dirks, 1948)

The one recurring element in all farce and accentuated comedy is the preposterous pace at which events move. The trap has been sprung and sprung again before escape is possible. Farce has the speed of fantasy, and Eric Bentley observed in his essay that its rapid pace is more than a technicality: it is a psychological necessity. It marks the nature of the experience. The idea that farce is accelerated tragedy is echoed in the 1966 programme by Eugène Ionesco: 'Take a tragedy, speed up the movement, and you will have a comedy. Empty the characters of psychological content, and again you will have a comedy: make the characters exclusively "social beings" — i.e., captives of the social machinery — and once more you will have a comedy, or perhaps a tragicomedy.' Feydeau's golden rule was to throw two of his characters together as quickly as possible when they should under no circumstances meet each other — a rule which, Achard points out, is followed instinctively by Sophocles, Shakespeare and Molière.

It is style that divides tragedy from comedy, but a fusion of both, a shift of emphasis, and the result can be equally exciting. Molière, '*le premier farceur de France*', always stood on the precipice of the tragic, and perhaps slipped over in *Le Misanthrope*. Alceste is the lover who refuses to hide in a sack or under a table. In the twentieth century, black farce from Roger Vitrac's *Victor, ou les enfants au pouvoir* (1928) to Anouilh's use of the Labiche and Feydeau stereotypes for shocking ends in *Ardèle au la Marguérite* (1949) and *La Valse des toréadors* (1952) has recently extended the genre, and their familiar *ingénues* and *femmes fatales* all play on the edge of the abyss. The mode of farce in Beckett and Ionesco is adopted essentially in order to lower the defences of their audiences before the attack on their values is mounted. In this way the absurd submerges its profundity in froth. The confectionery of farce has its place in serious drama, even if we are still surprised by the acrobatic juxtaposition of contrary responses associated with black comedy. Michel de Ghelderode's 'savage masquerades', Arrabal's frivolous treatment of horrors, Genêt's insulting devices of parody and burlesque, Ionesco's disturbing use of human puppetry: in all these the laughter is in the *Commedia* tradition of doing violence against society and the accepted mores, carried to an illogical extreme.

It is surprising that T. S. Eliot as long ago as 1918 and without experience of these plays, diagnosed the tone and mode of Marlowe's *The Jew of Malta* as those of savage farce. Today's familiarity with black comedy may also help us to make a correct judgment on those incongruous middle scenes in *Doctor Faustus*. In the past they have been discounted as Marlowe's inferior workmanship, or else not his work at all. The editor of the Revels Plays edition (1962), for example, decided that the 'tragic' Faustus is 'a very different Faustus from the cheerful anti-papist wonder-worker of the scenes at Rome, at the imperial court, and at Vanholt. This second Faustus is the creation, surely, of another author.' But if the seeming lack of unity of tone is the reason for disquiet, Clifford Williams's recent production (1968) for the Royal Shakespeare Company, with Eric Porter playing Faustus as a tragic fool, suggests that Marlowe knew better than the scholars what his stage was capable of supporting. The business of selling your soul to the devil is in any case a bad joke, and in keeping with the medieval lunatic vision of the Seven Deadly Sins exhibited by Lucifer. Boxing the Pope's ear and having sex with a demon are akin to signing a name in blood and having the mind 'delighted' by a dance of comic devils before they drag you off to hell.

The element of black farce is ancient in English drama. It is found in the Mystery Cycles, and obtrudes in such a play as Thomas Preston's *Cambises* (1569), 'a lamentable tragedy mixed full of pleasant mirth', the last provided by comic characters like Hob and Lob, Huf, Ruf and Snuf. It reappears powerfully in the tragedies of Shakespeare, Tourneur, Webster, Marston and Middleton. It is seen in the clowning of *King Lear*'s Poor Tom, who cannot separate body and soul, but in one breath wishes 'to prevent the fiend and to kill vermin' – very like Beckett's Didi who cannot think about his immortal soul for the flea in his hat. The grotesque dance of death in Tourneur's *The Revenger's Tragedy* (1607) and the cavorting of the madmen in Webster's *The Duchess of Malfi* (1613) colour the sober view of mortality in these plays. It is a savage joke when Vendice of *The Revenger's Tragedy* kills his enemy the Duke by having him satisfy his lust on the poisoned skull of his mistress 'dressed up in tires'. First Vendice meditates with conventional bitterness upon the skull:

> Have I not fitted the old surfeiter
> With a quaint piece of beauty? Age and bare bone
> Are e'er ally'd in action. Here's an eye
> Able to tempt a great man – to serve God;
> A pretty hanging lip, that has forgot now to dissemble:
> Methinks this mouth should make a swearer tremble,
> A drunkard clasp his teeth.

Then with a surge of ironic humour Tourneur has Vendice tempt the old lecher:

DUKE: Well done, hast brought her? what lady is't?
VENDICE: Faith, my lord, a country lady, a little bashful at first, as most of them are; but after the first kiss, my lord, the worst is past with them. Your grace knows now what you have to do; sh' has somewhat a grave look with her, but –   (III.v)

The same caustic humour is at the centre of Pirandello's jests: Enrico Quarto counterfeits his insanity to his own and our amusement until the shocking moment comes when he finds that he is trapped forever within his own masquerade.

Although in farce and comedy the audience usually knows everything, the impact of performance is always unforeseen. Nahum Tate's preface to *A Duke and No Duke* (1693) is apt: 'There are no rules to be prescribed for that sort of wit, no patterns to copy, 'tis altogether the creature of imagination.' But in any analysis, the quality of comic style, and thus its meaning, rests finally upon the comic actor for whom also there are no rules to be prescribed. It is probably true that a comedian is born and not made: he inherits a mystery. His power is unpredictable, like the clowns and fools of old. A play which embodies the spirit of jest owes everything to the figures on its stage who embody that spirit.

In *The Two Gentlemen of Verona*, Speed makes his appearance casually in order to cast a gently ironic light over the action, as when in II.i he mocks Valentine's performance as a lover. Feste, who is both at the heart of *Twelfth Night*'s spirit and also the play's objective commentator from without, has an even less obtrusive presence in the action which allows him to oversee the vanities of all the lovers from start to finish. The fool has a perennial function in comic drama, as William Willeford's recent examination of him in *The Fool and His Scepter* (1969) suggests. The book is a reminder that we must approach Shakespeare's fools on their own terms as Shakespeare himself did, and an invitation to recall the importance of the fool throughout our history. We have also to recognize the relevance of his role in the contemporary theatrical scene.

We know the fool in many roles. In *King Lear*, he can make his appearance in the middle of tragedy itself, and leave us in the throes with a topsy-turvy, non-committal 'And I'll go to bed at noon'. Or, like the Greek phallophorus, the Plautine slave, and the Italian Arlecchino in his motley, knavish, stupid and obscenely flaunting the phallus, he can jest at the social order and remind us of its permanent element of hidden chaos. Or, innocent in a world of self-interest, he may appear like Chaplin, fastidious in his rags, or like Keaton, dead-pan among the horrors of war in *The General*, and show us sanity in madness through the wildest of laughter. 'The fact is that the more ways a man is deluded, the happier he is, if folly is any judge': so wrote Erasmus in 1511.

The fool is our distorting mirror, and we willingly allow him the freedom to reflect our grotesque other selves; so he moves independently of our space and time, and unruffled assumes a primitive and magical licence to strip us naked. When Harpo Marx apes Groucho's gestures as if he were a mirror in *Duck Soup*, Harpo is demonstrating the fool's power of reflecting our stupidity. In Pirandello's *Right You Are If You Think So*, the *raisonneur* Laudisi, temporarily adopting the fool's position for the audience's enlightenment, discusses his own sanity with his mirror-image, significantly to no avail. Oliver Hardy is as big a fool as Stan Laurel, the equal he thinks inferior to himself: although any fool can see he is wrong. And it is abundantly evident that the apparent sanity of Didi in *Waiting for Godot* is as madly foolish as the apparent folly of Gogo his opposite. Speaking for us, the Fool sees himself and his folly in Lear, until the King himself in his madness acquires the fool's own vision, and the Fool is no longer needed on stage to point to what is ridiculous.

Fools are free of law and order, and free of the terrors of reality. In the theatre we regularly need to share their freedom and enjoy the dramatic release they provide. If it is true that they act in accordance with what Willeford calls 'a fundamental apperception' that is alive in everyone, their function on the stage or the screen, in the circus or in life is to supply some of the ingredients of a fundamental ritual which will never die. It is the ancient ritual of Dionysus, the ritual of irreverence and demonic laughter. Keaton in *Limelight* with his collapsing piano (like Grock before him) and W. C. Fields in *The Bank Dick* in his disintegrating car demonstrate by their imperturbability the startling nature of the phenomena about us, and prove that only a touch of the fool can preserve us from their vicissitudes. We remember Eliot's 'Man cannot stand very much reality'. Chaplin in *The Pilgrim*, trapped on the border between a United States marshal on one side and Mexican bandits on the other, can only waddle off with one foot in each country, belonging to neither. In the Republic of Fools all men are equal, and its empire embraces every habitation of man. Through the eyes of the fool we see intermittently that the world is one big practical joke.

The outstanding virtue of the fool is that he is understandable at all levels. The Fool in *Lear* is our spiritual guide, for his relationship with the audience is far more direct and obvious than his relationship with the King. When Hamlet is playing the madman, there are times when he seems to have stepped outside the frame of the action, but we the audience always know that he is no fool. The modern tradition of Harlequin is to be traced from Duburau the whitefaced pierrot of the Théâtre des Funambules, to Lecoq, Barrault, Marcel Marceau and Jacques Tati. In yet another tradition, Grock is to be balanced with Grimaldi, Keaton with Dan Leno. The time is now ripe to place into the pattern such figures of absurdist drama as Jarry's prototypical clown Père Ubu, and Beckett's universal clownish varieties as represented by Didi, Gogo, Pozzo and Lucky, with their universal names. Drama will always return to the condition of the circus to re-enact its indispensable ritual of folly, and find its dwelling in that sublime genre, the comic.

Erasmus also noted that one desirable form of folly is present 'whenever an amiable dotage of the mind at once frees the spirit from carking cares and anoints it with a complex delight'. What he goes on to say seems to predict the impulse behind comic theatre:

> This kind of madness . . . can bring a delight above the common both to those who are seized by it and to those who look on but are not mad in the same way. This variety of madness is much more widespread than people generally realize. Thus one madman laughs at another, turn about, and they minister to each other's mutual pleasure.
>
> (*The Praise of Folly*, trans. H. H. Hudson, pp. 51–3)

This notion may not be as eccentric as it appears: the comic stage of tradition reflects its audience like a distorting mirror, induces laughter and then laughs back at those who laugh at it. When the stage does not immediately mirror its audience, it often mirrors itself and serves the same function by proliferating its images.

In the basic patterns of the *Commedia dell'arte scenarii*, both the scene and the characters are arranged in the echoing symmetry of family houses set about an imaginary stage piazza. The masks of the company are themselves determined by pairs: two old men, *vecchii*, and two *zanni*, a fool for a fool. In Flaminio Scala's company of 1615, there were also two *inamorati*, male lovers, two *inamorate*, female lovers, and two *servette*. If the masters fall in love, so must the servants. Kathleen Lea writes, 'If Oratio duels with the Captain, Pedrolino must challenge Arlecchino. If Silvio goes to commit suicide, Zanni must make his will too. The bulk of the dialogue in the plays is in burlesque of the ravings, salutations, and protests of their betters' (*Italian Popular Comedy*, p. 66). Many of the plots of the *Commedia*, with the obvious help of the masks, take up Plautine themes of twins and doubles: Pantalone finds his double in his own wife's arms, or is locked out of his own house, until he hardly knows his own identity. Messages and money are entrusted to the wrong twin, until the whole company is in a state of hopeless misunderstanding. Naturally, elopement by doubles in the darkness proves catastrophic. Sometimes even the pairs come in pairs, as in Shakespeare's *The Comedy of Errors*, which echoes the *Commedia's Zanni incredibile con quatro simili*, which echoes Plautus's *Menaechmi*. But in this lively tradition even the desire for doubling does not need twins: in Goldoni's *The Servant of Two Masters* (1743), Truffaldino doubles for himself in a ludicrously improbable situation.

Commedia patterns of action are replete with repetitions, as if its peculiar world were a hall of mirrors. As in *A Midsummer Night's Dream*, choosing a partner can seem as arbitrary as dropping a little juice in the eye, so in the *Commedia* partners for life are paired off as easily as partners for a dance. In *As You Like It*, amorous rivalry is like a merry-go-round in which Phebe loves Rosalind, Silvius loves Phebe and Rosalind loves Orlando; so in the *Commedia* Angiola loves Cintio, who loves Celia, who loves Oratio, who loves Angiola, and thus we return to the beginning. When Rosalind chides Phebe in III.v for not valuing 'a good man's love', no doubt she speaks from the heart who cannot discard her doublet and hose to win her Orlando; but she does not reckon with the unwelcome result of treating so scornfully the scornful mistress of the courtly school.

ROSALIND: Cry the man mercy, love him, take his offer,
  Foul is most foul, being foul to be a scoffer,
  So take her to thee, shepherd: fare you well.
PHEBE: Sweet youth, I pray you chide a year together,
  I had rather hear you chide than this man woo.
ROSALIND: He's fallen in love with your foulness, and she'll fall in love with my anger!

Rosalind tries to leave, but Phebe chases after her, and Silvius chases after Phebe, so that all three inseparably circle the stage in a chain of undying love. The comic stage erupts in reduplication.

These repetitions are at the core of all *Commedia* business, for in the countless *lazzi* which make up the action of the plays, one character bounces off another until no one can mistake the source of laughter as it grows louder and louder. When, choked with sobs, Pulcinella cannot speak the sad news he brings his lovelorn master, this only makes the unrequited lover more distraught; and this in turn reduces Pulcinella to wilder crying, and the report is never spoken. As the Capitano more and more vehemently swears vengeance on the hapless Zanni on one side of the stage, Zanni on his side pleads more and more for the mercy of God, the Capitano and the spectator. When Pedrolino eats a dish of macaroni to console himself in his grief, his tears are so infectious that both Arlecchino and Burattino burst into tears too, and must likewise console themselves with macaroni, until all three are furiously crying and stuffing together over the same dish. When Aurelia and Flaminia quarrel in the street, Flaminia settles the matter by giving her a cuff and departing; but at that moment Pantalone enters and is struck by Aurelia's retaliatory blow; and so the *lazzi* proceeds through the whole company until the miserable Zanni, who is last, has no one else to hit.

These instances contain the very elements of comedy, and this last perfect little pattern was later seen in a wide range of comedies: in Sheridan's *The Rivals*, II.i, Sir Antony scolds his son Captain Absolute, who in turn scolds his servant Fag, who in turn abuses the Errand Boy: '*exit kicking and beating him*'. The Errand Boy has no one to kick, of course. Upon the unwelcome departure of her Colonel in Chekhov's *Three Sisters*, act II, Masha releases her anger on the old servant Anfisa, who in turn vents her spleen by mimicking poor brother Andrey as she answers his call: a more subtle sequence. In such repetitions, man is represented as a mechanical thing, behaving, as Bergson would say, by habit. At the same time, the pain of witnessing man as a robot is happily diminished by the same repetition that occasions it.

The frequency of mirror- and echo-effects in comedy suggests that they are fundamental to its form and style. Following the *Commedia*, Molière traces an exquisitely comic pattern of lovers in *Le Bourgeois Gentilhomme*, III.x (1670). In this, his stage analogue of a lover's quarrel is almost entirely visual: the words supply a choreographic notation for a dance whose gestures and movements are a balletic epitome of love's caprices. Cléonte is in love with Lucile, and his valet Covielle is in love with her maid Nicole. Together, master and servant represent all men as they first chafe under the imaginary offence given them by the indifference of the girls: arms folded firmly, heads in the air, the two men turn an angry shoulder when approached. With each renewed appeal, the girls circle their lovers to create the pattern of a chase:

LUCILE: Je veux vous dire, Cléonte, le sujet qui m'a fait ce matin éviter votre abord.

CLEONTE: Non, je ne veux rien écouter.
NICOLE: Je te veux apprendre la cause qui nous a fait passer si vite.
COVIELLE: Je ne veux rien entendre.
LUCILE: Sachez que ce matin...
CLEONTE: Non, vous dis-je.
NICOLE: Apprends que...
COVIELLE: Non, traîtresse!

LUCILE: I want to tell you, Cléonte, the reason why I avoided you this morning.
CLEONTE: No, I shan't listen.
NICOLE: I want to tell you the reason why we went by so quickly.
COVIELLE: I don't want to know.
LUCILE: You see, this morning...
CLEONTE: No, I said.
NICOLE: You see...
COVIELLE: No, traitress!

The dialogue breaks up into a rapid series of short expletive words and phrases, and the dance proceeds towards and away, forward and back, the pace increasing, the pitch rising, until Lucile stops in her tracks:

Hé bien! puisque vous ne voulez pas m'écouter, demeurez dans votre pensée, et faites ce qu'il vous plaira.

All right! Since you won't listen to me, go on thinking as you do, and do whatever you please.

Nicole of course echoes her, and now the dance is reversed, the men chasing the girls to a new peak, until it is Cléonte who stops short:

Hé bien! puisque vous vous souciez si peu de me tirer de peine, et de vous justifier du traitement indigne que vous avez fait à ma flamme, vous me voyez, ingrate, pour la dernière fois.

All right! Since you care so little to put an end to my anxiety, and to justify the unworthy way you treat my feeling for you, this is the last time you'll set eyes on me, heartless girl!

Covielle echoes his master and the dance is on again.

The echoing device ridicules the sentiments, but the joke is re-doubled when the parrotting accents of the servants mindlessly coarsen and exaggerate the high-flown passions of the principals, social differences undercutting what is left of any sincerity of feeling. Molière's neat puppet-show, perfect of its kind, is a composite of the verbal parody and stage burlesque to which pure comedy aspires.

The echo/mirror tradition in Western comedy can be traced to the present day. In Farquhar's *The Beaux' Stratagem* (1707), Aimwell addresses the lovely Dorinda with all sincerity, while Archer, playing his servant, works to seduce Mrs Sullen in baser fashion. Farquhar is often thought of as a sentimentalist for including an honest Aimwell, but the presence of a mirror in dishonest Archer must reduce the hero and increase the play's objectivity. In Gay's *The Beggar's Opera* (1728), the rivals for Macheath are Polly and Lucy, a frantic pair who divide his attention by this ironic air:

> POLLY: Hither, dear husband, turn your eyes.
> LUCY: Bestow one glance to cheer me.
> POLLY: Think with that look, thy Polly dies.
> LUCY: O shun me not – but hear me.
> POLLY: 'Tis Polly sues.
> LUCY: 'Tis Lucy speaks . . . etc.

This effect of repetition is more pronounced when sung to music. Mozart's *Così fan tutte* (1790) makes its musical jokes by having two pairs of lovers echo each other's sentiments with a delightful cynicism in the witty pointing and the pace. In Gilbert's *Patience, or Bunthorne's Bride* (1881), twenty love-sick maidens stem our flow of tears by the sheer proliferation of their rapture. In Wilde's *The Importance of Being Earnest* (1895) act II, the parallel quarrels of Jack Worthing with Algernon, and Gwendolen with Cecily, are another exercise of stylistic brilliance in the mockery of courtship. The characters speak like automata who repeat each other, so that their movements and gestures in exact symmetry repeat each other like their words. The perfect matching of the honeymoon couples on the hotel balconies in Coward's *Private Lives*, Act I (1930), and the ingenious simultaneous images of the two, then three, anxious couples in Alan Ayckbourn's classically composed farce *How the Other Half Loves* (1970) are extensions of the same mode. The deliberate repetitions in French plays of the absurd, like Beckett's *En attendant Godot* and Ionesco's *La Leçon*, doubtless take their inspiration from the *Commedia* tradition and French farce.

Many sub-genres of comedy regularly achieve a satirical edge by overplaying, and this element of exaggeration makes its appearance as parody in the language and burlesque in the acting. Burlesque is properly a genre in its own right, vulgarizing serious forms of drama by mockery, or larding commonplace situations with false dignity; since the sixteenth century it has frequently taken the form of a rehearsal-play. But the impulse of ridicule behind burlesque has always insidiously worked its reductive way through all kinds of comedy from Shakespeare to Chekhov, the extreme of naturalism.

The obvious burlesque scenes in Shakespeare apart (the play of the Nine Worthies in *Love's Labour's Lost*, Pyramus and Thisbe in *A Midsummer Night's Dream*, the mock-pastoral of Silvius and Phebe in *As You Like It*, each of which illuminates the theme of the whole by its extravagance), the burlesque element asserts itself time and again, subtly distinguished in style from the lyrical norm of its context. We hear the characteristic tone when Rosalind as Ganymede, boy-girl dressed as boy, presents herself to Orlando as his true love Rosalind, boy speaking as girl; for the mask she assumes is one of language:

ROSALIND: . . . ask me what you will, I will grant it.
ORLANDO: Then love me, Rosalind.
ROSALIND: Yes, faith, I will, Fridays and Saturdays and all.
ORLANDO: And wilt thou have me?
ROSALIND: Ay, and twenty such.   (*As You Like It*, IV.i)

Rosalind speaks here as she desires to speak, in her own person, like any girl who wishes to spite the proprieties, but dares not do so without some subterfuge such as Rosalind is now enjoying. Yet in her superior position, Rosalind is half mocking Orlando, and her words are frivolous and high-flown, her breezy gestures implicit in the lines. In the pretended wedding ceremony which follows, however, with a doubtful, laughing Celia playing the priest, Rosalind's high spirits almost betray her mask, and once or twice we see it slip as she speaks in her true voice:

I do take thee, Orlando, for my husband: there's a girl goes before the priest, and certainly a woman's thought runs before her actions.

The last line is as good as a hurried aside to the audience, and she quickly recovers her poise. But when Rosalind is alone again with Celia, she speaks lines with equal passion and her game rebounds upon herself, for the audience can see that she has been parodying her own mind: 'I'll go find a shadow, and sigh till he come.' In many of Shakespeare's comic characters who are not to be taken quite at face value, like Orsino and Olivia in *Twelfth Night*, we find similar touches of excess.

The impossibility of rendering many lines of *Cymbeline* for a serious response must lead us to consider the possibility that this mongrel and troublesome play is also in many respects a burlesque. Granville-Barker's diagnosis of it as 'sophisticated artlessness' and J. C. Maxwell's 'candid recognition of its odd combination of its incongruous elements' both point to the work of a burlesquer, of a playwright who could not stomach the new vogue for *Philaster*. Imogen's lines to Cloten's headless body, which she thinks her husband's, are hard to take seriously, but they are quite successful as burlesque. The joke is accentuated by Shakespeare's requirement that she feel her way from his foot to the bloody stump of his neck:

> I know the shape of's leg; this is his hand;
> His foot Mercurial; his Martial thigh:
> The brawns of Hercules; but his Jovial face —
> Murder in heaven? How? 'Tis gone. (IV.ii)

The absolute perfection of Imogen, the villainy of Iachimo and the inflexibility of Posthumus (particularly during the scene of reunion with his wife, v.v, when he strikes her to the ground as she tries to reveal her true identity) fit well into the same design. It is tempting to note the likeness between the tone of *Cymbeline* and the lines of such later poetasters as Nathaniel Lee, so apt for parody at the hands of Fielding. In *Nero* (1674), the dead Octavia is mourned by her brother Britannicus thus:

> Trust me, thy Sweetness I shall ne'er forget;
> Stiff with my Sorrows, on thy Tomb I'll sit,
> Till I at last into cold Marble turn,
> And with my pious Figure grace thy Urn.

Lee did not know how to understate a hero's grief; Shakespeare chose not to.

The burlesque touch has been felt on the English stage from the beginnings — one thinks of Noah or Joseph in the Mystery Cycles. In Elizabethan drama there are obvious instances like Beaumont's *The Knight of the Burning Pestle* (*c.* 1607) mocking earlier forms of drama, or Jonson's fifth act of *Cynthia's Revels* (1600) burlesquing his competitors' work. Middleton's exuberant city comedies are granted an exceptional vitality for the cheating and wenching of their characters by the wild exaggeration of their language. In *A Mad World, My Masters* (1600) Master Penitent Brothel's moments of bad verse simply add to the high spirits of his seduction of Mistress Harebrain:

> There shot a star from heaven;
> I dare not yet behold my happiness,
> The splendour is so glorious and so piercing.   (III.ii)

The even worse jingle with which the young rogue Witgood closes *A Trick to Catch the Old One* (*c.* 1606):

> And here for ever I disclaim
> The cause of youth's undoing, game,
> Chiefly dice, those true outlanders,
> That shake out beggars, thieves, and panders,
> Soul-wasting surfeits, sinful riots,
> Quean's evils, doctors' diets   (v.ii)

gaily underscores the mock reformation which ridicules all moralistic curtain speeches.

One of the finest moments of comedy in Congreve's *The Way of the World* (1700) is pure burlesque, that of the assignation between the 'old peeled wall' Lady Wishfort and the servant Waitwell, 'disguised as for Sir Rowland'. Not only is the man putting on the act of his life, aping every gallant he has seen or imagined, trying every turn of wit within his powers, but the lady too acts her part to the point of intoxication. The audience can especially enjoy the joke because it knows that all the professions of decorum by this superannuated coquette are false to what it has seen of her alone in her boudoir.

LADY WISHFORT: Dear Sir Rowland, I am confounded with confusion at the retrospection of my own rudeness! I have more pardons to ask than the Pope distributes in the Year of Jubilee. But I hope, where there is likely to be so near an alliance, we may unbend the severity of decorum and dispense with a little ceremony.

WAITWELL: My impatience, madam, is the effect of my transport; and till I have the possession of your adorable person, I am tantalized on a rack, and do but hang, madam, on the tenter of expectation.

LADY WISHFORT: You have an excess of gallantry, Sir Rowland, and press things to a conclusion with a most prevailing vehemence. But a day or two for decency of marriage –

WAITWELL: For decency of funeral, madam! The delay will break my heart.   (IV.xii)

The irony of this courtship is marked by the grotesque disguising – Waitwell with an unaccustomed full-bottomed wig and fop's clothing, the sweep of an outrageous hat as he bows deep to the floor; Wishfort with her over-painted face and its rash of beauty-spots on the chalk. Their words, however, belie them both. Wishfort's alliterative mouthing of malappropriate pruderies, accompanied by the coquettish writhing of her torso, is well matched by Waitwell's fantastic gestures of transport, his wink at the house when he speaks of her adorable person and his wonderfully overblown figure of racking and hanging.

The burlesque here is obviously set in contrast with the more modest exchanges of feeling in the play, and the scene serves its corrective purpose. In Farquhar's love-scenes a year or so later, something new is happening. The commonplace of Farquhar criticism is that he is the first of the sentimental comedians, his comedy self-defeating in its inconsistency; that he is at best a professional bowing to the box-office; and that this explains what is taken to be the saccharine of the passionate sentiment and sexual innuendo in his situations. This opinion persists in the face of a variety of evidence to the contrary: the literary historians must find their author 'transitional'. In his best-known play *The Beaux' Stratagem* (1707), the heroes are two penurious gentlemen who for once must live by their wits, particularly their tongues; the scene is set in the bawdy countryside and abounds in Jonsonian, even Rabelaisian, characters – a jolly fat innkeeper, his pretty barmaid daughter, a snobbish squire, an Irish priest, clownish highwaymen. The idea is hardly credible that an audience can assume some simple moral position for the author from the abrupt turn-about reformations of the last act, any more than they can for Middleton ('adventurers for four acts, humbugs for one').

A new note of parody in the style in any case dispels the notion that the sentiment is passionate. It is Archer, the principal hunter, who constantly undercuts a romantic response, and he does so by flamboyant word and gesture. He kisses Cherry, the pretty barmaid, with, 'Death and fire! her lips are honeycombs' (the language quite inappropriate to the object), and on her retort, 'And I wish there had been bees too, to have stung you for your impudence', he presses the parody further: 'There's a swarm of Cupids, my little Venus, that has done the business much better' (act I). There can be no taking these allusions at face value while the poor girl is side-stepping his attentions.

The point is that the well-born ladies are given the same treatment. Aimwell, the second hunter, praises his Dorinda:

like Ceres in her harvest, corn, wine and oil, milk and honey, gardens, groves, and purling streams, played on her plenteous face.   (III.ii)

If this is genuine, Archer's riposte is quick: 'Her face! her pocket, you mean; the corn, wine and oil, lies there. In short, she has ten thousand pound, that's the English on't.' Even Aimwell learns to play the game, and after feigning sickness in order to insinuate himself into Dorinda's presence, he 'recovers', grasps her hand and utters more mock poetry:

> Sure I have pass'd the gulf of silent death,
> And now I land on the Elysian Shore!   (IV.i)

When he finally kisses the girl, it is Mrs Sullen's turn to be the critic: 'So, so so! I knew where the fit would end!' The degree of sincerity the audience is to perceive in Aimwell is questionable, to say the least.

We are on surer ground with Archer, and the sensuality of his outrageous comparison of Mrs Sullen with her portrait is all a travesty, designed for one unmistakable purpose. Since we know this, Farquhar tempts us to laughter on every line:

Your eyes, indeed, are featured there; but where's the sparkling moisture, shining fluid, in which they swim? The picture, indeed, has young dimples; but where's the swarm of killing Cupids that should ambush there? The lips too are figured out; but where's the carnation dew, the pouting ripeness, that tempts the taste in the original?   (IV.i)

Cherry's swarm of Cupids, we note, descend again. And when Archer finally attempts the seduction in Mrs Sullen's bedchamber, this too is done to the tune of rapturous lines:

> Lilies unfold their white, their fragrant charms,
> When the warm sun thus darts into their arms.   (V.ii)

Farquhar is not so swayed by his feelings that he does not remember to match the darting line to the stage direction '*runs to her*', and to have the lady dodge around the bed with a shriek. Archer may be warm like the sun, but the lilies remain uncommonly stubborn.

Parody-burlesque almost emerges as the norm of style for the English comic stage. It is irrepressible throughout the early years of the nineteenth-century domestic drama. Thus the villain Lawyer Cribbs of Barnum's *The Drunkard* (1844), one of the 'delirium tremens dramas' popular on both sides of the Atlantic, skirts laughter with his stock phraseology:

Now is he started on the road to ruin. He had the taste for drink already — it needed but a gentle push to send him tottering over the edge of sobriety into the abyss of dipsomania. Ha! Ha! Ha!

This is part of the world of exuberant theatricality from which Shaw more often than not borrowed a style for the Reverend Morell and Eugene Marchbanks, his Ramsdens and his Tavys. *Arms and the Man* (1894) dallies with the burlesque mode in every scene. Raina opens the play with an Eleonora Duse reverie on her balcony, '*intensely conscious of the beauty of the night, and of the fact that her own youth and beauty are part of it*', until it is broken by the inflated rhythms of her mother's announcement, 'Sergius is the hero of the hour, the idol of the regiment!' In their ecstasy they '*kiss one another frantically*'. This burlesque of military hero-worship is the beginning of the comic process by which Raina's idealism is undone, together with any pretensions to jingoism the audience may share. Raina's scene in the second act with the returning warrior Sergius might have been written for comic opera (and did, indeed, suffer the fate of becoming *The Chocolate Soldier*):

I think we two have found the higher love. When I think of you, I feel that I could never do a base deed, or think an ignoble thought.

Inflated by burlesque, all that follows must be anticlimax, but at the moment when we feel the emotional lurch, the intellectual operation begins. Deflating Sergius obliquely deflates Raina, and simultaneously punctures the audience's own illusions about military glory. When Shaw slyly slips in and out of the burlesque manner, it is always to some purpose.

This discussion began with the caveat that the identification of genre and style in a play is of paramount importance for director or critic. Without its recognition, all kinds of critical absurdities result. How else to explain Jan Kott's perverse judgment that the burlesque playlet of Pyramus and Thisbe in *A Midsummer Night's Dream* is there to tell us that 'the world is cruel for young lovers'? By his humourless verdicts on this play Kott shows that he has, literally, no eye for style. Style is a mark of the inner coherence of the whole play experience. Richard Wollheim argues cogently in *Art and Its Objects* that style is devised to express (and the theatre would add to control) the limited range of emotions the artifact is to evoke. To neglect that control is to fragment and destroy the response possible to it. This is particularly important in those plays in which one genre overlaps another. Extremes of tragedy and farce present little problem: actor and spectator know what is expected of them. But in plays like *Measure for Measure, Cymbeline, Le Misanthrope, Peer Gynt, The Wild Duck* and the host of plays of mixed genre which follows the naturalistic movement in the theatre, the problem of balancing the generic elements to achieve a new coherence of style becomes acute.

The critical problems associated with the study of Shakespeare's comedies — their great range of styles and forms, the variety and mixture of their moods, the levels of realism or farce they assume, whether an audience must laugh *with* or *at* a character like Falstaff or Rosalind — are problems of stylistic coherence. They can be approached only from the particular, with the aid of perceptual analysis. If at a later time we venture to pass from the particular to the general, there will be little to gain and possibly a lot to lose. For the particular we look to the details which bombard the spectator, forcing him to laugh or, rather, giving him the freedom to laugh, a release from his own reality and sometimes also from the created reality of the play. All this without destroying that reality, that base-point from which all drama must take off.

Two small moments from *Romeo and Juliet* and *As You Like It* make the point. In both, Juliet and Rosalind have difficulty in saying goodbye to their lovers. The balcony scene (II.ii) is a lyrical duet as in opera: it sings of a mood and transfixes the audience as it transfixes the lovers. There is no 'action', the scene does not further the plot, the drama does not 'go' anywhere; instead, it extends a familiar feeling of young love to a point of rapture that comes close to sentimentality. The scene is in imminent danger of over-reaching, and risks laughter after 160 lines of sustained lyricism. Then comes the unerring Shakespearian touch which is both absolutely in character and exactly designed to regain control of our responses. Juliet says 'A thousand times good night!' and exits, but returns immediately to search for another excuse to stay. Now her tone is happily prosaic after all the poetry, and the line, 'I have forgot why I did call thee back', is almost dampening. Is this anticlimactic? Only if we respond with derision. But when an audience laughs on that line, as it usually does, it laughs with the contentment of recognition, relieved that the girl is human after all, able to believe that her heights of feeling can be common property. Shakespeare has released the spectator so that he may measure the idealism of the situation against his own earthly reality, and within the framework of the play he believes in Juliet's love. The reality of the stage is made substantial by a moment of comedy.

The comparable instance was written two or three years later, from *As You Like It*, but the context is clearly different. To cheer their spirits, Rosalind proposes that she and Celia 'devise sports', and puts the question that is addressed as much to us as to Celia: 'What think you of falling in love?' Celia's answer is ours too — as long as falling in love is treated as sport and not taken too seriously. 'Love no man in good earnest', she says, or you could be more miserable than before. All this suggests that the tone and image of the action an audience receives lack the intensity of tragedy, and set us up in a special way to receive Rosalind's tumble with the ambivalence of comedy. A few minutes later, Rosalind finds an object for her admiration in Orlando, who, appropriately for the young male lead, overthrows Charles the wrestler, and Rosalind is naturally smitten immediately. Already she has forgotten the first rule: to flirt, but not to fall in love. Our invitation to sympathize lightly with the coquettish side of the girl is thus already coloured by our wish to laugh a little at her lack of self-control.

Then Shakespeare, by a deft piece of stagecraft, clinches the matter. Rosalind runs back to Orlando as he stands stammering an aside, and directs a second aside at us:

> He calls us back! My pride fell with my fortunes —
> I'll ask him what he would. Did you call, sir?
> Sir, you have wrestled well and overthrown
> More than your enemies. (I.ii)

In case we missed the manner in which the two asides put into

Brechtian perspective the viewpoints of the silly young people, in a sense giving us two little plays simultaneously, Celia, the voice of propriety and anxious for the behaviour of her cousin as elsewhere in the play, compels our objectivity even further with her pettish, 'Will you go, coz?' It is too late: Rosalind has lost her heart, and some of our sympathy too. Strangely, we shall be able to enjoy Rosalind's lapses of control in the rest of the play with the more affection. It is not merely that Rosalind is in two minds; the audience is too, able to understand how sport has turned into earnest and at the same time compelled to keep its distance from Shakespeare's amorous victim.

The juxtaposition of these two instances, one from tragedy and one from comedy, was deliberate. Obviously the context for each is different, and exerts its own control of our responses, but essentially the comedic element operates equally whatever the genre of the play. Perhaps in the tragedy we laugh more *with* than at Juliet, in the comedy more *at* than with Rosalind. Here is implied that 'audience equation' mentioned before, by which the image of the stage action reflects more or less irreverence towards reality, and this irreverence is maintained by the degree of laughter. In Shakespeare, the intellect is always at work in the tragedies and the feelings in the comedies, and of overwhelming importance for the impact of a particular play is the interaction of the emotive with the cerebral. Our quest is the identifiable role of the audience in the process of performance, and the kind of illumination of human nature and behaviour that the best comedy brings is made doubly sure when first the sympathies are engaged.

This much may seem trite. We know that the mixing of heart and mind has always been acceptable to audiences, even if theory disapproves. The interesting problem is to estimate the proportions of the mixture according to the intensity of each ingredient. An examination of the curious role of Edgar in *King Lear*, the tragically wronged son of the Duke of Gloucester, runs no risk of invoking the wispy notion of comic relief. Edgar plays many parts in this great tragedy, but after he assumes the part of Poor Tom, his function seems designed to throw essentially comic light on the twin protagonists, Lear and Gloucester. Once the Elizabethan audience accepts his disguises and watches his teasing of the two old men in their distress, it is no longer required to be disturbed by his own story, and takes him on trust as a comic chorus of a kind more extreme than the Fool himself.

Edgar's first entrance as the Bedlam beggar is the performance of a lifetime, and the audience recognizes it for the pretence that it is. Only those on stage are deceived, and Lear's reaction is sublime:

> Didst thou give all to thy daughters?
> And art thou come to this? (III.iv)

He sees himself in Edgar, appalling in his nakedness. We must here pity Lear as he forsakes his dignity and his divinity, but it cannot escape us that the joke is on him. The more blatant trick is played on Gloucester the blind man, and in case it is thought that the grim humour of the heath is misread, the scene of Dover Cliff (IV.vi) should confirm it. To perpetrate the second fantastic deception, the actor playing Edgar must mime the steepness of the cliff-top by a crazy piece of over-acting that will convince his father that they are climbing. Yet we observe that Gloucester feels, and we know, that the ground is flat. Edgar's trickery works two ways: not only do we see the excess of the joke, but he does such a good job of imagining the sensations of vertigo that another part of us senses the tension in the mind of the would-be suicide. When the blind man falls flat on his face, Edgar has saved him from the ultimate in despair by convincing him that the gods have worked a miracle. We know, however, that it is Edgar's private miracle, his role-playing miracle, his joke miracle. Perhaps it would have been a worse joke to have escaped from one hell into another by jumping off a cliff. Yet do we laugh? With this touch of the absurd, Shakespeare pushes us to the extreme verge of laughter and simultaneously plunges us into the depths of compassion for human suffering.

The comic ambivalence of the Edgar scenes in *Lear* are more than dialectical in their opposite viewpoints on God and man: they are dialectical for the senses too, carefully ambivalent as theatrical communication. This delicate balance is even more acute in those plays which come nearer to the comic mode. *Troilus and Cressida* is a comedy whose atmosphere remains close to tragedy and apparent realism, a prime example of the mongrel kind, mixing kings and clowns, weaving lechery and love with the atrocious Trojan War which never seems to end, confusing the serious analysis of military politics with cynical laughter, and summed up in Thersites's perfect pun when he damns those who 'war/whore for a placket'. The play was not performed, it is thought, for three hundred years until 1907, and was a flop at that. Following this, a few rare performances, and then after World War II a rush of major productions all highly acceptable to the cold-war audiences. It is now entrenched in the Shakespeare repertory, and without debating the reasons for so long a neglect of a masterpiece, we can be clear that the mood of an anti-war play, one which treats heroism and romantic love with astringent honesty, found its audience in our own disillusioned age. Its particular brand of realism at last chimed with the spirit of the audience, and the equation was completed.

It is obvious that if Troilus is no hero (at the end he loses his girl and his horse), if Shakespeare's war is unheroic (he starts at year seven, and at the end it is still inconclusive, both sides claiming victory), if Helen the cause of the war has become Nell the whore, if the love scenes are unromantic (ugly Pandarus is always watching), Cressida is the strangest sort of heroine. She has troubled the critics down the years, but to type her as a lustful opportunist is to ignore a multitude of subtle double values attaching to her. Shakespeare could not have changed her destiny, but in view of Chaucer's sympathetic treatment of her, and in the knowledge that no dramatist of merit, least of all Shakespeare, returns a received idea in quite the way he receives it, she is an urgent case for perceptual analysis. We may find that in Cressida we have a quality which remarkably resembles modern anti-heroism, fraught with ambiguities as in Ann Whitefield in *Man and Superman*, Mother Courage in Brecht's play, Blanche Dubois in *A Streetcar Named Desire* and Ruth in Pinter's *The Homecoming*. Cressida is neither a whore nor a symbol of frail womanhood, but a realistic girl who must adapt to each new vicissitude or perish.

The attack on Cressida by those who wish to degrade her begins in the early scenes in which she turns aside the pander's blandishments with the only weapon at her disposal, her native wit. This certainly denies her ignorance of men, but not her innocence: she is no sheltered Victorian flower, but neither is she a modern bachelor girl. Nevertheless, at the end of her first scene she steps outside the play in non-illusory fashion, and speaks as her own chorus in the infamous terms of her sonnet,

> Men prize the thing ungain'd more than it is.   (I.ii)

When she utters that notorious confession, 'Yet hold I off', there are those who jump to pronounce her 'a Daphne who enjoys the chase'. Yet this advice echoes the words of every mother to her daughter, indeed, of every girl to herself. 'Yet hold I off' has been the realistic position to adopt from the beginning of time. Her punishment is to be handed over to the Greek Diomedes who seems to take his advice from *Playboy* magazine and who, as someone has said, cares for horses and women in that order. Her destiny is recorded, but her progress there is not. It is characteristic of Shakespeare to keep his audience in doubt and refuse it easy gratification: Cressida is a good example of what Brecht called 'complex seeing', of the balanced comic perspective.

The scene for which her critics damn her finally is that in which she kisses no less than five Greek generals (IV.v), surely the work of a born wanton. But with Cressida herself we must ask, 'In kissing do you render or receive?' For kissing is a two-way exchange, and we should look again at what must happen on the stage.

The Greek army is drawn up in full armour in order to witness the duel between Hector and Ajax. The trumpet blows in anticipation of Hector's proud entrance, but only Cressida appears, an initial irony. There is a festive spirit in the air, and into this formidable group of nine or more laughing soldiers is thrust little Cressida the hostage. Her own father Calchas the traitor priest stands by, intensifying the concept. The image on the stage is that of a woman in a man's world, a victim, a spoil of war. The image could be that of any war in which atrocities are committed by the military upon the civilian population. King Agamemnon salutes her, perhaps formally, with a kiss, and the foxy Ulysses suggests that they all kiss her. He organizes it like a game, as the stylizing of the rhyming couplets indicates. But how is this staged? Do the Greek heroes stand in line as in a cafeteria and get their kisses one by one? No, Cressida must be passed down the line of men. Does she skip joyfully from one to another as some critics imply? Her stubborn silence for half the scene suggests that she is manhandled. The soldiers' jokes are a teasing cruelty, and only when the cuckold Menelaus tries to take his kiss does she draw upon her wit in self-defence and shows that she too has an opinion about the unworthy cause of the war. When Ulysses has his turn, she makes him beg, and he in return refuses. Who won this skirmish, the men or the girl? Physically, maybe, it is the men, but in our eyes it is the girl. She is dubbed a daughter of the game only by an older man who has met his match in a pert young girl.

This is a scene which cannot be interpreted apart from the medium it is designed for, without estimating the tone established by what we see, without acknowledging the presence of an audience other than the on-stage audience of Greeks. An on-stage audience in Shakespeare, like the lords who watch in astonishment when Macbeth confronts Banquo's ghost, like the Venetian senators who witness Desdemona struck by Othello, always adds a dimension of irony to the scene, and reminds us that we must see both what it sees and more. In the kissing scene in *Troilus and Cressida*, the double values are shockingly disenchanting: Greek heroes are debased, chivalry is mocked, a war machine is seen to roll over the insignificant protests of the individual. The play is a dark comedy and not a tragedy; its sensations are intense by comparison with Shakespeare's romantic comedies; it is a play in which we are involved with the disintegration of society in war-time, but partly in the personal terms of a young girl's attempts to cope with an impossible situation. It remains a comedy because our eyes are not allowed to become blurred. At the same time Cressida is in parallel with the infamous Helen of Troy in a more domestic version. Neither is worth spilling blood for.

In *Shakespeare and the Common Understanding*, Norman Rabkin maintains that it is in the mainstream of human experience to have to live with irresolvable paradoxes, and that this is what Shakespeare is concerned to remind us of. 'We learn with Hamlet', for example, 'the tragic coexistence of two opposed ideals of behaviour', and he asserts that this is not a matter of genre:

The technique of presenting a pair of opposed ideals or groups of ideals and putting a double valuation on each is the basis of Shakespeare's comedy as well as his tragedy, and it is clearly the source of a good deal of his power. It is a mode of vision, not an ideology ... The meaning is more an area of turbulence than a sententious moral.　　　　　(pp. 12, 55)

It is possible to have a good deal of sympathy with this view. From the coexistence of radically opposed literary ideas it is not a great step to the coexistence of radically opposed theatrical feelings. But if these are to be communicated in the theatre and re-experienced as part of the working of a play without being mutually destructive, it is incumbent on the playwright to see that they are balanced.

The balance must be on the stage, and should be in the mind of the audience, a quality generated by the sanity and objectivity of the artist. A generation ago S. L. Bethell wrote of the multiconsciousness of the Elizabethan audience, by which it could be both detached by the ritualistic element of Shakespearian theatre, and at the same time involved by the regular insistence of his moments of realism. By this the Elizabethan spectator was granted an imaginative expansion of his perceptions and sensibilities. Nowadays we deploy the Brechtian terminology, like *Verfremdungseffekt*, the effect of estranging what is already familiar. Somewhere in between lies another delicate balance associated with Chekhov. But the equation must be more than a stylistic balance between the recognizable reality of a play's theme and the unreal spirit of its stage, the two mutually exclusive in some way. It must be more than a balancing of attitudes in the mind of the spectator, so that the impulse to advance held in counterpoise with the impulse to withdraw produces a comic catharsis through mutually exclusive criticism and sympathy. We should not be content with the idea of exclusive, oppositional drives as an answer to the way an audience resolves the contrary elements of comedy. Performance requires a conjunction of those energies released by actor and specta- tor, so that, when the most potent comedy is working irresistibly, the two are at one. In the best comedy of Shakespeare, more of the in- congruities of life are presented, and every time we receive some fresh comic illumination, we are being taught to arrive at an adjusted understanding of the human condition. We mature in compromise.

The comic view is as necessary to our social well-being as the tragic view is to our spiritual life. As a genre or a style, comedy offers what Susanne Langer would call a heightening of our vital rhythm. Comedy, she declares, 'expresses the continuous balance of sheer vitality that belongs to society and is exemplified briefly in each in- dividual' (p. 333). To borrow a fundamental notion from E. H. Gombrich's *Art and Illusion*: whether in tragedy or in comedy, style is always a way of seeing, and the history of style is therefore the history of human perception.

4

Conditions of performance

This chapter returns to the notion of a play as an historical event. The discipline of studying a play is absolutely subject to understanding its original conditions of performance. The chorus of voices today should remind us that the student of drama has already moved away from the 'new critical' position which regarded a literary work as a self-contained artifact, to be satisfactorily understood and evaluated from its inner workings. The new critics have been of service in teaching us to eschew the impressionism and generalities of the belles lettrists, and to look closely at the way words interact to make their meaning and impact. Their emphasis on the intrinsic worth of literature was timely, and suited well with the needs of a modest verbal entity like a lyric poem. But the drama always resisted the idea of itself as an impersonal operation, having its existence *in vacuo*, and did not yield to a purely semantic analysis and the assumption of determined moral values. The inadequate operation of reading a play this way has shamefully limited our understanding of major dramatic fields like those of the Greek Old Comedy, Plautus and his street plays, medieval cycles, the *Commedia dell'arte*, the Restoration comedy and the Victorian domestic drama; no doubt other, more familiar, areas remain critically undernourished.

In *Shakespeare's Plays in Performance*, John Russell Brown reminds us that if you apply literary perceptions and values to the drama, and use specifically literary methods of criticism, you naturally enough arrive at literary judgments. He believes that in the future a more valid Shakespearian criticism will increasingly use records of performance in order to define the experience of a play. A knowledge of a play's elements of performance must bring us nearer to a complete dramatic criticism. The full theatrical implications of a dramatic text are only to be discovered by such records of performance, which are 'responses to the essential facts of dramatic illusion' (p. 231). We could go further and insist that the study of records of performance is always likely to produce a more valid judgment than a merely literary criticism of a play, because performance has proof of viability in the genre's own medium, and no other approach can supply a substitute for this.

On the other side of the Atlantic, Bernard Beckerman insists in *Dynamics of Drama* that drama is not made of words, but of activities:

Unfortunately, dramatic theory has not sufficiently addressed itself to a close analysis of theatrical activity, primarily because it has seen theatre as a composition of words rather than of activities. It has tended to split motion from action, and then to concentrate upon the discussion of action. This seems to be a serious error, because, in failing to concern itself fully with activity before examining the concept of action, dramatic criticism and theory are ignoring the foundation of theatrical art.   (p. 13)

Beckerman arrives at the point where he asserts that the medium of a play is not language but human presence, and that we must return to the source of drama, the theatre itself.

This sense of a play as an activity and not a latent possibility, an interchange of energies and not a dormant dream, adds to the belief that drama exists in its realization and not in its intention. Since the activity of the theatre is designed expressly to touch and involve an audience, a segment of society, that audience and that society must in part control the kind of activity found in the theatre. Since society gets the theatre it deserves, its drama therefore tells us a great deal about the people who go there, why they go and what happens to them. What happens to them, of course, is the play experience, the grail which a drama student seeks, and to recover the power of life embodied in a play is the best reason for studying it. This is another argument why we turn to the play in its own medium and its own period.

The occasion of a play is of fundamental importance, and clearly it is not helpful to bring principles of judgment from a ritual performance of the ancient Greeks to a commercial theatre such as Shakespeare's. There may be some justice in believing that early Victorian melodrama, with its rigid conventions, also offered its popular audiences a manner of ritual experience, and even that this quality persists into the dramatic manifestations of the mass media in our century. But it is only academic to find a likeness between the manner in which a villain of melodrama played to his audience and the manner in which the amateur Herod of the medieval cycles played to his. A decision why people went to the theatre to see a particular play is needed at the outset, whether for worship or entertainment or something else, in whatever proportions.

Further, a knowledge of the class composition of an audience is sharply relevant to an understanding of the purposes of its theatre. One should not expect to find the content and manner of the Restoration drama, designed as it is for so narrow an élite audience, to have too much in common with the qualities of late Georgian plays, whose houses were ten times as big and whose audiences were as mixed. Similarly, the ceremonious temple ritual *noh* plays of Japan took their extreme idealism and aesthetic refinement in part from the feudal aristocracy for whom they were performed: their tradition of characterization and play-structure became formalized to a point of exceptional finesse, subtlety and sophistication, a static, oratorical majesty of style matching a refined code of symbolic gestures and intonations, the verbal expression fastidious and restrained. With fierce energies and wild passions, the *kabuki* of a later age acquired its broader vitality, its violent emotions and slapstick elements, from its broader, popular audience.

Richard Southern in *The Seven Ages of the Theatre* distinguishes between the creative arts, in which there need be no contact between the creator and his audience, and the performing arts, in which it is essential that the performer comes into direct personal contact with his audience:

You can enjoy Picasso at an exhibition in Stockholm while Picasso himself is on the coast of the Mediterranean, but you can only enjoy Sir Laurence Olivier when Sir Laurence himself performs in your presence, before you and an assembled audience in the self-same building. This coming into direct personal contact is part of the player's art and, with the relentless element of the One Occasion, must be appreciated for any true understanding of the essence of the theatre.   (p. 23)

Southern's 'one particular occasion', in all its importance, is difficult to assess even the day after. Already so recent a mode of experience as that of the Edwardian problem drama escapes us: it is now hard to understand the furore that attended the opening of *En attendant Godot* in 1953. How much more difficult is the task of the student of drama who must make a leap back to a former age.

We ask to know about the conditions of performance of a play in order to gain some sense of those governing factors of convention, stage and audience which guide us to the mode of experience the play's first audience underwent. In particular what chance do we have in trying to recreate imaginatively the theatre of the Greeks, the Middle Ages, the Elizabethans, the Restoration? Different as one is from another, all these share the communal conditions of open staging; but those who unselfconsciously go to a play are naturally unable to recognize conventions they take for granted, and we are today so implicitly a public of consumers that the participatory mode of experience defeats our power of imagination. This chapter will therefore isolate some general, but essential, problems about earlier modes of performance which must be resolved if their vitality is to be appraised.

If we believe that drama is a reactive art, we must be plagued by the question how, in a theatre the size of the ancient Greek, some 400 feet across and seating a number between the 17,000 of the Theatre of Dionysus and the 56,700 of the Theatre of Ephesus, any kind of worthwhile experience was possible to the spectators. Sheer size and scale seem to be one of the modal factors to be weighed. The Greek *theatron* meant a 'place for seeing', and, collectively, the spectators themselves, those who watch; however, the act of seeing was not at the heart of this occasion, we can be sure, and the absence of visual detail in Greek tragedy supports this. But scale remains. That the number of the chorus was far greater than that of the actors proper, that the chorus's song and the animation of its dance in sheer force of sense impressions dominated the static, cothurnus-shod principals, encourage the idea that this was not a narrative drama with choric interpolations, but a choric drama with narrative interpolations. The masked actors remained remote and impersonal, while the chorus, in closer touch with the audience, was relatively free to reinforce and expand its centrally visual and aural impact.

The question remains: in this size of theatre could a Greek audience have a ritual experience with all the implications of homogeneous participation, a communal sharing between actor and audience? A first assumption must be that it is not size that is the modal factor after all, even if this insists upon an austere grandeur of aural presentation. From this and other early religious drama it is arguable that the secret of the experience is to be found in the quality of 'roundness' – the great circular 78-foot *orchestra* at the centre of all, the near-roundness of the vast arena itself. There may be a special virtue for an audience watching any activity 'in the round': in such a situation a spectator shares and enjoys the focus of the action with the actor himself. This explains physically, at least, why the chorus repeatedly reproduces and extends the deepest thoughts of all Greek citizens. In this spirit the chorus becomes the play, and the audience the chorus, teaching and self-teaching without didacticism, because the lesson is impressed by the players on the feelings of those who share them. The chorus merely articulates by ritualistic means, therefore, what the spectators wish to have articulated, and what in more intimate circumstances they would have wanted to say for themselves.

A study of conditions of performance in Greek times, it seems, dissolves into a consideration of its mode of apprehension, making evaluation possible. We are not finally measuring the breadth of an auditorium, but the depth of a response whose fervour can be felt in the weight and rhythm of the lines. A similar transference of judgment from the physical to the subjective and aesthetic will be, though less obviously, one way of understanding the drama of any theatre.

The three centuries of life in which the English mystery cycles flourished (the Festival of Corpus Christi was decreed by Pope Urban IV in 1264; the York cycle was played until it was proscribed in 1569) was an astonishing length of time for one dramatic form to be sustained and perfected. Only the Oriental theatre lived as long, and a similar refinement of technique in the various arts of the stage may not have been impossible. Here were nearly twelve generations of a drama so intimately linked with its many small communities that its social role must have been all-pervasive. Chapter I touched on the fact that most research, understandably, has been done into its origins in Church ritual, and various attempts have been made to determine its genre retrospectively ('the Elizabethan theatre was the crowning glory of the medieval experiment'). And in spite of many contemporary attempts at reviving the Mystery Plays, the medieval theatre experience, with its simplicity and intimacy of playing and response, remains misty. The living relationship between stage and audience is still the fundamental object of interest, however, and a good deal of external evidence is open to examination.

The pressures of a harsh environment we can see with Pieter Breugel's eyes; the rigours of a rooted faith are recognizable in the sinister panels of Hieronymus Bosch. The illiteracy of a popular audience, and its unsophisticated view of the scriptures, guide us to other virtues in the plays. Add to this a crowded city, the special holiday, the air of festival, the June warmth, the year-long culmina-

tion of effort by the guild actors, every man well-known in his lo-
cality, and all the unique ingredients of a shared activity seem to be
present. Even an element of lively competition was felt, as in the
Greek festivals: one guild competing with another in the decoration
of its pageant or mansion, one Herod or Jesus striving to outdo the
next. The severity of the appointed critics ('the moste connyng discrete and able plaiers within this Citie' are indicated in the Council
Book of York, 3 April 1476, with instruction 'to serche, here, and
examen all the plaiers and plaies and pagentes') would have been
nothing compared with the intimate judgment of the citizens themselves.

It is a commonplace that the great theme of these plays matched
that of the Greeks: profound in purpose, vast in conception, the
mystery cycles explored the whole story of Christian man's moral
adventure on earth. Yet the conditions of their performance were
different in essential ways. The medieval crowds did not expect to
have their emotions conducted like a huge symphony assembled in
one place: it was individualized in many smaller groups pressing
round a pageant wagon in a street, or a 'mansion' in the market
square. This relationship of the spectator with the stage wholly
changed the ritual shaping of the drama. Now the medieval citizen
could see and inspect the celestial adornment of heaven in gold and
blue, the spectacle of hell-mouth belching smoke; he could admire or
criticize the gilt mask of the Father, tremble or not at Satan's 'serpent
form with yellow hair upon his head', recognize Herod's gloves red
with the blood of the Innocents, and at the same time know the
local source of the props and effects. Now gesture, movement and
facial expression (only the supernatural figures, it seems, wore masks),
as well as the more subtle music of the voice possible in intimate
playing, added to the impact in the tight focal circle. The impersonality of a dancing chorus was replaced by the individuality of a performer meeting a more individual response.

The details of the mystery play scripts constantly reveal these
multifarious, often contradictory, conditions: homiletic speech,
admonitory and moralizing, on the one hand, touches of local dia-
lect appealing for another level of attention on the other; the awesome
dignity of God's address to his angels or Christ's to the crowd set
against the humour in Satan, Adam, Noah's Wife, Joseph, Dame
Percula and many more; the sweep and power of a deep religious
pathos felt in the scenes of crucifixion, sharpened by the many details

of medieval cruelty and violence. And this drama of ranging contrasts was played by its actors for high stylization at one moment, and with a pointed and realistic by-play with the spectators at their feet at the next. Spectacle with simplicity, symbolism with realism, grandeur with familiarity, lofty characters with lowly, were all encouraged by the liberties of open and open-air staging. A heritage indeed for the Elizabethans, but an independent mode.

With all its freedoms, the medieval drama was nevertheless constricted by certain circumstances of its playing: the rarity of the annual event, the religious occasion, the circumscribed Biblical content of the action, the dogmatic predetermination of every development in the story. In this lay both a strength and a weakness: the medieval drama had the powerful expectations of a ritualistic and repeated event, but it lacked the joy of the unexpected. The world of the Italian *Commedia dell'arte* was created, and survived for so long, because such restrictions were removed. The basic operating conditions of the early *Commedia* may be summed up in a word: freedom. To be sure, it met with municipal attack, as at Bologna where women, young men, children, priests and friars were forbidden to witness the plays. But it was itinerant, adaptable to any audience, flexible in every way; it was quite 'illegitimate', and free to grow.

The *Commedia* also enjoyed the focal intimacy of the Greek roundness and the smaller audiences of the medieval drama: thus nonillusory playing to known spectators was still at the heart of the experience. However, the response of the viewer to an undetermined 'plot', and the reaction of the player to a solicited and hard-earned response, provided a new source of growth and new rules for building a play. Chapter 3 discussed the virtues of spontaneity in an improvised play, one in which the actors were the authors and performance grew from their reaction to each other through the channel of the audience. In a drama of spontaneity and improvisation before a fully participating audience, the mask animates the body, and in turn the body further defines the expression of the mask. The riotous spirit of the *Commedia*'s stage is directly attributable to the shared freedom which the mask lent both actor and spectator: the reduction and rejection of reality became an end in itself. The long history of this form and its amazing proliferation across Europe can be explained by these conditions of playing: they made of the *Commedia* the third great mode of Western drama. Its decline began not only when Goldoni tried to control and limit performance by means of a written dialogue, but also when the troupes found themselves in increasing demand by noble patrons unwilling to watch alfresco. It died when it left the public piazza, which was the natural extension of the piazza setting of the booth stage, and was destroyed when housed in such glorious monstrosities as Palladio's theatre at Vicenza. The *Commedia* had no future when it lost touch with its true audience, its vital conditions of performance, and became civilized.

It is little wonder that the popular Elizabethan stage, the *corrales* of the Golden Age in Spain and even the Court theatre of Louis XIV in France borrowed freely from this kind of street theatre. Signs of the *Commedia dell'arte* are everywhere in Shakespeare's comedies. In Madrid, an Italian troupe set up an early example of the Spanish *corrales* in 1574. Molière's debt to the style and content of the *Commedia* is well known: the balletic qualities of his stage, his ability to use farce in the service of comedy, the frontal attack of actor upon spectator, take life and energy from the Italian tradition.

In England, the architecture of the London theatres sought that quality of roundness which allowed the full involvement of the audience, a high homogeneity of response and a new ritualism of effect. In such circumstances a king could seem to speak for mankind, and every spectator be a Hamlet for the nonce. But in sensing the Elizabethan mode it is not of this that one thinks first. A new and far greater range and flexibility of response was made possible by the exceptional size and depth of the Elizabethan platform in relation to the house. With its many playing areas – in part a development from the medieval tradition of multiple staging, in part a commonsense exploiting of a rich opportunity – the stage platform of the new playhouses encouraged a dramatic dialogue and scene structure of exciting tonal variation. From this stage grows Shakespeare's own craft of simultaneous staging, whereby attention may be demanded for two or more actions at the same time, with all this means for ironic interplay in the word-choice of the dialogue and the scoring of the performance. We shall see later how the practice of moving a character into or out of his play was also prompted by these playing conditions. Only in the modern theatre have such provocative effects been attempted again, after Pirandello and Brecht pioneered the release from the constraints of realism.

In *Endeavors of Art*, Madeleine Doran enriched our study of form in Elizabethan drama by stressing its power to induce a double mode of perception. The historical perspective she insisted upon was an aesthetic one, since the Renaissance playwrights, like any others, were bound to work within a context, a frame, of artistic reference. The playwright's frame of reference 'must have consisted, not merely of the ideas of artistic purpose and form to which he could give a name, but also of the tastes, interests, assumptions, and attitudes to which his age would have predisposed him whether he thought about them or not'. One age differs from another in its art 'because the artists have different modes of imaginative beholding'. With this we readily agree, and would wish to extend the notion to include the spectators who are part of the playwright's frame of reference.

This approach applies most obviously to our muddled concept of Elizabethan tragicomedy. The tragicomic mixtures found throughout the period in a vexing variety of patterns reflect what Doran deduces as 'a sophisticated end product of Renaissance delight in variety and resistance to the simplicity of classical form'. When today we look for neo-Aristotelian satisfactions of unity in a work according to modern criteria of the interweaving of parts and the balance of effect, we may overlook the fact that few Elizabethans were willing to sacrifice their delight in variety. At best the result was what Doran called 'a kind of multiple unity of many parts' — a touch of despair here — but it was exactly this motley omnifariousness that gave an Elizabethan play its spirit. 'It was bustling, lively, and generous. The motto seems to have been never to throw anything away that could possibly be tucked in somewhere. One of the reasons for Shakespeare's superiority to his fellows was that he had a genius for finding a way to bring all this variety into harmonious relationship.'

Madeleine Doran's argument may bring us closer to the life of the Elizabethan stage and reveal its disturbing ability to stimulate any spectator who submitted himself to the experience. Asked whether they were 'comedians', the Player in Middleton's *The Mayor of Queenborough* replied without hesitation,

We are, sir; comedians, tragedians, tragi-comedians, comi-tragedians, pastorists, humourists, clownists, satirists: we have them, sir, from the hug to the smile, from the smile to the laugh, from the laugh to the handkerchief.   (v.i)

And to this a physical style of playing in depth to engage an audience, and scene after scene in Shakespeare teases us with the complications of ironic action, calling for double and triple responses, constantly ambivalent in laying one meaning upon another, setting attitude against attitude, superimposing a smile upon a tear, impudence upon profundity.

The scene in which the Nurse brings Juliet the news of the arrangements for her marriage with Romeo (II.v) demonstrates simply how this double-level playing works. It is striking that the audience has just heard from Romeo's own lips the message the Nurse is bringing, and yet Shakespeare perversely treats us to a long, and at first highly lyrical, solo of conventional lovesickness from Juliet as she waits for the Nurse to arrive. Her subject is time, she is in suspense, but there is none for us. Of course in some sympathy we see and hear her agitation:

> The clock struck nine when I did send the Nurse,
> In half an hour she promised to return,
> Perchance she cannot meet him; that's not so:
> Oh she is lame, love's heralds should be thoughts,
> Which ten times faster glide than the sun's beams.

But why does Shakespeare take up valuable stage time for a confessional soliloquy here? We hardly need further promptings of sympathy for the girl, and, although our affection for her remains warm as we watch her anxious performance downstage, we quickly discover that such is not the scene's intention at all. Juliet's fears, idealistic in tone but at the same time expressed in jerky sentences, are chiefly there for comedy: a hit at romantic excess, a reminder of the amusing difference between the old and the young, a strangely cool and objective look at our heroine in the throes.

The notion of Shakespeare's ironic intention is reinforced when the Nurse at last makes her entrance – upstage, of course, so that Juliet must run to meet her:

> O God she comes, O honey Nurse what news?

After Shakespeare's implicit anticipation of the image of the old woman as 'unwieldy, slow, heavy, and pale as lead', Juliet's lines are alive with her youth and excitement. But the Nurse is made to prolong the agony, and moves with exaggerated slowness down the stage, the girl at her heels:

> NURSE: I am aweary, give me leave a while,
>   Fie how my bones ache, what a jaunce have I?
> JULIET: I would thou hadst my bones, and I thy news.

As the Nurse gives her orders to her servant, catches her breath, attends to herself, hobbles away pursued by Juliet, perhaps on the open stage of the Elizabethan platform a wink at the audience would appropriately remind us that her performance is all pretence — else what is the proximity good for? This comic delay continues for some fifty aching lines after the entrance of the Nurse, and while the device helps transmit to us some idea of Juliet's suspense, its chief purpose must be to have us share the pleasure of tormenting the girl as the old woman is doing. Three-dimensional stage space takes on unpredictable meaning when it is put to good use in context, and the Elizabethan response to Juliet's plight is deliberately ambivalent. Laced with comic double values in which we enjoy teasing and being teased simultaneously, this sweet story of young love gains strength and muscle in its objectivity.

In the mature plays, Shakespeare's instinct to capture the double values of his stage becomes sharper still. Antony's speech in the Forum in *Julius Caesar*, III.ii has all the force of simplicity — not in the rhetorical tricks he plays on the citizens, but in the distinction between the reaction to Antony of the on-stage audience and our own. On the open platform Antony's address must be upstage facing the audience both on and off the stage; indeed, individuals in the crowd of supers playing Roman citizens seem to drop their initial comments into our ear like asides, and looking upstage with them we seem to swell their number. On Tyrone Guthrie stages today the play is often staged as if we were intended to be the Roman crowd ourselves. But this is a false invoking of 'participation': such pretense cannot be sustained for long when the ear contradicts the eye.

We soon perceive, as the on-stage audience cannot, what chicanery Antony is perpetrating with his repeated innuendoes, his emotional deceit and his dissembling as Caesar's chief mourner. By the time we hear the citizens' cries of

> — They were traitors: honourable men!
> — They were villains, murderers.
> — Revenge! — About! — Seek! — Burn! Fire —
>   Kill! — Slay! Let not a traitor live.
> — Pluck down benches.
> — Pluck down forms, windows, anything.

we have dissociated ourselves from our apparent representatives on the stage. In part prepared by Brutus's earlier logic, the offstage audience sees the on-stage audience as a mob by making an intelligent rejection of the irrational outcry. Any hesitant deductions about Antony's motives are finally confirmed when we hear Antony, at last alone on the stage, utter anarchical sentiments in a new and uglier tone of voice:

> Now let it work: mischief, thou art afoot,
> Take thou what course thou wilt!

This speech in turn is immediately illustrated, as so often in Shakespeare, by action: the rioters set upon an innocent bystander, Cinna the poet, and mob violence rules. In this manner the Elizabethan stage granted its audience two sets of ears: it simultaneously heard Antony both as a politician and as a man, and was compelled to recognize the difference.

When Shakespeare put Elizabethan stage conditions to full use in a scene having many centres of interest, it defies descriptive analysis, like any image too various in colour and tone, shape and size. Such a scene is that of Banquo's ghost, *Macbeth*, III.iv; but let us try to follow the sequence of affective stage images, avoiding what Dr Johnson called 'the cant of those who judge by principles rather than by perception'. The formality of the ceremonial music, the presence of the throne and the laden banqueting table, and the colourful processional entrance of the King and Queen and their court as they circle the stage, immediately establish this as a public occasion: all in extreme contrast with the slinking movements and the whispers in the dark of the Murderers' scene it follows. The only doubtful note might be struck by the music of the 'hoboys', which carry sinister and supernatural, as well as decorous, implications. Macbeth's voice initially matches the pageantry, 'bright and jovial' as his Lady had enjoined him, a public voice, very much in command:

> You know your own degrees, sit down:
> At first and last, the hearty welcome.

Lady Macbeth 'keeps her state', overlooking all from her throne upstage: already her separation from the feast lends us another pair of eyes with which to see – this is to be a performance she has planned and will oversee. But Macbeth is to receive three bloody visits, each providing another, more urgent centre of interest in which Macbeth the private man will be seen in public surroundings. The King is in constant motion ('ourself will mingle with society'), and finds it easy to keep half an eye upon the other door – watching, perhaps, for Banquo or news of him. His first visit is from the Murderer who despatched his rival. 'There's blood upon thy face' breaks into the public line, 'we'll drink a measure / The table round', with a sharp change of tone. Macbeth draws the Murderer apart and downstage toward us, the better for the spectators, but not the guests, to witness the double performance, the conspiratorial manner, of the King. Upon the disastrous information about Fleance and the response 'Then comes my fit again', we see also a third Macbeth, the even more secret man, and the tension between host and guests is implicit and anticipated. From her place of vantage Lady Macbeth also sees her husband's other self, and returns him with sibilant whispers to his duty:

> You do not give the cheer: the feast is sold
> That is not often vouch'd, while 'tis a-making.

Meanwhile the Ghost 'with twenty trenched gashes on his head' has taken Macbeth's place at the table, but there are 15 ironic lines before Macbeth sees him as we do: an appalling delay during which Macbeth resumes his ceremonial manner and dares to mention Banquo's absence. In non-illusory drama we do not have to believe in ghosts to see what Macbeth sees, nor the guests to see another face on their leader. They are on their feet ('Gentlemen rise, his Highness is not well') and the short lines suggest the disruption of the scene; perhaps the music stops abruptly.

All eyes are on Macbeth, Macbeth's on Banquo. The tension between the King and his lords is now explicit, and when order returns, we watch the interplay of word and glance between guest and guest, Macbeth and Lady Macbeth. The presence of strangers emphasizes the depth of the King's hypocrisy. It takes all the Lady's time to seat the company again, and to regain control over her husband. But she has not seen the Ghost, and she is steadily losing him to his private horrors. The variations in the pace of Macbeth's speech after the Ghost has left point to his complete disturbance, and we see his strained smile covering the forced evasions of his toast to the absent Banquo – this bravado at the very moment when the Ghost is making his second appearance. It is as if Macbeth is summoning his nemesis ('Would he were here'), and Shakespeare makes use of the reappearance completely to unnerve him and finally to disrupt the banquet. This time the guests rise compulsively and the party breaks up in total disarray. They depart in a manner quite at odds with their grand entrance, and the Queen has lost all authority, the beginning of her personal collapse. She can only accept the situation feebly: 'Stand not upon the order of your going.' The Macbeths finally slump forlorn and alone over the shambles of their feast, each suffering a personal defeat. And the dawn rises: 'What is the night?' — 'Almost at odds with morning'.

This review of the development of the scene can barely touch the way the Elizabethan stage lends itself physically to accentuating the tensions in the action. The audience has the privilege of watching Lady Macbeth as she watches her plans for deceit break up: we understand her and yet are pleased to see her stretched by events now all but beyond her. We also watch Macbeth in his contest with the Murderer and the Ghost, bloody reminders both of his 'saucy doubts and fears', and we see these develop to the point of his open exhaustion of spirit:

It will have blood they say:
Blood will have blood.

Again we understand, even with a degree of compassion, the words confirming, pointing and enlarging the gory stage images we have seen; and yet we vicariously enjoy the working of providence as the murderer is brought low. We also watch the struggle, increasingly beyond bounds, between the man and the woman, a hopeless clash between a shallow and a profound mind to keep private and public matters separate.

Yet, obliquely, an indispensable group on the stage, the uneasy guests, torn between formality and fear, insures that the private shall become public. As they represent the world's eyes, tension between them and the Queen, and between them and the King, becomes intolerable. Again, we see what they see, see how murder must out, see the precarious edge that Macbeth is treading both as a monarch and as an immortal soul. The Elizabethan stage enables such complexities to work with ease, and they fully engage us in a drama which is at once realistic in its observation of human behaviour and imaginative in its representation of wider significances: in Dr Johnson's words, remarking 'general properties and large appearances'.

The Greek, medieval and Renaissance theatres have a common ele-

ment of immeasurable importance: they grew from, and were nourished by, unified communities. Their writers enjoyed the favours
of an essentially homogeneous audience which also embodied a fair
range of social attitudes while gathered together in one place;
unfortunately, this magic context for good playwriting may be a thing
of the past. The theatre today rarely finds such conditions even for
playing, and certainly not for playwriting: cinema unhappily pre-
cludes the basis of any reactive dramatic experience, and in television
there is at best only a pretended rapport between the studio and
the living-room. In being completed before any spectator need see it,
the film may have more in common with the art of painting than with
the stage. The dramatic activity of the twentieth century betrays
a desperate search for new forms of playmaking and staging, in the
uncertain hope of accommodating the fragmented nature of contemporary theatre-going.

The diversity of life and style on the medieval stage, in Jacobean
comedy, in Shakespeare, the mixture of voices and attitudes and
motives, lent richness to the circumscribed themes of Renaissance
drama, and is part of their creative energy and their genius. Only two
or three times in the history of English theatre since Shakespeare have
playwrights faced a homogeneous audience again. In each case homogeneity prompted an eruption and development of a successful genre;
in each case, however, the audience was also socially limited,
denying the playwright some of the vitality that goes with range.
Such an eruption occurred with the exuberant court comedy of the
Restoration after 1660, the flourishing of comic opera and satirical
burlesque just before the Licensing Act of 1737 which closed all
theatres except Covent Garden and Drury Lane, and the positive
explosion of 'illegitimate' burletta and domestic melodrama in the
first half of the nineteenth century. To these we might add the plays
of the short-lived Irish dramatic movement at Dublin's Abbey
Theatre. All else is borrowed, derivative, largely untrue to its
theatre and audience: one thinks of the forced, false theatre of heroic
tragedy, of the quasi-Elizabethan verse drama of the Romantic
poets, of the Edwardian domestic and social moralities, and the
pallid verse dramatists of the 1930s and 40s. But this is not the
place for a potted history.

Restoration comedy admirably illustrates how particular conditions combine to create a viable mode of theatre. If we believe with
McLuhan that games are extensions of social man, then a primary

example of such a game is to be found in the kind of social theatre which took its life from the court of Charles II, from the narrow world of his courtiers and their women. The early rules of this particular game were elastic: Etherege was more concerned with the audience's perception of social manners, Wycherley with social mores; Etherege was a delicate still-life painter, Wycherley a skilled manipulator of puppets in the flesh. But because of an unusually close rapport between author, stage and audience, Restoration comedy was nevertheless alive with interplay between all parties: its best texts were devised like an electric circuit in which performance threw the switch.

Playhouses were of the smallest. In the beginning the King's and the Duke's Men actually adapted walled and roofed tennis courts with their penthouse corridors (inside dimensions some 96 by 32 feet), the net line which divided the service from the hazard side exactly dividing the play and the audience. Ten years later, the interior dimensions of the Dorset Garden Theatre of 1671 (about 137 by 53 feet) and Wren's design for Drury Lane in 1674 (112 by 36 feet) were still comparably small. The spectators were artificially illuminated by the same candles which lit the actors, so that both actor and audience had the sensation of being in the same friendly room. The actors played far out on the apron forestage and almost as much in the centre of the house amongst the spectators as in the larger Elizabethan public theatres.

In these confined circumstances the audience behaved as if it were in a private party, enjoying private jokes. By today's standards it would be considered very badly behaved indeed, showing a total disrespect for the art of drama. Was this then a 'bad' house for a new playwright to write for? On the contrary, the lively life of the pit mirrored the spirit of the stage, and the stage was an extension of the house. A Restoration audience was arguably the best in the world.

This factor of the spectator's attitude to the play points essentially to the mode of the Restoration experience. It would seem that box, pit and gallery had a life of their own and were often in competition with the play itself. Spectators certainly played a role, not only in the auditorium, but back-stage too — a role not unlike that of the actors themselves. In his *Restoration Theatre* Montague Summers usefully collected evidence which touches in the picture of the world of the new playhouse in those early years. Henri Misson in his *Memoires* suggests the general attitude of irreverence towards the play in the intimate conditions of the Theatre Royal in 1698: 'Men of quality, particularly the younger sort, some ladies of reputation and virtue, and abundance of damsels that haunt for prey, sit all together in this place, higgledy-piggledy, chatter, toy, play, hear, hear not.' Several entries in Pepys's *Diary* hint at the familiar back-stage activity notoriously attributed to gentlemen and actresses: in 1668 he

did see Beck Marshal come dressed, off of the stage, and looks mighty fine, and pretty, and noble: and also Nell, in her boy's clothes, mighty pretty. But, Lord! their confidence! and how many men do hover about them as soon as they come off the stage, and how confident they are in their talk!

In prologue and epilogue, Wycherley seems to suggest that the players accepted this state of affairs willingly:

> You good men o' th' Exchange, on whom alone
> We must depend, when sparks to sea are gone;
> Into the pit already you are come,
> 'Tis but a step more to our tyring-room.
>
> (Epilogue, *The Gentleman-Dancing-Master*, 1672)

> We set no guards upon our tyring-room,
> But when with flying colours, there you come,
> We patiently you see, give up to you
> Our poets, virgins, nay, our matrons too.
>
> (Prologue, *The Country Wife*, 1675)

The players were less happy when the spectators used the stage itself for self-display, as many a prologue intimates:

> But that this play may in its pomp appear,
> Pray let our stage from thronging beaux be clear.
> For what e'er cost we're at, what e'er we do,
> In scenes, dress, dances; yet there's many a beau,
> Will think himself a much more taking show.
> How often have you curs'd these new beau-skreens,
> That stand betwixt the audience and the scenes?
> I asked one of 'em t' other day – Pray, sir,
> Why d'ye the stage before the box prefer?
> He answer'd – my shape, my leg, I there display,
> They speak much finer things than I can say.
>
> (Settle, *The Fairy-Queen*, 1692)

As late as 1711 Richard Steele describes how one beau

getting into one of the side-boxes on the stage before the curtain drew, was disposed to shew the whole audience his activity by leaping over the spikes; he passed from thence to one of the ent'ring doors, where he took snuff with a tolerable good grace, display'd his fine cloaths, made two or three feint passes at the curtain with his cane, than fac'd about and appeared at the other door; here he affected to survey the whole house, bow'd and smil'd at random, and then shew'd his teeth (which were some of them indeed very white); after this he retir'd behind the curtain, and obliged us with several views of his person from every opening.   (*The Spectator*, no. 240)

In spite of all this, the presence in the playhouse of another ingredient ensured that the auditorium itself was the scene of the main performance. The pit and boxes were graced by orange wenches and other ladies of easy virtue in vizards, and these found themselves in competition with well-born ladies who adopted the vizard that they should not be deprived of their sport. Many playwrights testify to the diversionary attraction this caused. Thus the character of the spark Brittle in a play of Thomas Betterton's:

'Tis the pleasantest thing in the whole world to see a flock of wild gallants fluttering about two or three ladies in vizard masks, and then they talk to 'em so wantonly, and so loud, that they put the very players out of countenance — 'Tis better entertainment, than any part of the play can be.   (*The Amorous Widow*, 1670)

In one play Thomas Shadwell recreates the atmosphere of the pit by having several of his characters speak discursively:

—What should we do at this damned playhouse?
—What ladies are here in the boxes? Really, I never come to a play but on account of seeing the ladies.
—I cannot find my mistress; but I'll divert myself with a vizard in the meantime.
—What, not a word! All over in disguise! Silence for your folly, and a vizard for your ill face.
—Gad! some whore, I warrant you, or chambermaid in her lady's old clothes.
(He sits down and lolls in the orange-wench's lap)
—She must be a woman of quality; she has right point.

—'Faith! she earns all the clothes on her back by lying on 't; some punk
lately turned out of keeping, her livery not quite worn out.

(*A True Widow*, 1678)

Thomas D'Urfey sums the matter up neatly in another prologue:

> Another to compleat his daily task,
> Fluster'd with claret, seizes on a mask,
> Hisses the play, steals off with punk i' the dark,
> He damns the poet, but she claps the spark.

(*A Commonwealth of Women*, 1685)

Here was a playhouse serving either what Macaulay, in *The
Comic Dramatists of the Restoration* (1841), thought of almost as a
bordello, or what Tom Brown, in his *Amusements Serious and
Comical, Calculated for the Meridian of London* (1700), saw as a
'land of enchantment': 'The playhouse is an enchanted island, where
nothing appears in reality what it is, nor what it should be.' Certainly,
any dramatic theory of illusory communication is quite unable to take
account of its temper; yet the evidence from the plays is so abundant
that it cannot be ignored. The evidence insists upon an answer to the
big central questions: what kind of play would emerge in this heated
climate? Was this not a 'bad' audience? Only if rapt attention or
a state of hypnosis is all that matters for performance, and perception
is thought to depend only on signals from the text itself. We recall
Brecht's appalled description of the spectators in the theatre of
illusion:

We see somewhat motionless figures in a peculiar condition: they seem
strenuously to be tensing all their muscles, except where these are flabby
and exhausted. They scarcely communicate with each other; their relations
are those of a lot of sleepers ... True, their eyes are open, but they stare
rather than see, just as they listen rather than hear. They look at the stage
as if in a trance. (*A Short Organum for the Theatre*, trans. J. Willett)

Restoration playing conditions were bad only if it is thought that a
play must suppress the life of its playhouse and not respond to it.
In the private parties of the Restoration theatre, an actor could share
the fun and an author be one of the guests, their mouthpiece and their
critic.

There is one other key physical factor which must supplement
the picture of the Restoration playhouse experience. The script had to

match the self-conscious acting of the young women who appeared on the London stage for the first time in a regular way, vying for favours, one suspects, with the vizards in the pit.

In Shakespeare's time boy actors playing the female parts were essentially role-playing, as Rosalind's epilogue to *As You Like It* makes clear when she begs applause:

If I were a woman, I would kiss as many of you as had beards that pleas'd me, complexions that lik'd me, and breaths that I defi'd not: and I am sure, as many as have good beards, or good faces, or sweet breaths, will for my kind offer, when I make curtsy, bid me farewell.

The amusing absence of sexuality in this reminds us that Shakespeare was exercised by the transvestite element in his comedies to show in a variety of ways only what women *would* do had they the liberty of men. He was perforce obliged to reveal the hearts and minds of his female characters, not their persons, and it was left to a later age to show what women actually looked like and what they actually did.

In 1629 French actresses played at the Blackfriars Theatre, and they were hissed out of town. In 1660 young women off the streets met the need of the new court theatres. A prologue of Thomas Jordan's for the King's Company records the occasion:

> I come, unknown to any of the rest
> To tell you news, I saw the lady drest;
> The woman plays today, mistake me not,
> No man in gown, or page in petticoat.
>
> (*A Royal Arbour of Loyal Poesie*)

Playing to the audience came on apace in such intimate circumstances, as Richand Steele seems to complain years later:

I, who know nothing of women but from seeing plays, can give great guesses at the whole structure of the fair sex, by being innocently placed in the pit, and insulted by the petticoats of their dancers; the advantages of whose pretty persons are a great help to a dull play. When a poet flags in writing lusciously, a pretty girl can move lasciviously, and have the same good consequences for the author.   (*The Spectator*, no. 51, 1711)

In the mid-eighteenth century, the actor Thomas Wilkes remarked the continuing freedom of the exchange between actress and spectator:

It is very common for young performers, the ladies in particular, in scenes which require the greatest exertion of the natural powers, and in the very warmth and pathos of a sentiment, to bestow frequent side-glances on the audience, demanding their applause, more for their beauty of person or elegance of dress than for their just acting.

(*A General View of the Stage*, 1759)

There speaks a professional in the best sense.

Because of the presence of women on the stage, not only were scenes more lubricious, but over half the plays written between 1660 and 1700 contained 'breeches parts', whereby the girls could show a little more of their legs than their ankles. Elizabeth Boutel, a favourite of the town, spoke this epilogue of John Corye's:

> As woman let me with the men prevail,
> And with the ladies as I look like male.
> 'Tis worth your money that such legs appear;
> These are not to be seen so cheap elsewhere:
> In short, commend this play, or by this light,
> We will not sup with one of you tonight.

(*The Generous Enemies; or, The Ridiculous Lovers*, 1671)

Not only did the presence of actresses on the stage start a search for plays old and new which would exploit them, but the whole structure and tone of comedy suffered a sea-change.

When the student knows of these conditions of playing, it is impossible to read the lines which open Wycherley's *The Gentleman-Dancing-Master*, or others like them, without some sense of their pertinence to the occasion:

HIPPOLITA: To confine a woman just in her rambling age! take away her liberty at the very time she shou'd use it! O barbarous aunt! O unnatural father! to shut up a poor girl at fourteen, and hinder her budding: all things are ripen'd by the sun; to shut up a poor girl at fourteen! —

Self-advertisement had never gone this far before, in the swish of the skirts and the pout of the lips, and in the twinkle in the eye. The theme is picked up on the other side of the stage. Not to be outdone, her maid echoes Hippolita's performance:

PRUE: 'Tis true, miss, two poor creatures as we are!
HIPPOLITA: Not suffer'd to see a play in a twelve-month! —

PRUE: Nor to go to Ponchinello nor Paradise! –
HIPPOLITA: Nor to take a ramble to the Park nor Mulberry-gar'n! –
PRUE: Nor to Tatnam-Court nor Islington! –

And so they continue to list the places of entertainment and assignation which everybody knew, each mention no doubt raising a roar of approval. The game was on, and all concerned had already absorbed the rules.

If there is a difference in style between, say, Wycherley and Congreve, it is not necessarily because of a generation's development in dramaturgy: in many ways Wycherley enjoyed a better sense of the stage. We must look to the difference between their regard for their function as playwrights and their attitude to the audience. A generation has passed, and at the centre of things a pert Elizabeth Boutel has been replaced by an exquisite Anne Bracegirdle. Both playwrights, however, see the role of their theatre as part of a social celebration: the sense of *coterie* playgoing and play-making is present in both. Both kinds of actress deem it necessary in performance to flirt with their audience, and the audience still expects the familiarity. Performance analysis remains to be done on all this unusual material.

For example, the physical proximity of the actor to the audience, together with the festive nature of the occasion, developed the aside from what seems a trivial stage convention to a technical device of exceptional variety and subtlety, whereby an ambiguously innocent creature from the country like Margery Pinchwife not only suggests double intentions in her part, but also supports *doubles entendres* in her lines according to how far the personality of the actress is encouraged to burst out of her characterization. Similarly, rakes like Dorimant, Horner or Archer may seem morally indefensible at one moment, but at the next charmers who are the envy of every male and a challenge to every female in the audience. The art of the 'implicit aside' is felt behind every line in the comedies, especially those designed for the leading ladies and gentlemen, and any wit aspiring to be a poet in this theatre would be a fool not to make the most of the accepted mode of performance.

One has only to read Colley Cibber's delightful chapters on the 'theatrical characters of the principal actors' in his *Apology* for what he calls 'lively strokes of nature' in order to relish the Restoration spirit of performance. One of his favourites was Mrs Mountfort in the part of Melantha in Dryden's *Marriage à la Mode* (1672):

Melantha is as finished an impertinent, as ever fluttered in a drawing-room, and seems to contain the most compleat system of female foppery, that could possibly be crowded into the tortured form of a fine lady. Her language, dress, motion, manners, soul, and body, are in a continual hurry to be something more, than is necessary, or commendable.

When she attacks a gallant who calls upon her, she

pours upon him her whole artillery of airs, eyes, and motion; down goes her dainty, diving body, to the ground, as if she were sinking under the conscious load of her own attractions; then launches into a flood of fine language, and compliment, still playing her chest forward in fifty falls and risings, like a swan upon waving water.   (chapter v)

It is not a matter for despair, therefore, that such plays do not deal in good and evil and the state of one's soul. We may regret with one critic that the plays are confined to 'a miserably limited set of attitudes', but we can hardly accept that their quality lacks 'the essential stuff of human experience'. We may find with another critic that 'love did not exist' for these characters, and yet reflect that it may be as inappropriate to expect the amorous passion from Donald Duck. The mode of Restoration comedy is closest to that of social farce, and criticism must cease to apologize for it in terms of depth psychology, satirical intention, or whatever gives it literary respectability. Better by far acknowledge its beautiful absence of emotion, its perfectly calculated aesthetic distancing and the precision of the game it plays, and so arrive at unique and extraordinary insights into our enduring social proclivities.

The conditions set up by mass, popular audiences offer a conspicuous contrast. If the Restoration created a most unusual drama because of its audience's limited size, the nineteenth century created another because of its audience's excessive size. The period saw a rapid growth in the number of theatres in England, in the size of the average auditorium and in the number of plays written and produced (between 1700–50 and 1850–1900 the number increased by ten times from 2,000 to 20,000). But the truly significant increase came in the number of working-class people who regularly attended the legitimate and the illegitimate theatre, the stock companies and the penny gaffs (over a hundred of these in the poorer sections of London). The upper and middle classes deserted the drama for the opera, and in the early days only a Kemble or a Kean could lure them back. The size of the major theatres encouraged a new degree of spectacle on the stage and a new style of ranting, or 'projecting', from the players, while the new and simpler homogeneity of the large audiences for domestic drama and melodrama called for strong, emotional plots and broad stereotypes of characterization. The study of drama in the early years of Victoria's reign is essentially the study of an unprecedented social event, one which determined a whole new code of stage conventions.

The key to the conventional signals of Victorian domestic drama is to be found in the audiences who went to see it. The manager was at the spectator's mercy as never before, and he denied his patrons their rights at his peril. 'Patrons' seems a misnomer: they were largely poor and illiterate, dwelling in city slums. Nevertheless, in their world of theatre, if not outside, they had a fanatical sense of justice and injustice, and found vice where they wanted to: among the upper classes, wealthy merchants and squires, and representatives of the law. The downtrodden, the widows and orphans, working men on hard times and defenceless country girls, all those who worked for a pittance, formed the new tribe of heroes and heroines. They were joined by sailors of the Queen's navy, but, interestingly, not her soldiers. In the theatres which the new audience made its own, playgoers could express their feelings with cries of rage or shouts of joy as nowhere else, and they did. Theatrical rapport was complete: the noise of the audience was matched by that of the players as they roared back, and the clamour of both mingled with the calls of food sellers and the bawling of drunks.

Here then was another 'bad' audience whose homogeneity was good for theatrical vitality. Applause took the form of stamping and shouting, and was to be heard intermittently throughout the performance. The actors expected it, themselves calling for a response after a moral sentiment or after making a 'point' with a striking moment in the action of the play or a deft stroke of characterization, usually marking it by taking big steps to one side of the scene or towards the house. This might be thought to shatter the frame of illusion, breaking convention, were it not part of the convention itself. When the pit rose, as it did at Henry Irving's entrance as Mathias in *The Bells* in 1871, the roar of excitement was a necessary release for the audience. So Gordon Craig believed: Irving would stand as if measuring the length and volume of applause by shifting his right foot; then, by carefully judging his moment as the noise began to weaken, he clipped it short by seeming to wake from a long ordeal.

The hurricane of applause at Irving's entrance was no interruption ... It was a torrent while it lasted. Power responded to power ... for though Irving endured and did not accept the applause he deliberately called it out of the spectators. It was necessary *to them* – not to him; it was something they had to experience, or to be rid of, or rather released from, before they could exactly take in what he was going to give them.

(*Henry Irving*, p. 54)

The case was not essentially different for the villain. Hissing was his applause, if he had done his job well, and in the performance of Bill Sykes in the scene of Nancy's murder in *Oliver Twist*, hissing would extend to cursing, as John Hollingshead's graphic description tells:

Nancy was always dragged round the stage by her hair, and after this effort Sikes (*sic*) always looked up defiantly at the gallery, as he was doubtless told to do in the marked prompt copy. He was always answered by one loud and fearful curse, yelled by the whole mass like a Handel Festival chorus. The curse was answered by Sikes dragging Nancy twice round the stage, and then, like Ajax, defying the lightning. The simultaneous yell then became louder and more blasphemous. Finally when Sikes, working up to a well-rehearsed climax, smeared Nancy with red-ochre, and taking her by the hair (a most powerful wig) seemed to dash her brains out on the stage, no explosion of dynamite invented by the modern anarchist, no language ever dreamt of in Bedlam could equal the outburst. A thousand enraged voices, which sounded like ten thousand, with the roar of a dozen escaped menageries, filled the theatre and deafened the audience, and when the smiling ruffian came forward and bowed, their voices, in thorough plain English, expressed a fierce determination to tear his sanguinary entrails from his sanguinary body.

(*My Lifetime*, pp. 189–90)

Professional showmanship was more at work here than any theory of the drama; but it worked.

This kind of response to villainy suggests that the feelings of the Victorian audience were an untrustworthy mixture of moral indignation and vicarious pleasure. It loved its villains with a hate which, in its intensity, belongs to a childhood world. The theatre offered it the passing joys of complete and unsophisticated involvement in the direct and exciting experience, while all the time it knew well enough that it was only watching a performance. Indeed, it is hard to separate reality from make-believe at critical moments: playing the drunkard in a typical temperance play *The Bottle* (1847), the actor O. Smith, as Henry Baker records,

upset a cup of liquor; with a cry of horror he cast himself upon the stage and ravenously licked the spilled drink. It was one of those daring bits of business that only a strong actor, confident in his own powers, would have dared attempt; had it been weakly done it would have raised a laugh; as he did it, it sent a shudder through the house.

(*History of the London Stage*, 1904)

It is hard, therefore, for modern criticism to separate the element of burlesque from the illusory in these plays: modern revivals usually achieve only the former. In truth, the themes of melodrama are also ambivalent. In the simple moral patterns of these plays, Victorian evangelism preached a system of rewards and punishments which had little to do with the real world outside. Like a balance-sheet, vice would be punished and virtue, an entirely practical consideration, would be rewarded, so that the audience could be confident that all the misery and suffering of the protagonists would be worth it in the end. If the playgoers could not discover providence working on their side in their day-to-day lives, they expected it in the playhouse. And yet they knew they were indulging a lie, and enjoyed every minute of it.

It follows that our guides to audience perception on the Victorian stage are bold and simple, and outrageously so: there was no final illusion of reality. Characterization was uncomplicated, with never a sense of development, and marked by the clearest signals. The heavy villain immediately revealed himself in black – black cloak, black opera hat, black moustache; with his cane he always fell into the class of 'toff' or 'swell'. His female counterpart, all but a scarlet woman, would be overdressed in gaudy colours, ribbons and ear rings. By contrast, the doll-like heroine was always dressed in white, the symbol of purity and innocence (Agnes Fitzarden in William Moncrieff's *The Lear of Private Life* has four changes, of which three are white), and always with a bonnet; when the bonnet was lost or dangling by a careless ribbon and the poor girl's hair was in disarray, it could be safely assumed that she was in deep distress and imminent danger of assault upon her virtue; at the curtain call, the hat would be on and every hair again in place, praise be. If the hero was in a state of moral degradation (as in the temperance plays), his costume would magically change to rags like one who had seen better days, and a little blue chalk would appear on his cheeks to suggest by his unshaven looks the depths to which he had fallen. This was the nearest approximation to character development that this drama afforded.

The moral condition of the characters would also be simply delineated by their surroundings, a plain choice between virtue and vice. If the painted backcloth insisted that they were in street or tavern, the natural abodes of vice, they were in trouble. An ageing widow and her pretty daughter found starving and weeping in a modest country cottage or city garret, both emblems of virtue, were still on the path of righteousness.

In her wretched garret in a poor district of New York city, Mary Middleton of P. T. Barnum's successful temperance play *The Drunkard* (1844) sits shivering in an old shawl. She has been deserted by her husband, who, tempted by one Lawyer Cribbs, took to drink. Mary's dress is in rags, but it remains pristine white, so the audience knows that all yet remains well. Her music plays – the sad strings of a single violin. The wind howls outside, and perhaps at her repeated mention of the appalling state of the weather, the audience adds its voice to the noises-off. A knock is heard, which pretty Mary assumes immediately to be that of her errant husband; however, the audience has already heard the villain's theme, and knows better. Sure enough, enter Cribbs, a villain of the deepest dye, come to place temptation in her way now that her fortunes are at their lowest. Every spectator in the house recognizes the pattern of his own wayward condition. A hiss and a growl from the crowd and a leer and a threat from Cribbs, and he launches into the buttered smooth tones of his familiar piece.

CRIBBS: Your pardon for my intrusion at this untimely hour, but friends are welcome at all times and seasons, eh? So, so, you persist in remaining in these miserable quarters. When I last saw you, I advised a change.

MARY: Alas, sir, you know too well my wretched reasons for remaining here, But why do you come at this strange hour? Have you brought joyful tidings of my Edward?

CRIBBS: I must persist in it – you would do well to remove elsewhere.

MARY: Return to the village I will not. I must remain in New York and find my husband.

CRIBBS: This is a strange infatuation. He has others to console him whose soft attentions he prefers to yours.

MARY: What do you mean, sir?

CRIBBS: That there are many women — not of the most respectable class — who are always ready to receive presents from wild young men, and are not very particular in the liberties that may be taken in exchange.

MARY: Man, man, why dost thou degrade the form and sense Heaven hast bestowed on thee by falsehood?

Her words acquire an evangelical eloquence; but observe — at the very moment when suspense is running high and the threat to Mary's virtue imminent, the scene is stopped dead by the careful timing of her appeal to conscience. It has all been heard before, but it comes up fresh as paint. There follows a concatenation of cheers, sobs and curses, which act upon the audience as an almost physical release, tidily underscoring Mary's irreproachable sentiment about mankind. We may despise both the form and the content of this sort of theatre, but it exemplifies the pure strength of a simple aesthetic perfectly suiting its function.

The balletic gestures and poses that accompanied the powerful signals of the melodrama were the glory of the Victorian stage. The Edinburgh magazine *Theatre*, published in mid-century, is one of a number of sources of information on how the stage appeared to the naked eye. In its series *The Way to the Stage, or How to Become an Actor and Get an Engagement*, the apprentice thespian learned that, for example, he must kneel when declaring his love: 'Kneeling is often necessary in all suppliant passions, but it is only necessary to bend one knee in cases of love, desire, etc., which must never be the one that is next the audience' — a nice subtlety. Anger has 'the mouth open, and drawn on each side towards the ears, showing the teeth in a gnashing posture' — no doubt for the distant projection of the image. Grief 'sudden and violent, expresses itself by beating the head or forehead, tearing the hair, catching the breath as if choking; also by screaming, weeping, stamping, lifting the eyes from time to time to heaven, and hurrying backwards and forwards.'

Eyes and teeth have other duties. Despair,

bends the eyebrows downward, clouds the forehead, rolls the eyes, and sometimes bites the lips, and gnashes with the teeth. The heart is supposed to be too much hardened to suffer the tears to flow, yet the eyeballs must be red and inflamed. When despair is supposed to drive the actor to distraction and self-murder it can be seldom or ever overacted.

Dotage, Infirm or Old Age introduced new elements: it 'shows itself by hollowness of eyes and cheeks, dimness of sight, deafness and tremor of voice, hams weak, knees tottering, hands or head paralytic, hollow coughing, frequent expectoration, breathless wheezing, occasional groaning, and the body stooping under an insupportable load of years'. Props had their place in all this, and for Wonder and Amazement they were indispensable: 'If the hands hold anything at the time when the object of wonder appears, they immediately let it drop, unconsciously: the whole body fixes in a contracted, stooping posture, the mouth open, and the hands held open.'

It is no wonder that so many tableaux or 'pictures' (the term most often used in the old acting editions) are to be found as show-stoppers at the beginning, the climax and the end of a scene. Darting to one side, staggering back, pleading to high heaven, falling into a chair, sinking to the earth, standing transfixed to the spot, even making one's way across the stage upon one's knees – all suggest the clichés of the penny novels of the time transformed into living action. Yet they also indicate a vigorous, lusty and almost acrobatic display designed for immediate meaning within a convention familiar to author, actor and audience.

The point of this chapter has been to suggest where, in the matrix of external physical factors which shape a play, one seeks the telltale perceptions, those which show and explain its quality. They are those which cannot be passed over without risking unscholarly irrelevance. How can Synge's *Playboy* be understood without knowledge of the political tensions of the Irish dramatic movement? Or Jonson's *Bartholomew Fair* without the social structure of Jacobean society? Or Etherege's *The Man of Mode* without the spatial relationships of the Restoration stage?

Every theatre experience has its own *modus operandi*. Tradition in the theatre is constantly being modified as any one of many new influences is felt. Often they are those of the individual talent: it is possible to recognize the innovative and repercussive qualities in the work of such men as Ben Jonson, Molière or Brecht; Garrick, Stanislavsky or Meyerhold. Often a shift of mode can be directly related to the success of a particular play: Beaumont and Fletcher's *Philaster*,

Buckingham's *The Rehearsal*, Ibsen's *A Doll's House*, the play not necessarily outstanding but merely apropos, the audience and its theatre ripe for the occasion, the idea opportune. If the moment is not apt, disaster may follow, and the strange history of such delayed masterpieces as those of *Troilus and Cressida, Tartuffe, The Way of the World, Danton's Death, A Month in the Country* and *Ubu Roi* can be explained no other way.

The bulk of the history of theatre is an account of how the various parties to the play, audience, actors, author, chime with the best features of the physical theatre and the development of its conventions. It was Charles Macklin who first played Shylock for sympathy in 1741, but in retaining the conventional red wig of the comedian, he balanced the eighteenth century's new interest in the psychological depth of Shakespeare's characters with its continuing belief that the Jew was comic. Edmund Kean removed the red wig, replaced it with a black one and presented an authentic Shylock to match the new realistic approach to the classics of the stage. Finally, when Henry Irving in 1879 cut the scenes of the rings and the whole of the comedy of the last act following his exit in the role, *The Merchant* was at last a tragedy.

When Colley Cibber complained of the steady loss of the stage apron during the eighteenth century, he was complaining of the loss of a vital convention:

It must be observ'd then, that the area, or platform of the old stage, projected about four foot forwarder, in a semi-oval figure, parallel to the benches of the pit ... By this original form, the usual station of the actors, in almost every scene, was advanc'd at least ten foot nearer to the audience, than they now can be ... When the actors were in possession of that forwarder space, to advance upon, the voice was more in the centre of the house, so that the most distant ear had scarce the least doubt, or difficulty in hearing what fell from the weakest utterance: all objects were thus drawn nearer to the sense ... nor was the minutest motion of a feature (properly changing with the passion, or humour it suited) ever lost, as they frequently must be in the obscurity of too great a distance.

(*An Apology*, chapter XII)

We can now point to this physical change, even though it was brought about merely by a demand for more seats ('To all this a master of a company may say, I now receive ten pounds more, than could have been taken formerly, in every full house!') as a major reason for the loss of intimacy and the game-spirit of Restoration comedy.

Today the theatre is everywhere in search of its physically appropriate mode. Scientifically conscious of behaviourist psychology, the communication arts, theatre research and the evolution of the stage, managers, actors and playgoers are engaged in a most important public debate, its findings tested in practice every time a play is done in an old or a new theatre. The Tyrone Guthrie playhouses built at Stratford in Ontario, Chichester in Sussex and Minneapolis in Minnesota are symptomatic. The decision of the British National Theatre to have two stages, one a picture-frame and the other an open stage, suggests that the final choice is not yet made. Nor is the issue merely a physical one. Playing in a frame or in a circle affects the whole discipline of the actor and the choice of play he makes; but the decision will radically determine the kind of experience that audiences expect of their theatre-going, and therefore the skills of the playwright, the role of the manager, the function of the theatre in society and the whole future of the drama.

In spite of doubts and hesitations, the trend is towards open staging. Its advocates believe that this physical form offers actor and spectator the biggest opportunity to join in the most flexible and yet the most intense of possible experiences. Art is not progressive, and there is in this assumption some idealistic sense that a return to the participatory and non-illusory drama of the Elizabethans is possible.

The work of Vitruvius, who early attempted to reconstruct on paper the stages of Greece and Rome, was rediscovered in the sixteenth century, and the avid Renaissance architects readily seized upon his idea of a great central *porta regia*, all but a proscenium arch. This influence was in direct conflict with the native Elizabethan tradition of the open platform. In Jonson's Induction to *The Magnetic Lady* (1632), Damplay praises the work of the architectural master, but with a smack at Inigo Jones and his Italian scene magic for the court masques, the Boy asserts that the local product is best:

Sir, all our work is done without a portal – or Vitruvius. *In foro*, as a true comedy should be.

In foro is the English way: in the market-place, at the exchange, where actors and playgoers were theoretically interchangeable, the actors at one with the spectators, the spectators not above climbing on to the stage; where the 'realism' of the representation was never the first consideration, if it was considered at all; where the conventional rules of the game were at their most elastic, and carried within themselves infinite possibilities for imaginative extension; where actors could be in character one moment and impersonally choric the next, playing and role-playing.

Ambidexter, the prototypical comic Vice in Thomas Preston's popular *Cambises* (1569) – that native concoction of tragic ranting and farcical knock-about – demonstrated how he could and would 'play with each hand', both to the other characters on the stage and to the audience close around him. This is the theatre of the blatant aside, of the direct address which could embrace a whole house. This is the drama of eye-to-eye prologues, sly inductions and heated soliloquies. This theatre seems to encourage action both remote and near, plays and plays-within-plays, wheels within wheels which are exactly suited to arena performance. In this theatre plot matters less than the intensity of a spectator's involvement with the player at his work, less than the pace and rhythm which follows his identification with the actor and his action. This is the theatre of double meanings and double values, in which the real and the unreal are balanced on the stage for a perfect equation with the audience's suspension of disbelief, arousing and deeply satisfying. Bertolt Brecht would have welcomed this theatre; Shakespeare made it his own.

It is the theatre in which the rhythms of physical sensation coincide with imaginative sentiment: on the stage, the body with the word; in the audience, perception with conception. Iago invokes hell,

> I have't: it is engender'd: hell, and night,
> Must bring this monstrous birth, to the world's light,

at the very moment when the storm breaks over Cyprus with a roll of Elizabethan thunder, cannon-ball in a trough, and word-building creates the high-wrought flood. Macbeth invokes evil,

> come, seeling night,
> Scarf up the tender eye of pitiful day,
> And with thy bloody and invisible hand
> Cancel and tear to pieces that great bond,
> Which keeps me pale,

at the very moment when his hired assassins, 'night's black agents' of whom he speaks, creep upon the stage in readiness to do their worst. Lear roars with unfocused rage, all but a madman,

I will do such things,
What they are yet, I know not, but they shall be
The terrors of the earth,

at the very moment when a strange new voice is heard ominously in reply, symbolizing the unknown '*storm and tempest*' of the text, grand and impersonal.

Shakespeare's theatre engenders characters like Edmund the bastard in *Lear*, nearly but not quite an Iago because of the overwhelming force of that first soliloquy:

Thou Nature art my goddess, to thy law
My services are bound, wherefore should I
Stand in the plague of custom, and permit
The curiosity of nations, to deprive me?

'Why bastard? Wherefore base?' – the appeal is direct, the questions insistent, the visual proximity and open honesty supplying a modifying force which no audience can resist and which keeps him alive as a character to the end of the play. The Globe platform is the natural haunt of Hamlet the double man, the accomplished actor who plays his parts to Claudius, Polonius, Rosencrantz and Guildenstern, and also another man, our familiar who repeatedly comes forward on the intimate stage to speak his troubled mind into our ear.

Some of these concerns of actor and action in relation to the audience and its response call for separate treatment in the next chapter. Meanwhile, there is one central point to hold in mind: any theatre which denies its own nature risks self-destruction. Richard Southern is a warm advocate of the open stage because of its freedom from the restriction of theatrical illusion: 'Here poetry is not out of place. In an open-stage theatre, the illusion that you are *not* in a theatre is hard to create; the anti-illusion that that is just where you are and that it is a reality is equally hard to suppress' (*The Seven Ages of the Theatre*, p. 288). It is the place where fancy and invention remain the law because the fact of place cannot be dismissed from the mind.

5
Acting and role-playing

We are so accustomed to seeing actors impersonating 'characters' as realistically as possible, trying to the utmost of their bent to convince us of the living actuality of the figures they represent, that we forget that conviction of reality is only one, relatively minor, purpose the actor may pursue. Realism in characterization is so recent an objective for the actor that it does not seem unfair to see it as merely a period convention like any other; it is important, but only in so far as it belongs to our time. Realistic acting was a direct result of the naturalistic movement in the theatre after Ibsen, and of the continuing expectations of the film and television media long after the stage had dropped them. As a convention, it has already passed into history because of the greater needs of a succession of dramatic movements from symbolism, expressionism and the absurd, which called for abstract characterization, to the forms of epic theatre in Brecht and Genêt, who required the actor to play freely in and out of character. The actor's role is returning to its former function, which was not first that of impersonation, but nearer to that of interpreter and spokesman.

It is necessary to take the perspective view. The actor has the double advantage of being human like his spectators, looking like them, able to represent and demonstrate their feelings, and at the same time capable of impersonating the creatures of an unreal fiction, giving a kind of life to the figures of pure fantasy. Thornton Wilder believed that because the theatre is the most human and closest to life of all the arts, it therefore permits an extreme degree of distortion. This paradoxical notion may account for the abuse of the audience permitted the boy players in the Induction to Jonson's *Cynthia's Revels* (1600), and other plays like it, and may suggest an answer to the puzzle of the manner in which the Elizabethan audience viewed and accepted boy players at all, whether acting in a burlesque style or realistically. The actor can sweep us into another world, and yet keep a foothold on reality. In the highly stylized theatres of the Greeks, the Middle Ages and the Renaissance, of the Sanskrit and Oriental theatres, in all of man's most exhilarating drama, the conventional leap into that imaginative other world has always been extreme, risking loss of reality, dangerously irrational.

Pantomime, dumb-show or ballet is performance which tells a story by dance or gesture without words. Since any of these completely embodies the idea of drama as a pretence, to witness it is to recognize the fictive nature of dramatic representation, of a pretence which knows it is a pretence. No matter how exquisite the art of a Marcel Marceau, it can never attain realism. Pantomime is at the heart of the tradition of theatre, yet demonstrative acting, though it may range between the artificiality of dance and the conviction of real behaviour, can never complete a final verisimilitude. The norm of gestic communication was established by the giant gestures of Greek actors static in their *cothurni*, the patterned dancing of the Greek chorus, the dignified performance of priests in medieval liturgies.

The miming of Mary Magdalen in the tenth century liturgical scene of the three Marys, together with her chanting, suggest a certain ritualistic manner clearly adopted to elevate and interpret the action:

MAGDALEN (*here she turns to the men with her arms extended*): O my brothers! (*Here to the women*) O my sisters! Where is my hope? (*Here she beats her breast*) Where is my consolation? (*Here she raises her hands*) Where is my whole well-being? (*Here, head inclined, she throws herself at Christ's feet*) O my Master!

The solemn directions to accompany the *Quem Quaeritis* given in the *Concordia Regularis* by Ethelwold Bishop of Winchester also suggest a style of acting which is fundamentally demonstrative. When the Angel reveals the empty tomb to the women, it is done as if exhibiting the meaning symbolically:

Let him rise, and lift the veil, and show them the place bare of the cross, but only the cloths laid there in which the cross was wrapped. And when they have seen this, let them set down the thuribles which they bare in that same sepulchre, and take the cloth, and hold it up in the face of the clergy, and as if to demonstrate that the Lord has risen and is no longer wrapped therein, let them sing the anthem *Surrexit Dominus de sepulchro*, and lay the cloth upon the altar.

It may not be fanciful to hear an echo of this in 'The Street Scene' (1938), Brecht's celebrated seminal discussion on how a man at a street-corner mimes an accident he has just witnessed: 'The demonstrator acts the behaviour of driver or victim or both in such a way that the bystanders are able to form an opinion about the accident'. If discussion follows, Brecht says, the demonstration could be repeated and transformed so that an alienation-effect occurs: 'The demonstrator achieves it by paying exact attention this time to his movements, executing them carefully, probably in slow motion; in this way he alienates the little sub-incident, emphasizes its importance, makes it worthy of notice' (*Brecht on Theatre*, trans. J. Willett, pp. 121–6). Brecht is insisting that imitation has its limits: style of performance must always justify its purpose.

To begin at the beginning: the actor stimulates his audience's leap of imagination by his performance, the physical act of doing something itself initiating the thinking process for the spectator. The work of the actor is therefore uniquely creative, and Tyrone Guthrie claimed that the actor had

> a far more creative task than the orchestral player. This is because the script of a play reveals so much less of its author's intention than does the score of a symphony. This may seem paradoxical, because every literate person can read the text of a play whereas to be able to read a full symphonic score is an accomplishment.   (*A Life in the Theatre*, p. 123)

Not such a paradox, since the actor's skill exceeds that of mere literacy, and the accomplished reader of a play will constantly assume the actor's role as he reads. Bernard Grebanier takes the argument a stage further when he asserts,

> In a drama of even the feeblest psychological insight our interpretation of the things said is subject to what is actually being thought ... Thus, when we analyze a drama, we must first place emphasis on the thing being done, next, the thing being thought, and – in view of these – last, the thing being said. In our daily living, could we always manage to gauge people with the same precedence we should be living with perfect discretion.   (*The Heart of Hamlet*, p. 134)

A play in this way conveys meaning which is partly stated by what is done, partly completed by the thinking of the audience. The actor seems to thrust a dagger into his breast, the audience completes his death. Iago says to Othello, 'My lord, you know I love you', the audience knows better.

On the stage, doing is meaning and acting is communication by a cooperative wish. But upon investigation, the mystery grows, as Richard Southern suggests:

If you *do* something or *perform* something – speak, move, play an instrument – you can embody in that action whatever you have to say. But it is important to emphasize at the beginning that the secret of the theatre does not lie in the thing done but rather in something that arises from the manner of doing. Drama may be *the thing done*, but theatre is *doing*. Theatre is an act.   (*The Seven Ages of the Theatre*, p. 22)

Susanne Langer spelled this out in more detail:

Once we recognize that drama is neither dance nor literature, nor a democracy of various arts functioning together, but is poetry in the mode of action, the relations of all its elements to each other and to the whole work become clear: the primacy of the script, which furnishes the commanding form; the use of the stage, with or without representational scenery, to delimit the 'world' in which the virtual action exists; the need of making the scene a 'place,' so that often the designer produces a plastic illusion that is secondary here, but primary in the art of architecture; the use of music and sometimes of dance to keep the fictitious history apart from actuality and insure its artistic abstraction; the nature of dramatic time, which is 'musical' instead of practical time, and sometimes becomes strikingly evident – another secondary illusion in poetry, but the primary one of music. The guiding principle in the use of so many transient borrowed illusions is the making of an *appearance*, not under normal circumstances, like a pretence or social convention, but under the circumstances of the play.   (*Feeling and Form*, pp. 332–3)

This principle of drama as a mode of human activity built upon appearances and sufficient to its own laws explains such a statement as Shaw's: 'Iago does not exist – all we have is what he says.' Try again: the *Oresteia* does not exist – all we have is what it does.

In other ways, the principle also explains the emphasis on the physical even in the most realistic school of playwriting. The teaching of Stanislavsky constantly returns to what is done as a way of suggesting what is thought: 'An actor must speak to the eye, not to the ear.' For Stanislavsky physical action was a symptom of, a clue to, the larger action of the mind, both for the actor himself ('In a psychological action there is always something physical') and for the audience ('The "small truth" of physical actions stirs the "great truth" of thoughts, emotions, experiences'). The greatest theoretical exponent of naturalistic acting would thus accept that performance is like the iceberg. Even in drama at its most realistic, what is seen is there to hint at what is not, and imagination completes the process.

The actor's personal equipment contributes to the sharpness and intensity of the message an audience is asked to receive and complete. It also in part determines the kind of message, its relative degree of fantasy or realism. The actor can basically present only what is seen and heard: his person and his voice. When the spectator looks at the stage, he does not see a character – he sees a man or a woman, youth or age, a smile or a frown, an arm raised or a finger extended, a figure walking or dancing. Nor does he hear words – he hears song or speech, a low tone or a light one, a whisper or a shout, quick speaking or slow, rhythm or silence itself. The actor may adjust all or any of these resources in rapid succession in order to convey the message to his audience, to make it reflect or have it relax. We attend to the actor's face and figure, with or without mask and costume; his gesture and movement, with or without props; his voice and its tone, rhythm and pace – even a change of pace must signal a new perception, as when Romeo hesitates before he rejects Tybalt's challenge, or when Hamlet is suddenly disinclined to kill Claudius at prayer. All these sensitive attributes speak to us before we take in the meaning of the words the actor utters.

They may begin to hint at character, but, more importantly, they guide us to an immediate sense of the *role* the actor is to play. For voice, face and figure, and how far they obscure or reveal the true personality of the player, are also the surest guides to the convention adopted for the play, the convention prompted by the mood and content of the drama, its actual stage conditions and its actual audience. The actor answers to the needs of the play experience, and these may belong largely to the conventions of the period of the play, but there is always some modification to be made for the actuality of the present. For one reason or another, in performance there is constant interaction between the actor's real personality and his role. One would not wish it otherwise, for it is this which keeps the stage improvisatory, immediate, personal and alive to its audience. An actor's resources are always at the service of the theatre experience, which implies the peculiar business of impressing and engaging the spectator.

It troubles modern dramatic criticism that bonny Prince Hal must reject Falstaff, that Hamlet must play both the prince and the madman, that Cleopatra must change from a hussy to a queen: the Elizabethan role-playing actors would have found no inconsistency in such parts. Neither would the Greek actor who had to play both male and female at the drop of a mask have felt this schizophrenia of character and role. In both instances none of the theatrically unnatural demands of realism were being made upon the actor. Madeleine Doran notes this feature of Elizabethan characters as failure of coherence or, in Kenneth Burke's terminology, lack of 'repetitive form':

That they operated by no formal theory of individuality of character, except perhaps the humour theory, is shown by the frequent failure of coherence of character – what we might call the failure of repetitive form ... This of itself need not mean a lack of expressive energy, for although that is the quality, the sense of living wholeness, we recognize in the depiction of all successful individual characters, it may be present merely in intensely realized situations and fail of that first sense of cohesion. (*Endeavors of Art*, p. 233)

Even when new standards of realistic acting are being set, as after the eighteenth century, the ambiguities of non-illusory characterization produced performances of powerful depth from the best actors. In *Macbeth and the Players*, Dennis Bartholomeusz's recent study of the stage history of *Macbeth*, he shows how the complexity of character in the principals is revealed by the range of performance which Shakespeare's text admits. Watching Edmund Kean's performance, his audience was forced to decide about Macbeth's stature, whether heroic or like a dwarfish thief. From Macready's performance, the audience might assume both, since his superstitious Macbeth changed from the erect, martial figure of the first act to the common thief of the last. An abiding question in this play is whether Macbeth should dominate or be dominated by his wife: again, Macready could show that Shakespeare intended both. Macready's Macbeth was a man who at the last could command Seyton in imperious tones and yet drop immediately to the colloquial 'How does your patient, doctor?' In the artistry of a major interpreter in the modern theatre, the double values of an Elizabethan role could seem single.

More remarkable still is the modern revelation of double intentions in Lady Macbeth. It was Mrs Siddons who started a train of new and enlightening interpretations. Her personal beauty, together with her sense of Shakespeare's indication of Lady Macbeth's sensibility, brought a tenderness to the role that made credible her husband's capitulation to her: 'a creature who fascinated not Macbeth only but the audiences at Drury Lane and Covent Garden as well', Bartholomeusz reports. It was the subtlety of her voice which enabled her to bring out 'the varied and complex pattern of tone and feeling already there in Shakespeare's verse' (p. 105). In particular, she reproduced the quality of Lady Macbeth's possession when her full deep voice dropped to 'O, never shall sun that morrow see', or when her 'We fail' was spoken with a soft fatalism, incidentally anticipating modern academic discussion of Senecan stoicism in Shakespeare. Thus when she says, 'You lack the season of all natures, sleep' after the trials of the banquet scene, she seemed to be as much in need of rest as Macbeth himself.

What of Helen Faucit's very feminine Lady Macbeth, an interpretation marked by having her seem to faint in actuality after the murder of Duncan? This business was usually performed as a pretence to distract attention from her husband's embarrassment; now it stressed her sensibility to murder. 'Plucking the nipple' must have come across with extraordinary force on the lips of this actress, much more than if she had approached the part as a scold and a harridan. What of the practical and domestic lady of Ellen Terry, who began to speak more and more mechanically as she lost her grip on practical affairs? What of Mrs Patrick Campbell's temptress? Or Lillah McCarthy's fragile and shallow beauty? Or Vivien Leigh's vixen? Bartholomeusz's study shows us the total spectrum of the part, for if any one reading works in the theatre without distortion of the original text, it is arguably a valid aspect of Shakespeare's multi-faceted heroine: Lady Macbeth can embody all these qualities. If they seem mutually contradictory, it is only because we today expect a consistent performance within a naturalistic convention which was not then anticipated. Furthermore, it is right to wonder whether a boy actor could convey so many sides of one character. The Elizabethan answer must be: only if he were role-playing and not merely impersonating.

The notion of Elizabethan characterization as a presentation of varied *personae* all having the same face is yet to be grasped by modern actors. Strindberg asks that the characters of his dream plays 'split, double, multiply, vanish, solidify, blur, clarify' – but fragmentation of character is not what non-illusory drama calls for, rather a wider range of presented attitudes and poses. Shakespeare's characterization is more akin to Brecht's *Gesten*, by which feelings are pointed and externalized without trying for consistency; in Brecht, man is shown in a series of changing, contradictory images whose unity comes 'despite, or rather by means of, interruptions and jumps' (John Willett, *The Theatre of Bertolt Brecht*, p. 175).

The same range of language which determines complexity of character in Shakespeare is also the guide to the range of vocal roles expected of his actors. It is the same Henry V who must utter the rousing rhetorical verse before Harfleur who speaks in quiet prose in another role before the camp fires of Agincourt; the same man who can swear defiance to the French as charms us and Kate at the French court: the same character in different roles. In the first act of *Hamlet*, Polonius is the father who sends his son on his journey with incontestable words of wisdom, perhaps to offer a contrast with Claudius in the absence of King Hamlet himself; but the same figure must also serve his turn as the comic meddler of a politician who demonstrates the rottenness of Denmark and provides a foil for the meanderings of the Prince – until his first sober image returns in death and his character to solidity and realism through the grief of Ophelia and Laertes. The Macbeth and Lady Macbeth who can converse urgently on equal terms before the murder of Duncan have moved far apart into different worlds after it, the Lady's clipped verse still suggesting her grip on affairs, while Macbeth's incantatory reverie is the speech of a man lost in phantasmagoric apprehension. On the same stage Lear can be his early imperious self, absorbed in his own play, while the Fool is free to pass outside the action and fling his ironic doggerel to the critical audience.

In the Elizabethan theatre, the range of forms and vocal tones is closely related to the role-playing required of the actor and the separate modes of apprehension required of the audience. Peter Brook has written recently of the 'rough' theatre which he believes is freed of the tyrannous unity of style: 'A popular audience usually has no difficulty in accepting inconsistencies of accent and dress, or in darting between mime and dialogue, realism and suggestion. They follow the line of story, unaware in fact that somewhere there is a set of standards which are being broken' (*The Empty Space*, p. 60).

Brook goes on to claim that the Elizabethan was the greatest of the rough theatres.

We have too long neglected the physical voice of poetry in our admiration for its music, or word-play, or wit. Milton was rooted in another culture when he wrote that 'Books are the flat score of the spoken word, a mere latter-day convenience for preserving the fiery magic from generation to generation'. The fiery magic on the stage of the seventeenth century meant, not first an increase in the semantic meaning of the text, but an enriching and invigorating of the actor's personality through the language he was given to speak. The mere noise is important, and every glorious metaphor; but its muscular impulses, the physical voice on the stage, first recreate life in abundance through the agency of a role-playing actor. As such vigorous speech, familiar or remote, personal or impersonal, penetrates the less conscious mind of an audience, it is guided to a range of responses which have little to do with the demands of realism.

In chapter 3 it was argued that the improvisational element is essential in all live theatre. It is now possible to see that the actor's sense of creativity prompted by the presence and response of an audience is of greater moment than the haphazard outcome of some social game. It can involve the discipline and the freedom of a script. At the heart of performance, improvisation is intimately associated with the assumption of a role. At its simplest, as Stanislavsky believed, 'A character is a new human being born of the elements of the actor himself united with those of the character conceived by the author of the play' (Sonia Moore, *The Stanislavski System*, p. 33). Even self-absorbed actors of the modern realistic tradition dare not dispense with spontaneity: Stanislavsky cautiously accepts that, although the lines are fixed, there must be creative moments when an actor is essentially improvising in contact with an audience, when he must be inventive.

The case for non-illusory role-playing must go farther. Just as the wearing of a mask in part suppresses one personality, the actor's, to substitute another, the character's, without completely denying either, so the impulse to improvise is generated at the very moment of performance by the merging of actor and character, and the living tissues of both are preserved in the conjunction. The text is not a high wire from which the actor is in danger of falling, but a trampoline from which he constantly springs and returns.

The Polish director Jerzy Grotowski, of the Institute for Research into Acting at Wroclaw, has by experiment attempted to reduce the actor/audience relationship to its essentials, stripping away all the superfluous encrustations of the commercial theatre – set and décor, costume and make-up. In his book *Towards a Poor Theatre*, he has described how this encourages the actor to make a total gift of himself to the audience, bringing him into a kind of communion with the spectator. Grotowski sees the players as one ensemble, the audience as another: when the two are integrated, a play has begun. 'What is achieved is total acceptance of one man by another.' In this way theatre is an encounter: the actor's lines are his point of departure, his performance is human contact, the whole operation is something growing and organic. In an interview Grotowski stated, 'In each of our productions we set up a different relationship between actors and audience. In *Doctor Faustus*, the spectators are the guests; in *The Constant Prince*, they are the onlookers. But I think the essential thing is that the actor must not act for the audience, he must act *vis-à-vis* with the spectators.' Grotowski is trying for an ideal balance, perhaps impossible of achievement, between the actor's self-discipline and his spontaneity in performance.

Both Stanislavsky and Grotowski have worked within a tradition which separates the worlds of actor and audience; both worked to close the gap between. What if there were no such separation? The spontaneity that belonged to the *Commedia* and to the open stages of the Renaissance was of a different order.

A *Commedia dell'arte* performance was built up by one stereotyped antic after another, links in a chain. Its enduring tricks were of the 'circus' kind: the *lazzi* of 'joy' or 'recognition' or 'falling asleep', of bumping one another in the dark, of covering some victim with soot or flour, or Pantalone looking for the spectacles still on his nose, of Harlequin catching and eating a fly or trying to tickle himself to death. All these tricks had one thing in common: their success was dependent upon the audience. They could be justified and built up to heights of the ridiculous only with the approval of those who watched them. Duchartre reports that a famous Harlequin of the eighteenth century, Riccoboni, thought the improvisatory method ensured that, however old the jokes, they could never grow stale: 'Impromptu comedy throws the whole weight of the performance on the acting, with the result that the same scenario may be treated in various ways and seem to be a different play each time' (*The Italian Comedy*, p. 32). This freshness is directly related to the one variable factor in the theatre equation – the changing audience.

When in *The Servant of Two Masters* (1743) Goldoni, with the utmost care, places Truffaldino in the precarious position of serving two dinners to two different people in two different rooms all at the same time, he more or less leaves the rest to the nature of theatre, actor playing to audience. In the same way, if two interacting clowns decided to take their mutual performance to a peak of madness, the only limitation was imposed by the exhaustion of their audience.

Something of this happy pattern of appeal to the audience is present in the coney-catching scene between Autolycus and the Shepherd in *The Winter's Tale*, IV.iii: the thief must perform outrageously like one in the throes of death in order to pick the Shepherd's pocket, then make a lightning recovery in order to shake off the benefactor who will not desist from helping him. The scene in which Pistol is forced to eat Fluellen's leek in *Henry V*, V.i rises in a comic series of threats and protests to the point where Pistol gulps that great line which expresses the incontrovertible termination of the business by discarding nearly all its punctuation:

By this leek, I will most horribly revenge I eat and eat I swear —

In *Twelfth Night*, III.iv, critics may dispute the dramatic logic of having Sir Andrew the effeminate man matched in a duel with Viola the mock man, but it is what every spectator desires: they are made for each other. Having most elaborately set up the event, Shakespeare has no need to write the scene of their confrontation: *'They draw'* is the bare stage direction. With the fear of God in the pair of them, he lets the *lazzi* of the duel develop as they may, confident that the audience will work upon the actors, and the actors upon the audience, to provide the rest. The scene takes fantastic paths unknown, as poetic comedy will.

We may not believe that all of Hamlet's advice to the Players (III.ii) is Shakespeare's own (his groundlings 'capable of nothing'?). 'Let those that play your clowns speak no more than is set down for them' is especially not the advice of a practising playwright, and R. G. Collingwood would agree: 'Tell the performer that he must perform the thing exactly as it is written, and he knows you are talking nonsense. He knows that however much he tries to obey you there are still countless points he must decide for himself. And the author knows it too' (*The Principles of Art*, p. 320). But the improvisatory element in Shakespeare's comedy is usually more directly related to the tone and gesture implicit in the script because he wrote as an actor might himself write.

Shakespeare seems to have exactly anticipated the shape of the performance in Trinculo's lines as he comes upon Caliban crouching on the stage in *The Tempest*, II.ii:

What have we here? a man or a fish? Dead or alive? A fish: he smells like a fish; a very ancient and fish-like smell; a kind of not of the newest Poor-John. A strange fish!

To achieve the fullest laughter response from the audience, Trinculo will punctuate these lines with four 'takes' at each mention of fish – full-face glances at the audience, each a shade longer than the last and each a grimace more repelled by the smell. Thus by voice and expression Trinculo commands the spectator's assent to his discovery at the same time as each laugh, louder than the last, prompts a more exaggerated reaction to the smell. It is hardly a coincidence that, when a drunken Stephano comes upon both of them shaking under Caliban's gaberdine, the text supplies three asides which operate in precisely the same way as Trinculo's takes:

CALIBAN: Do not torment me: O!

STEPHANO: What's the matter? Have we devils here?

CALIBAN: The spirit torments me: O!

STEPHANO: This is some monster of the isle with four legs, who hath got, as I take it, an ague. Where the devil should he learn our language?

CALIBAN: Do not torment me, prithee; I'll bring my wood home faster.

STEPHANO: He's in his fit now and does not talk after the wisest.

Stephano's blurred reactions to Caliban's groans are partly in character as a drunken fool and partly those of any role in which a clown must enact the *lazzi* of meeting a monster with four legs.

Not unrelated are the host of playing opportunities buried lightly under the surface of the Pyramus and Thisbe burlesque of *A Midsummer Night's Dream*, V.i. Quince's stumbling recital of his prologue and his inability to 'stand upon points' is only the beginning of a long sequence of theatrical howlers implicit in the lines. Upon the entrance of the whole company in outrageous costumes, Quince's line, 'Gentles, perchance you wonder at this show' announces the five like an inept dumb-show, to which the mechanicals respond as befits their first appearance before an audience; Pyramus bold, Thisbe coy, the rest abashed. Apart from Wall's 'lime and hair' and their attendant problems, his sensibility, to which Theseus refers, is the cue for a range of realistic reactions to the passion of Bottom the lover and the fate that overcomes Thisbe: Wall happily confounds art with life. The repetitions of Bottom's line, 'Thou wall, O wall, O sweet and lovely wall', doubtless are there to remind Tom Snout, lost in admiration for Bottom's performance, not to neglect his duty with the chink, and 'Curs'd be thy stones' suggests that the two comics engage in an unscripted difference of opinion which persists throughout the subsequent meeting of the lovers. Thisbe's discomfort after kissing Wall's lime and hair, and the difficulties of the lovers in communicating through an over-sensitive and restless chink, are multiplied by the hamming of the lines. There is no need to go on: the traditional business of Lion's mousy roar, of Moonshine's having too many props to manage with two hands, of Quince's gesticulated prompting when Moonshine forgets his lines – all are provided for by Shakespeare. By the time that the lovers must die, the scene has so ascended into cloudcuckooland that the author need no longer guide their clowning as precisely as before: interminable speeches provide for the comedy of Pyramus's living death and Thisbe's unwilling recognition of his body. The endless variety of business which has accumulated in playing this scene over the years speaks enough for Shakespeare's careful planning.

In all such scenes the aside and the soliloquy are conventions inseparable from role-playing in non-illusory theatre: they persisted to the end of the nineteenth century when the naturalistic movement overtook the stage. These devices imply a complicity between actor and audience in the pleasure of putting on a play. The view that their apparent purpose was merely to inform the spectator of what was passing in a character's mind, like an interior monologue in the modern novel, is the mistake of superficial, anachronistic and literary thinking. The fundamental purpose of the aside or the soliloquy is to engage the spectator directly, to throw him a face-to-face challenge to agree or disagree: they are a reminder to all that a play is in progress. Anne Righter believes that such devices of extra-dramatic address became increasingly conventional by the time of Shakespeare, in that they consisted of speeches merely overheard by the audience without conscious intent on the part of the speaker. This can be decided only in relation to the contemporary theatrical context: in Elizabethan times there was no alternative convention of self-contained realism by which a soliloquy could seem awkward and selfconscious. However, Anne Righter accepts that 'The soliloquy continued through Elizabethan and Jacobean drama to imply a certain rapport with the audience, a rapport that was indefinite and deliberately vague, but which helps to explain both the usefulness of the convention and the disfavour with which it came to be regarded by the dramatists of a later age' (*Shakespeare and the Idea of the Play*, p. 56). A creative sharing of the action with the actor remained at the heart of the Elizabethan theatre experience.

Playing to the audience was natural to the open, non-illusory theatre, but we can only guess at the kind and intensity of the audience's response to the treatment. If it is hard for us to recreate the spirit in which an Elizabethan audience went to the theatre, it is harder still to imagine the forms their judgment took. The high rhetorical style, sawing the air, tearing a passion to tatters, seem ludicrous today, but in spite of Hamlet may have delighted the auditors. Again: today we grow very knowing if too many parts are doubled, but it was quite the thing when Tudor companies were small – and when standards of realism did not trouble the playgoer. In a useful chapter in *Literature and Drama* on the printing of plays, Stanley Wells records that a title page would often carry an assurance that not too many players were needed to mount the play. The manuscript of John Bale's *King John* (*c.* 1548) offers help with doubling in the text itself: 'Go out England and dress for Clergy'; 'Here go out Usurped Power and Private Wealth and Sedition; Usurped Power shall dress for the Pope, Private Wealth for a Cardinal, and Sedition for a Monk.' (Here the doubling actually makes a polemical point.) *The Conflict of Conscience* (1581) suggests quadrupling the parts: 'Prologue, Mathetes, Conscience, Paphinitius for one'; 'Satan, Tyrannye, Spirit, Horror, Eusebius for one'; 'Avarice, Suggestion, Gisbertus, Nuntius for one', and so on. Only a theatre of role-playing and improvisation could tolerate this for long.

A hundred years later, the Restoration stage is still improvisatory, its players still role-playing. At Drury Lane in 1675, *The Country Wife* created one of the best of all breeches scenes (III.ii). As a safeguard against her seduction, Margery Pinchwife has been dressed by her jealous husband as a boy, her own brother. At their first encounter in public at the 'New Exchange', Margery is harassed and flattered by the predatory Horner, who is no doubt winking at the audience the while, until she betrays her femininity with silly blushes and giggles. She is on the stage in a triple role, as a boy, a country hoyden and an actress. As Horner increasingly tests her sex with caressing words and hands, it is hard to know which of the three is responding to him: the ecstatic girl is passed from Horner to Harcourt, and from Harcourt to Dorilant, in a balletic chase about the stage behind her husband's back:

HORNER: Tell her, sweet little gentleman, for all your brother there, that you have revived the love I had for her at first sight in the playhouse.

MRS PINCHWIFE: But did you love her indeed, and indeed?

PINCHWIFE (*aside*): So, so. — Away, I say.

HORNER: Nay, stay. Yes, indeed, and indeed, pray do you tell her so, and give her this kiss from me. (*Kisses her.*)

PINCHWIFE (*aside*): O heavens! what do I suffer! Now 'tis too plain he knows her, and yet —

HORNER: And this, and this — (*Kisses her again.*)

MRS PINCHWIFE: What do you kiss me for? I am no woman.

PINCHWIFE (*aside*): So — there, 'tis out. — Come, I cannot, nor will stay any longer.

HORNER: Nay, they shall send your lady a kiss too. Here, Harcourt, Dorilant, will you not? (*They kiss her.*)

Hoist with his own petard, Pinchwife is in a frenzy which knows no bounds, his explosive asides registering the danger like a pressure valve. Cheered on by the audience, Horner grows increasingly more daring, until with a giddy smile Margery wholly loses her desire to remain incognito.

Another hundred years later, but perhaps with the diminished force of a slightly more realistic convention of playing, Kate Hardcastle and Marlow are still addressing faces and remarks to their audience in Goldsmith's *She Stoops to Conquer* at Covent Garden in 1773:

MARLOW: This pretty smooth dialogue has done for me. (*Exit.*)

MISS HARDCASTLE: Ha! ha! ha! Was there ever such a sober sentimental interview? I'm certain he scarce looked in my face the whole time. (act II)

He scarce looked in her face, since, apart from considerations of plotting, he was showing the house his distaste for sentimental young ladies. Throughout the scene of their first encounter, the pair of them are only pretending to be models of decorous, hypocritical society, and this not only suggests that each has two parts to play, but that the spectator has two plays to watch: the one on the surface in which Kate and Marlow do not hit it off, and the other which the actors share with the audience by asides and inflexions of voice.

When Kate is playing Cherry the barmaid, duplicity occurs again. We are in conspiracy with the heroine, so that a comment like the following offers a rebuff to Marlow at the same time as it carries a secret message for the audience's ears alone:

And who wants to be acquainted with you? I want no such acquaintance, not I. I'm sure you did not treat Miss Hardcastle that was here awhile ago in this obstropalous manner. (act III)

The speech loses its edge unless it is delivered straight at the audience. The playhouse was still small: Covent Garden did not enlarge its auditorium to 86 feet by 56 feet until 1782, and intimacy was still possible. In his impulse to return to the theatre of his favourites, Molière, Vanbrugh and Farquhar, Goldsmith created a superb comic situation which was in practice a natural vehicle for that spontaneity, or what he called 'liveliness', he so admired in the Restoration (*An History of England in a Series of Letters from a Nobleman to His Son*, Letter XVI).

Another hundred years, and the Victorian troupers were struggling to sustain the improvisational element in impossibly large theatres. It was too late: not until the twentieth century is a major playwright found encouraging extra-dramatic address. Pirandello's purpose is to tease his audience for its over-confidence in its material reality, and he resorted to the practice of reviving, quite out of period, structural devices which implied a modest improvisational technique. It is, however, a false and artificial spontaneity that he relied upon, and this is especially apparent in his trilogy of improvisational plays, plays 'of the theatre in the theatre', designed to dramatize the spectator's uncertain sense of reality and illusion.

At the opening of *Six Characters in Search of an Author* (1921), the Actors emerge from the auditorium, the world of the audience, speaking its language, behaving exactly as if a real rehearsal were about to begin. In this way expected reality is challenged by the Characters who follow them; when the feelings of the Characters are then reproduced with fierce intensity, they seem more real than the Actors themselves. In *Each in His Own Way* (1924), the characters Michele Rocca and Delia Morello must first play their parts in act I like normal creatures of the stage; but they are in fact characters in a play-within-a-play. In the interval they seem to emerge as from the audience itself which is gathering in the foyer of the theatre, and in the second act they continue to 'improvise' as if they were not characters at all. The disturbance caused when the 'real' Delia confronts her actress brings the whole play, significantly, to a premature conclusion. And in *Tonight We Improvise* (1930) the caricature of a director/author of an improvised play-within-a-play, one Dr Hinkfuss, starts a rebellion among his actors by his high-handed methods, leaving them free to step in and out of character, and the plot to take various directions. This apparent anarchy continues until the audience is completely in the dark as to whether the improvisation is controlled or not.

These inventive devices of Pirandello's are all to make an audience selfconscious participators to the point of total confusion. Nevertheless, such improvisation is no more than a trick to bridge a chasm between stage and audience which would have been quite foreign to the players and playgoers of the Renaissance. A play will not always spring to life by resurrecting a convention long dead.

It is the condition of drama that it needs human agents, the actors; it is the condition of acting that it needs to impersonate character, and for this the actor turns to the playwright for guidance. Between the conception in the mind of the author, the figure who presents himself on the stage and the character received by his audience, there is a side spectrum of perception. Utter objectivity is required of the playwright, for his is what in 1953 Eliot called the third voice of poetry: 'when he is saying, not what he would say in his own person, but only what he can say within the limits of one imaginary character addressing another imaginary character'. More recently, Peter Brook has written,

It is woefully difficult to write a play. A playwright is required by the very nature of drama to enter into the spirit of opposing characters. He is not a judge; he is a creator — and even if his first attempt at drama concerns only two people, whatever the style he is still required to live fully with them both. The job of shifting oneself totally from one character to another — a principle on which all of Shakespeare and all of Chekhov is built — is a superhuman task at any time. (*The Empty Space*, p. 31)

It is as if the author assumes a mask, many masks: he must be an actor himself.

The author plants the notion of objectivity in the actor's mind. For the actor also has finally to be impersonal in order to impersonate, although this requirement may be a short or a long step in his trans-mutation from actor to character: there are degrees of impersonation. The audiences for the early drama had no trouble in accepting an actor at any stage between the man they knew as a performer and the character they had to perceive.

It is sufficient to list the many plays of the sixteenth and seven-teenth centuries which use actors in direct address with a sublime indifference to modern rules of self-contained dramaturgy. Diccon, the mischievous Bedlam beggar in William Stevenson's *Gammer Gurton's Needle* (*c.* 1550), comments on the shindy he causes before or after every scene, in and out of character. His counterpart in Nicholas Udall's *Ralph Roister Doister* (*c.* 1553) is Matthew Merry-greek the parasite of Roman comedy made English, and he talks to the audience as easily as any jolly Vice in the popular tradition. Ten years later, the Vice appeared with equal facility in tragic material, like John Pikeryng's *The History of Horestes* (*c.* 1567), and in R. B.'s *Apius and Virginia* (*c.* 1567) Haphazard plays the Vice to the audience, stepping in and out of the play and at one point actually cautioning us to watch out for pickpockets.

Anne Righter believes that this double function on the part of cer-tain comic characters suggests that the English drama is becoming self-contained at this time, but it is arguable that such acting devices seek to encourage spectators to continue to respond consistently as self-concious participants in the act of playmaking, deliberately inhi-biting their role as mere onlookers. It is inescapable that the symptoms of this direct familiarity between stage and audience persist for many years: in Thomas Kyd's *The Spanish Tragedy* (*c.* 1589); Asper in Ben Jonson's *Every Man out of his Humour* (1599) who addresses the audience as 'Gracious and kind spectators'; the Tyre Man in *Jack Drum's Entertainment* (1600) and the Candle Lighter in *What You Will* (1601), John Marston's contributions to the war of the theatres; Mulligrub in his *The Dutch Courtesan* (1605) with Cocledemoy who is everything from presenter to Vice and coney-catcher; Quomodo in Thomas Middleton's city comedy *Michaelmas Term* (1605) and Quicksilver in *Eastward Ho* (1605) – and the clowns and fools in so many plays of Shakespeare. Throughout the period art and life remain delightfully confused.

This dual function of Elizabethan acting may explain why it is a commonplace of Shakespearian criticism that his characters do not for long remain consistently in character. Maurice Charney has recently restated the question:

What does being 'in character' mean? The need for dramatic persons to be consistent throughout their plays – as if the plays were slices of life – may be foreign to Shakespeare's art. Many speeches are the product of the occasion rather than the personal mood of the speaker, and any attempt to tie the speaker closely to his words may lead to dead ends, where the character is speaking not in his own behalf, but for the benefit of the play.

(*How to Read Shakespeare*, p. 86)

In support of this thinking, he quotes familiar lyrical lines from such unlikely characters as the bestial Caliban ('The isle is full of noises') and the drunken soldier Enobarbus ('The barge she sat in, like a burnish'd throne'). From another standpoint, G. Wilson Knight has refused the term 'character', complaining that a critic who adopts an ethic 'created to control the turbulence of actual life' is generally found to be 'unconsciously lifting the object of his attention from his setting and regarding him as actually alive' (*The Wheel of Fire*, p. 11).

These views are both right and wrong. Of course a character is a fiction, and whether seen in a technical or an interpretative light has only an existence limited by its play. Yet the actor lives, and for the audience continues to live, both in his own person and his impersonation, for as long as he stands upon the stage. Who knows? – we may take the impression he leaves out of the theatre with us. To this extent he is subject to all the inspection and analysis due to a real person. The paradox of great art is that a fiction can come alive. Nevertheless, it is for the actor himself by his manner on the stage to deny or encourage the right to treat him as a sublunary creature. By the level and quality of his playing, the actor indicates to the spectator how his characterization is to be evaluated.

The spectator in the theatre never stops to consider his own or the actor's role in the play: he takes for granted an actor's talent in spontaneity and accepts the role to be played. Once the actor is on stage, the mask is always half on. Once he fully dons his mask, assumes his character, a new set of rules comes into force. Character is another agency by which the actor reaches out to the audience, a strictly controlled guide to our image of the play's life. Mosca's magical third act soliloquy in Jonson's *Volpone* (1606) comes to mind:

I could skip
Out of my skin now, like a subtle snake,
I am so limber ...
and be here,
And there, and here, and yonder, all at once;
Present to any humour, all occasion;
And change a visor swifter than a thought!

In the extreme case of a drama whose actors actually wear masks, it is easier to see the control at work. In the drama of, say, the Greeks or the *Commedia dell'arte*, immediate and circumscribed recognition of an actor's role is *de rigueur* and essential to the response. The mask saves the need for basic character exposition: Agamemnon or Pantalone appears ('It's me again!') and the spectator properly anticipates a certain course of action from him. In the masked drama, the player will always follow the injunction of the mask: it would be most unsettling if he did not. Even in more realistic plays the early established traits of character cannot be reversed without placing in jeopardy the temporary conviction of illusion belonging to the occasion. Happily, some change is possible within the set limits, for an audience will convince itself that the figure on the stage has revealed more of itself, has 'developed'. The process of following a character through a play is very like – and can be as absorbing as – learning an unknown truth about an acquaintance one has known for some time, or discovering more about oneself.

No scenes in Shakespeare are better designed to reveal the character of the protagonist in fine detail, and at the same time make an audience aware of his changing mask, than *Macbeth*, II.ii–iii, those which follow the murder of Duncan. The trick is accomplished by setting on the stage character images presented at such different levels that the audience responds to Macbeth as if to a different creature. Macbeth and his lady grow more and more apart visually and vocally as the verse controls their separate reactions to the crime, Lady Macbeth quick, prosaic and urgent like her entrance, Macbeth slower and slower as he moves apart on the platform and speaks his growing preoccupation:

LADY MACBETH: Consider it not so deeply.
MACBETH: But wherefore could not I pronounce Amen?
I had most need of blessing, and Amen stuck in my throat.

Ideas of prayer, blessing, sleep and blood recur. By compulsive repetitions that now seem like obsessions, by intoning words which sing aloud of his pain, Macbeth moves towards us both physically and spiritually, until the knocking at the door brings man and wife together again. Lady Macbeth hurries him off, Macbeth dragging his feet.

When Macbeth next appears, he is in his nightgown as instructed, the perception suggesting an entrance from his bedchamber. Again he is presented sharply in contrast with another player who speaks and behaves as if in a different sphere, a stranger to the turmoil in Macbeth's mind. Macduff's outdoor costume, the polite normality of his attitude and his easily paced speech accentuate Macbeth's short, halting answers to his questions. As they pass upstage towards the horrendous door which hides the dead king ('This is the door!' from Macbeth), again the contrast between two characters helps the audience supply a dimension to Macbeth's terror. As the murderer waits for the skies to fall, Lennox's choric account of the prophecy of 'dire combustion, and confus'd events' delays the action, adds to suspense, enlarges the event and matches the monsters of Macbeth's mind. The murderer stands stock-still and we hold our breath. When Macduff finally appears at the chamber door, all the horror of regicide is heard on his tongue and seen in the figures panicking from their beds in white, 'like sprites' on doomsday. Noise and movement, bells and shouts, and a rapid series of entrances enact the frenzied image of a murder disclosed: all in preparation for the third image of the haunted man.

With his leading speeches, Macbeth once more draws all eyes to him. We know exactly how well he is sustaining his pretence of innocence, how tense are his nerves, and with delighted privilege hear the ironic ambiguity in

> Had I but died an hour before this chance,
> I had liv'd a blessed time

and the sardonic ambivalence in

> Here lay Duncan,
> His silver skin, lac'd with his golden blood,
> And his gash'd stabs, look'd like a breach in Nature,
> For Ruin's wasteful entrance.

He speaks with the hypocrisy and cold control of evil, and with the sincerity of profound feeling. Faced now with the knowing Banquo who heard the Witches, and the King's sons Malcolm and Donalbain, he speaks too reasonably the speech which declares his lack of reason, and as he confronts the crowd alone, the accusing presence of the on-stage audience is there to measure the extremity of his plight. The whole operation guides the audience to a belief in the development of Macbeth's character. Shakespeare's stratagem has insisted on his two faces for Lady Macbeth and two more for Macduff, and thereby with these encounters four for the protagonist.

The dubious success of masked drama in this century, in Cocteau's *Les Mariés de la Tour Eiffel* (1921), O'Neill's *The Great God Brown* (1926), Genêt's *The Blacks* (1958) and Arden's *The Happy Haven* (1960) – not counting partly masked plays like Pirandello's *Six Characters in Search of an Author* (1921), Anouilh's *Thieves' Carnival* (1938) and Brecht's *The Caucasian Chalk Circle* (1948) – points to the difficulty of introducing out of period a convention of self-conscious theatricality and engaging an audience in the paradoxical deception of simultaneous distancing and involvement. Ritualistic tricks with characters are not enough without a basis in ritualistic belief. Of these sporadic attempts at reviving the old convention, only Genêt's play has advanced the art of the theatre, because he conceived his work as a play-within-a-play and its parts as satirical mirror reflections of his audience's attitudes. Like the brothel in *The Balcony* (1956), the theatre for *The Blacks* was a house of illusions, and to have the audience admit as much permitted the free play of the artificial, the ceremonial and the ritualistic, of satire, invective and insult. Genêt succeeded in abolishing characters, he claimed, in favour of signs.

When Genêt employs actual masks in *The Blacks*, it is clearly within a convention that does not expect any realistic response. All initial perceptions are designed to destroy preconceptions of illusion. The black actors have shined their faces with boot polish, the white court is quite obviously masked: '*The mask is worn in such a way that the audience sees a wide black band all around it, and even the actor's kinky hair.*' The stage is provided with a master of ceremonies, and the audience is to be constantly aware of a play-within-a-play, a contrived performance, even a rehearsal play, as Archibald reminds it:

We embellish ourselves so as to please you. You are White. And spectators. This evening we shall perform for you.

We shall increase the distance that separates us – a distance that is basic – by our pomp, our manners, our insolence – for we are also actors.

The conscious performances of all the players and the distancing of the masks makes the play a *clownerie*.

The play's multi-levelled staging, the striking of varied attitudes, the variety of speech and song, and the structure of the play itself in which actors impersonate blacks impersonating blacks and whites, contribute to a fantastic edifice of ritualism. This provocative, unreal framework for the play permits an imaginative freedom of fierce statement and counterstatement. It permits a theatre which can enact extreme racial tensions, one in which blacks can scandalously vent their anger at whites, utter what blacks believe whites feel towards them and act out the consequences of the conflict – but all in a medium of make-believe. Which would be trivial, were it not for the fact that their anger is a reality. The actor's mask is carefully allowed to slip from time to time, as when Archibald cynically reminds the audience that it is only watching a performance, or when Virtue the prostitute accuses Village of losing his impersonality and enjoying his sexual assault on the whites, or when Newport News rushes in to report on the actual racial warfare supposedly taking place outside the theatre: these tactics have the effect of recalling the terrifying reality the play represents. In *The Blacks*, therefore, masks are used, not to identify individual characters in the traditional way, but to define whole racial positions, and 'character' has been successfully subordinated to the greater claims of the theatre experience.

Role-playing is the pivot of Shakespearian comedy, and nothing is more characteristic of its interest than the device of transvestism; nor is it more brilliantly exploited than in *As You Like It*. When Rosalind climbed into Ganymede's breeches – on whatever pretext – the Elizabethan audience had every right to expect a rapid extension of the comic mode.

> In my heart,
> Lie there what hidden woman's fear there will,
> We'll have a swashing and a martial outside,
> As many other mannish cowards have,
> That do outface it with their semblances. (I.iii)

Shakespeare is to grant his audience fantastic revelations of human behaviour, both male and female.

Once Rosalind is in breeches, Shakespeare repeatedly reminds us, not that she is a boy, which we can see, but that she is a girl, which we cannot.

I could find in my heart to disgrace my man's apparel, and to cry like a woman: but I must comfort the weaker vessel, as doublet and hose ought to show itself courageous to petticoat; therefore courage, good Aliena.

(II.iv)

The Rosalind who finds love-songs pinned to the trees in Arden behaves in a manner quite out of keeping with her clothes, and reveals her girlishness in a string of impetuous questions:

— Is it a man?
— I prithee who?
— Nay, but who is it?
— Nay, I prithee now, with most petitionary
    vehemence, tell me who it is. (III.ii)

The lines swell with Rosalind's growing excitement, until she can stand no more of Celia's teasing:

Good my complexion, dost thou think though I am caparison'd like a man, I have a doublet and hose in my disposition?

When she hears that the one who has penned his tedious homilies of love is none other than her own Orlando, and that he is here in the forest with her, the role-playing joke has been tuned to a perfect pitch. Her cry is spontaneous:

Alas the day, what shall I do with my doublet and hose?

The point is made: playing both boy and girl together has its advantages as a ruse, but it comes hard in reality, especially when a girl needs to muster all her feminine attributes for an Orlando. What shall she do? Her first impulse is to hide:

'Tis he, slink by, and note him.

In spite of Celia's proprieties, Shakespeare has other plans. It is not in Rosalind's nature to play the passive maiden, and she decides for action:

I will speak to him like a saucy lackey, and under that habit play the knave with him.

Begins that extraordinary game which only the Elizabethan mode of theatre could have admitted: Rosalind offers to teach Orlando how to love, half in mockery, half in her earnest desire to have him play the lover. Her mask will force him to assume one of his own. She finally seizes on a better idea: she will cure him of his love-sickness – perhaps to test his sincerity. She will do it by playing his Rosalind for him, as once before she says she cured a lover:

He was to imagine me his love, his mistress; and I set him every day to woo me: at which time would I being but a moonish youth, grieve, be effeminate, changeable, longing, and liking, proud, fantastical, apish, shallow, inconstant, full of tears, full of smiles; for every passion something, and for no passion truly any thing; as boys and women are for the most part, cattle of this colour.

'Boys and women': she is describing herself, no less, in her dual role. In effect, she will play herself, rapt in the throes of her own love. She and Orlando will be lovers, but, by the rules of the theatre, denied their fulfilment: the audience must imagine the rest. Rosalind will tease herself abominably in her need to stay by him: as Ganymede she will be a fake, a mere means to an end; in her own person as Rosalind she will be painfully thwarted; but the boy actor who will play both will have the best of the joke, and the Elizabethan audience is to share it.

There follows that striking sequence of comic scenes to which only a boy playing a girl playing a boy could give full dramatic meaning. Reminding the theatre audience of the rules, Ganymede with Rosalind's eyes will 'prove a busy actor' in the 'pageant truly play'd' by Silvius and Phebe, and he proceeds to lecture the cruel Phebe like a man, yet with the unrequited love of a girl.

> But mistress, know yourself, down on your knees
> And thank heaven, fasting, for a good man's love. (III.v)

Ganymede as the mock Rosalind castigates Orlando for being late, and at the same time speaks with the passion of the real Rosalind, the girl who is anxious lest her stratagem prove fruitless:

Why how now Orlando, where have you been all this while? You a lover? And you serve me such another trick never come in my sight more.
(IV.i)

Orlando, with his 'dear Rosalind' and his 'fair Rosalind', is joking at the expense of the mock Rosalind, but the real Rosalind is not laughing. However, she has tricked Orlando into role-playing too, and the masks and poses and tones the boy actor now adopts barely separate the triple image of Rosalind as she plays herself, Ganymede and her idea of Orlando's Rosalind. Then with characteristic impetuousness she plays parson, bride and groom, all three, and even then dares to follow the maiden with the matron, much to the amusement of Orlando and the horror of Celia.

Boy, girl, boy, girl — we listen to four for the price of one, unsure that any is real. But Shakespeare is not done yet. Brother Oliver is produced in IV.iii to show Rosalind Orlando's bloody napkin, and it is another Rosalind who faints away:

CELIA: Why how now Ganymede, sweet Ganymede.

OLIVER: Many will swoon when they do look on blood.

CELIA: There is more in it; Cousin Ganymede.

OLIVER::   Look, he recovers.

ROSALIND: I would I were at home.

CELIA: We'll lead you thither: I pray you will you take him by the arm.

OLIVER: Be of good cheer, youth: you a man? you lack a man's heart.

ROSALIND: I do so, I confess it: ah, sirrah, a body would think this was well counterfeited, I pray you tell your brother how well I counterfeited: heigh-ho.

OLIVER: This was not counterfeit, there is too great testimony in your complexion, that it was a passion of earnest.

ROSALIND: Counterfeit, I assure you.

OLIVER: Well, then, take a good heart, and counterfeit to be a man.

ROSALIND: So I do: but i' faith, I should have been a woman by right.

Rosalind's repeated insistence that she counterfeited her swoon underscores her genuine distress. Her grief unmasks the true Rosalind, and the audience is required at the last to make its greatest shift in perception.

The sequence in Shakespearian comedy of comparable subtlety is in *Twelfth Night*, I.v, a less staccato assault of contradictory feelings, a more delicate exposure of the female mind by little pulls and pushes of the heart. A certain double vision is expected of an audience watching the filigree of tone and attitude in the scene of Viola with Olivia, because it is uniquely a love scene between two boys playing girls, one dressed as the boy Cesario. The modern audience responds to an embarrassed Viola required to carry messages of love to her rival from the Orsino she wants for herself; the Elizabethan audience responded to a keener joke, a stage phenomenon that could have meaning only for those who had never seen a woman on the stage. The accent is placed squarely on the presentational behaviour of women.

When Viola must make verbal love to the woman she loathes, Shakespeare, by the usual device of putting her into doublet and hose, has trapped her into showing us two faces of woman. At the same time, the lady Olivia, the object of Orsino's attentions, is also trapped by her own sexual proclivities into showing us two more faces. The difference between them lies in our attitude: we have less sympathy with Olivia than we have with Viola because for Viola there is no recourse, so that we are placed in the central comic position of evaluating and measuring the thoughts of a woman in a ticklish sexual situation, not mechanically, but tested on our feelings. Here we should point to one or two moments in the scene of their first meeting which seem planned to induce the double values of comedy.

One such moment occurs before Viola has set foot on Olivia's stage. Near the start of the scene Olivia is demonstrating the excess of her mourning for her brother's death, determined inexorably to live like a nun. Her sighing and posing looks suspect from the beginning, but Feste is used to advise us to watch for inconsistent behaviour. 'Good Madonna', he begins, and his repetitions introduce a note of mock-sacred irony in the address:

CLOWN: Good Madonna, why mourn'st thou?
OLIVIA: Good fool, for my brother's death.
CLOWN: I think his soul is in hell, Madonna.
OLIVIA: I know his soul is in heaven, fool.
CLOWN: The more fool, Madonna, to mourn for your
  brother's soul, being in heaven.

In his customary way, Shakespeare tells us something and then shows it through the medium of his theatre. Before Feste she acts out her role as mourner, gathering some natural sympathy and some amusement at her fantasies as a nun. When a 'gentleman' is reported at her gate, her series of tell-tale questions suggests that her resolve is somewhat unsure:

— A gentleman? What gentleman?
— Marry, what is he?
— What kind o' man is he?
— What manner of man?
— Of what personage and years is he?

These questions hardly become a cloistress, but are prettily appropriate to a young girl. When she veils herself to receive the caller, we may ask how long she can hold out before the coquette usurps the *religieuse.*

Viola is forced to pay court to her rival, and, what is worse, it turns out that the rival enjoys playing practical jokes on those who court her. Is this to express her scorn for Orsino, or for all men? Viola has difficulties enough in playing the man as the boy actor strides in mouthing tidy iambic pentameters:

The honourable lady of the house, which is she? . . .
Most radiant, exquisite, and unmatchable beauty.

The actor bows and clears his throat a little, perhaps, before speaking these parodistic lines, for the whole performance here is burlesque, especially since Viola cannot see any beauty, matchable or otherwise, behind the row of veils. Olivia's veil has thus become, as we saw, one of both mourning and flirtation, exactly reproducing the double values in the lady. It follows that Viola's prepared speech quickly collapses when she does not know where to look, and verse slides into prose as she lamely concludes,

I pray you tell me if this be the lady of the house, for I never saw her. I would be loath to cast away my speech: for besides that it is excellently well penn'd, I have taken great pains to con it.

As Olivia and her ladies laugh at Viola, no doubt we are not intended to suffer too much with her. When her false words invite our laughter, we have taken Olivia's position:

VIOLA: I took great pains to study it, and 'tis poetical.
OLIVIA: It is the more like to be feigned.

Yet some ambivalence in our feeling towards Viola remains, and the contrast between their verbal tones provides the evidence. Since Viola as a boy is compelled to suppress her real feelings, they strike us as genuine against Olivia's easy self-display. When the moment is ripe, the lady will delight in teasing Viola with her beauty, confident that her features are her trump card — although she cannot know as we do that Viola's interest in her looks is merely the curiosity of jealousy.

If it is Olivia's tantalizing coquetry with her veil that catches the eye, it is the sincerity of Viola's response which lifts the burlesque of the boy actors to a warmer, lyrical level, and in so doing all but halts the action, perplexes the audience and changes our attitude towards her. The key to the new mode of performance lies in the speech Viola makes when Olivia finally removes her veil:

> 'Tis beauty truly blent, whose red and white
> Nature's own sweet and cunning hand laid on:
> Lady, you are the cruell'st she alive,
> If you will lead these graces to the grave,
> And leave the world no copy.

Words have turned to poetry, the lines have caught fire, and Viola seems to speak with the feelings of a man in Orsino's sorry plight, in sudden compassion for the man she loves, her speech no longer well penned nor apparently got by heart. From here on, the Olivia who removed her veil so confidently is quite deceived, taking Viola's place as the victim of a practical joke. Although still jocular, Olivia responds a trifle breathlessly to the young man's new tone, flattered beyond measure at his suggestion, as she thinks, that they should marry and have a family. More importantly, the audience no longer finds Viola merely funny. We hear in her voice her own deep desires for fulfilment, and sense that for one part of the girl love is not a daydream but a living, an active, a creative need.

This progress towards stripping both players of their masks is completed by the most beautiful and genuine piece of poetry in the play, Viola's willow cabin speech, and by Olivia's deliciously frank soliloquy after Viola has left, when she speaks and moves like an infatuated little girl. It is characteristic of Shakespeare in his golden comedies to advance towards a crisis, and do this many times, in which it is not only the protagonist who is lightly taken apart, but the spectator too. When Olivia has a vision of real love, when Viola cries out for pity as she speaks in imaginative sympathy with the one she loves,

> O you should not rest
> Between the elements of air and earth,
> But you should pity me,

the spectator must reconcile his mockery of girls who behave like puppets with his feeling for the humanity that lies behind the burlesque performances.

Thomas Wilkes's complaint about actresses who bestow frequent side-glances on their audience probably does not reflect the common opinion. Among the men and boys of the public and private theatres before the Commonwealth, and among the ladies of the court theatres after the Restoration, the mode of seventeenth-century role-playing is rich with addresses to the house explicit and implicit, soliloquies and asides, glances and 'takes', bows and curtsies, prologues and epilogues, ad-libs and all sorts of extra-dramatic signals. All indicate how comfortably close and warm was the relationship between stage and audience, all very much part of the experience of shared perform-ance. The popular theatre of the early Victorians was continuing this tradition when an actor stopped the show to make a point and receive applause out of character, when the young lead would rant a moral sentiment and at its peak wait for the vocal response of the house, or when the heavy villain challenged the audience with his cane and his snarling laughter.

Soon a conflicting tradition grew up: that the actor owed his first loyalty to the character he was playing and the author who wrote the play. In 1880 Squire Bancroft advertised his renovated Haymarket Theatre with this description: 'A rich and elaborate gold border, about 2 ft. broad, after the pattern of a picture-frame, is continued all round the proscenium, and carried even below the actor's feet — there can be no doubt the sense of illusion is increased.' In a theatre of total illusion, which became a reality with the advent of photo-graphic realism in the cinema in the twentieth century, consistency of behaviour was essential to ensure that the audience would believe in the actuality of the play. As the apron receded behind the pro-scenium arch, the actor retreated into the picture-frame. The house-lights gradually went out with the advent of gaslight after 1849 and the spectator was shut off from the actor by a curtain of darkness. Naturalistic theory dominated the art of drama and the stage became two-dimensional and non-participatory. The natural skills of role-playing were at last discredited.

If acting became more withdrawn, this does not mean that charac-ters also became two-dimensional. The nineteenth century saw a compensating attempt to supply depth to character, both to make an audience believe in its reality and to draw it into the illusory world of the picture-frame. By coincidence at this time, the novel was growing more empirical and the scientific method was applied to everything, including the mysteries of the mind. Shakespeare antedated Freud by centuries, Ibsen did so by years, but their characters lent themselves to what John Fernald has called the 'harmonic discord' in characterization: 'that is, certain kinds of characters can only be truly realized in depth, provided the more obvious elements of which they are composed are combined with other elements which are, apparently, contradictory to them' (*A Sense of Direction*, p. 93). Characterization in depth was common to all the great plays of the realistic movement: the actor of the new domestic drama had to learn to reproduce undercurrents and changes of feeling and in the new comedy to recognize a character as a hybrid creature not wholly laughable. Relationships between characters became similarly more ambiguous and like life: the instability of ordinary living was reflected in the restive shifts between characters in the best plays of Ibsen and Chekhov.

There is an essential difference between Shakespeare's luminous, presentational character contrasts and Ibsen's shading of values between echoing pairs. The image of a shrewish Katharina recoils from that of a docile Bianca in *The Taming of the Shrew*; by juxtaposition, the pathos and simple virtues of Lady Macduff deepen for us the vices of Lady Macbeth; or the irreverent adultery of Cleopatra is set off by the piety of Octavia. In Ibsen, however, the contrast must be thoughtfully pursued between the respective hypocrisies of Manders and Engstrand in *Ghosts*; the mistaken positions of Hjalmar and Gregers Werle are still being weighed at the end of *The Wild Duck*; or even Hedda's defiance and Thea's courage in *Hedda Gabler* can be seen as socially complementary. The structural patterns in plays of modern realism create a less clear-cut dialectic, and an audience will be challenged by the play only if it is magnetized by the reality of the play-world, the actor keeping his distance and the spectator reaching him only by some empathetic process.

The ambiguities with which an audience responds to a part like Mrs Alving's or Hedda Gabler's are like jury judgments in a real-life court drama, but a spectator can cut himself off from them by any personal, emotional or even intellectual barrier he cares to erect. The case is not the same with the satirical comedies of Bernard Shaw, especially those later pieces when he had cast off Ibsen and returned instinctively to a former mode of presentational theatre. Shaw returned to the patterns of melodrama and extravaganza to achieve a new biting edge in burlesque. As director at the Court Theatre, he also called for a presentational style of playing: 'Say it to the audience', he urged his actors, 'they'll be hearing it for the first time'. He orchestrated his dialogue for his actors and marked their scripts like passages of music – with *andante, allegro* and the like. He also believed that a play should be cast by voice:

In selecting the cast no regard should be given to whether the actors understand the play or not (players are not walking encyclopedias); but their ages and personalities should be suitable, and their voices should not be alike. The four principals should be soprano, alto, tenor, and bass. Vocal contrast is of the greatest importance ... The director must accordingly take care that every speech contrasts as strongly as possible in speed, tone, manner, and pitch with the one who provokes it, as if coming unexpected as a shock, surprise, stimulant, offence, amusement, or what not. It is for the author to make this possible; for in it lies the difference between dramatic dialogue and epic narrative.

(Martin Meisel, *Shaw and the Nineteenth Century Theatre*, p. 48)

Hesketh Pearson reported that Shaw asked for his plays to be declaimed in the flamboyant style, 'just as Shakespeare's should be':

The modern naturalistic method is out of place with them, and [Harley Granville] Barker had practically introduced this method to the English stage. Such plays as his own or John Galsworthy's were ideally suited to this style of production, but the rhetoric of Shaw or Shakespeare was beyond him. Both as player and producer Barker favoured restraint and under-acting, and by the time he had finished reading [*Androcles and the Lion*] we wondered whether the sight of a Roman emperor being chased by a lion was going to be comic or tragic. If Shaw had read the play there would never have been a doubt on the point.

(*The Listener*, 13 Nov. 1952)

Androcles and the Lion was produced in 1913, and we note that Pearson's reference point is Shakespeare.

Shaw's sense of acting was founded on Barry Sullivan, Ristori and Salvini, and he thought of a play as if it were opera: 'Sing it: make music of it.' Opera, Shaw claimed, taught him to shape his plays 'into recitatives, arias, duets, trios, ensemble finales, and bravura pieces to display the technical accomplishments of the executants'

(Meisel, p. 50). Opera and non-illusory drama both ask for the direct perception of performance *per se*. Such presentation makes of Shaw's comedy a pattern of postures and attitudes, and his characters have often been criticized for being more like caricatures than the characters of a modern realist. Nevertheless, it was this directness of style that ensured that the satirical shots he fired at his audiences were on target. 'My method of getting a play across the footlights is like a revolver shooting: every line has a bullet in it and comes with an explosion' (Meisel, p. 436).

It is not easy to clip a passage from the scintillating first act of *Man and Superman*, but this is a very normal sample:

TANNER: What do you intend to do about this will?

OCTAVIUS: May I make a suggestion?

RAMSDEN: Certainly, Octavius.

OCTAVIUS: Arnt we forgetting that Ann herself may have some wishes in this matter?

RAMSDEN: I quite intend that Annie's wishes shall be consulted in every reasonable way. But she is only a woman, and a young and in-experienced woman at that.

TANNER: Ramsden: I begin to pity you.

RAMSDEN (*hotly*):   I dont want to know how you feel towards me, Mr Tanner.

TANNER: Ann will do just exactly what she likes. And whats more, she'll force us to advise her to do it; and she'll put the blame on us if it turns out badly.

The satirical interplay is submerged in reading, but in performance consists in the position the audience is compelled to adopt *vis-à-vis* the three men. Tavy, the romantic *jeune premier* he seems to be, is the most apparently sympathetic of the three with his '*elegant suit of new mourning*', his '*frank clear eyes*' and all the rest, and it is he who makes the apparently sensitive suggestion that Ann Whitefield should be herself consulted about the choice of a guardian. 'Yes', we say, with equal chivalry. But Shaw is already springing his trap. It is Ramsden, dignified and respectable, who concurs, at first aligning us with liberal wisdom. But again Shaw has led us by the nose, since in the same breath Ramsden makes a smooth about-turn and modifies Tavy's generous motive by an appeal to masculine reason: Ann is only a woman. In 1903, the irrationality of this must strike every female and male in the audience as laughable, and Ramsden's liberal-ism is shown to be thoroughly mid-century. If all right-minded people in the audience now find Tanner to be their spokesman in his rebuttal of Ramsden's 'reasonableness', they too have been tricked. Tanner's actual reaction is one of horror at what might happen if the girl's natural ingenuity is supported by the law.

Tanner is defending himself against what he considers to be woman's predatory instinct, and Shaw has moved us in three quick steps from the romantic position to the objective and scientific. The complete reversal of sympathies from compassion for a bereaved young lady to unfeeling criticism comes as a surprise and a guilty delight for the audience, its laughter encouraged by the irresistible march of the lines towards the trumpeting of Tanner's conclusion in three loud blasts. In that laughter, Tavy's unworldly idealism and Roebuck Ramsden's liberal reason are demolished. Yet in his absurd self-humiliation as a mature male before a young girl, the laugh is on Jack Tanner too. Their three *Gesten* are well pointed – alienated – by an epic method that belongs to a longer tradition of the theatre.

In 1903 Shaw was already parting company with the naturalistic vogue in acting, by returning to a frank, declamatory style that was hardly in its grave. After Shaw and all those who joined him in the retreat from realism, the actor is again required to play a role other than merely to create a character. The actor playing Shaw, Pirandello, Brecht, Beckett, Genêt and other playwrights who have neglected the imperatives of illusion must acquire the style of an actor who is fundamentally an intermediary between his play and his public. He must learn a new acting technique which is as old as drama itself.

The idea of impersonal presentation is clarified by separating the modern notion of character from the ancient tradition of role. In an exchange of shots in *The Quarterly Review* of 1908 about the use of a supposed Elizabethan traverse curtain, William Archer asked of William Poel why Silence should not have been left sleeping in his chair at the end of the orchard scene in *II Henry IV*, v.iii as the curtain closed, instead of being carried to his bed. Poel's answer is the Elizabethan one:

But why? Carrying off a drunken man is good business on the stage. But the traverse was not required to shut off anything from the eye. If Silence had got up and walked out at the end of the scene, I don't believe the audience would have noticed it or minded. A scene is always over on the

Elizabethan stage when the speaking ends; what the actors did afterwards was done simply to suit their own convenience. If they were in sight of the audience, they were no longer looked upon as the characters but as the actors.

(Robert Speaight, *William Poel and the Elizabethan Revival*, p. 108)

No longer looked upon as characters, but as the actors: until Brecht, we found this thinking hard to follow. It is easy to recognize functions of characterization: the development of a King Lear, the changes and reversals that overcome Othello, the several moods of Hamlet; it is less easy to accept the dual role-playing of Prince Hal, Edgar in his several disguises, the Duke of Vienna who plays both man of state and man of God in *Measure for Measure*. The Elizabethan theatre expected variety from its performers, the variety of multi-personality. M. C. Bradbrook quotes *Euphues* (1578) in her Clark Lectures of 1968: 'He that always playeth one part bringeth loathsomeness to the ear. It is variety that moveth the mind of all men.'

Brecht's startling concept of the actor as critic of the play he is in, making of his performance a discussion with the audience he is addressing, is not new, except in its context of social realism. It dates back to Greek tragedy, in which Clytemnestra the adultress and murderess could also speak for all wives whose husbands had abandoned them in time of war. In Elizabethan times also, the dual task of the actor placed upon his audience a similar duty, that of separating actor from character, truth from falsehood, reality from pretence. The actor compelled a dialectic of response which added another dimension to whatever tension lay in the play proper. In weighing his sympathies, it was the spectator's privilege, as always, to oversee the whole presentation as evidence by which to make his own choices. Brecht's epic acting has simply revived the spectator's former function as participator, and the actor's as theatrical go-between.

The Spanish Tragedy, Kyd's popular revenge play, was crowded with incident, but it was nevertheless introduced by the wholly static Ghost of Don Andrea, the husband of Bellimperia killed in battle, who sits with the lifeless morality figure of Revenge watching the sensations on the stage below. They will 'serve for chorus in this tragedy'. They do indeed oversee the play, and have a word or two to say after each act, but their acknowledged effectiveness in performance comes of the strength of their link between reality and fantasy, audience and actor. The prophet Oseas who draws lessons for the audience from watching the corrupt people of Nineveh in *A Looking*

Glass for London and England (*c.* 1590) by Lodge and Greene is another such intermediary whose presence, for Anne Righter, 'provides the audience with an image of itself'. Yet Oseas

> is involved, unlike his counterparts in the gallery and pit, with the action of the drama on its own level. The events which he beholds from his throne are not, in his eyes, those of a play. Nor are the people to whom he speaks a theatre audience. At the command of God, he witnesses a series of real happenings, occurring now for the first time, and preaches to a future generation miraculously, and mysteriously, revealed.
>
> (*Shakespeare and the Idea of the Play*, p. 70)

If such plays appear to be primitive, the same impulse that set Don Andrea and Oseas on the stage to address the audience makes of Vindice the revenger in Tourneur's *The Revenger's Tragedy* (1607) – nearly a generation later – something of a stage chameleon. In 1912 Ashley Thorndike found him troubling: 'You are never sure of the actors. Each is one thing at one moment, and another at the next. Vindice, the malcontent, is a moralizing avenger, and also a degenerate' (*Webster and Tourneur*, p. 15). He is more: he is the presenter of the play and his own performer; he disguises himself as Piato the pander, then he becomes again the melancholy scholar hired to kill himself as Piato, and finally he has also to ape his enemies in the masque in the fifth act. If we wish to know the real Vindice, everything in the play seems to point to the fact that we are asking a totally irrelevant question: he tells us at the outset that he will be 'a man o' th' time'.

Against this background, and given Shakespeare's more experimental talents, it is not unlikely that the complexity of certain central characters in his plays was not due so much to their author's insights as a depth-psychologist as to the dual role they were frequently called upon to play.

Richard, Duke of Gloucester is Shakespeare's first consummate role-player. Elizabethan history portrayed him as every kind of rogue, able to hoodwink his victims without a conscience, a treacherous friend and a remorseless enemy. But Shakespeare avoids the crass sensationalism which his subject invites. If Richard in life was supposed to be a dissembler, Shakespeare's brilliant stroke of theatre is to have him take his audience into his confidence at all stages, so that we are perforce his conspirators.

> Why I can smile, and murder whiles I smile
> > (*III Henry VI*, III.ii)

suggests in reading a villain whose duplicity we can watch and judge with superior virtue, but when the lines are spoken straight to the audience, we must immediately consider where we stand. When he tells us frankly,

> I can add colours to the chameleon,
> Change shapes with Proteus for advantages,
> And set the murderous Machiavel to school,

he remains an actor who is still part of our world, so that we share his villainy when he steps back into the play. The tragedy of *Richard III*, in which Richard plays every part from wooer to saint, becomes a series of moral tests on the theatre's power of elasticity: how far can an audience be persuaded by mere convention to lend itself to villainy? Asked whether Richard could or should succeed in wooing Princess Anne (I.ii), our answer would be 'no'; in performance, we not only believe it, but we also desire it. In the scene of Richard's equally implausible appearance '*between two bishops*' before the Lord Mayor and citizens of London (III.vii) – a nearly blasphemous joke – we are, incredibly, able to savour his mock piety and laugh heartily at the Citizens' Amens.

Although Richard II talks of playing 'in one person many people' (*Richard II*, V.v) and by critics is thought of as the actor king, it is clear that he is no player king in the sense that he steps in and out of the action like Gloucester. And when the clever Bolingbroke becomes Henry IV, it is not he who is shown as the role-player, but his son. Is Hal the royal hypocrite because he announces his double role,

> I'll so offend, to make offence a skill;
> Redeeming time when men think least I will,
> > (*I Henry IV*, I.ii)

or is he still the presenter with a special and symbolic duty in a political play whose audience wished to see both the rake of legend and the statesman of renown? His opening soliloquy makes of him a chorus to his own play, as Schücking, Dover Wilson, Kittredge and others have said. Therefore he can be received as a cunning politician like his father only if the audience refuses to accept its part in the play.

Anne Righter is less concerned with the theatre than with the metaphor of acting, but she is right to recognize the importance of the tavern scene (II.iv) in which the Prince plays his father while Falstaff plays the son: ' "Banish plump Jack, and banish all the world" . . . is answered by Hal on three levels. "I do, I will." The words are spoken by Hal in the pretended character of his father, by the prince Falstaff himself knows, and by the future Henry V concealed here behind two masks' (p. 116). Add to this that the audience hears the 'I do' from the gay dog within the play, and the 'I will' from the actor without, and the fullness of this play-within-the-play emerges. Groans from Falstaff, cheers from the audience.

At times a happy self-consciousness of the playhouse produced laughter at the expense of the play itself. Doubtless Bottom in *A Midsummer Night's Dream*, IV.i, forgotten for ten minutes and left asleep on the stage after all the others have departed, achieved a laugh against the play on his line, 'When my cue comes, call me, and I will answer.' When Orlando burlesques his entrance with a special voice for his mock Rosalind in *As You Like It*, IV.i,

Good-day, and happiness, dear Rosalind,

Jaques makes a dry exit with a distinctly theatrical joke:

Nay then God buy you, and you talk in blank verse.

In mimicking Patroclus's imitations of Agamemnon and Nestor to their faces, Ulysses is playing a more integrated ironic joke. If his performance is at the expense of Patroclus, Agamemnon and Nestor, all three, it implies our collusion:

— Sometimes great Agamemnon,
  Thy topless deputation he puts on.
— Now play me Nestor; hum, and stroke thy beard.

(*Troilus and Cressida*, I.iii)

This is the same man who in the same scene can speak the justly acknowledged statesmanlike set-piece on degree, then step down to be the foxy Ulysses with his questionable tactics. How much of this theatrical jesting was present also in Cressida's two voices or Hamlet's work as his own choric commentator is a matter for judgment in performance. As characters in their plays they may seem deceitful, even insane; as players they offer the audience an extra set of eyes and ears.

In Othello, was Iago an obscurely motivated villain, passed over in promotion, suspicious of his superior officer with his wife, and so on? Or was he the figure of the devil himself ('I am your own forever'; 'I look down towards his feet'; 'I bleed, sir, but not kill'd'), guiding the audience and his victim to a vision of hell? We shall never know, nor will psycho-analysis tell us. When Shakespeare's drama has matured this far, the double action created by a role-player like Iago has permitted a symbolic drama for which the audience's span of imagination seems infinite.

At the end of *The Tempest*, v.i the Boatswain announces that the very ship which in the beginning we had believed irreparably 'split' is again 'tight, and yare, and bravely rigg'd, as when / We first put out to sea'. The audience is made aware, if it was not before, that Prospero has been duke, father and magician, and of these three the last made the play experience possible. Anne Righter writes,

In *The Tempest*, the process which began in *Pericles* reaches its final bewildering conclusion. The world becomes a shifting haze of illusions, some of them created deliberately by Prospero, others existing independently of his art. Prospero is like a dramatist, contriving a play, but he himself is actor in that drama as well, involved with the illusion on its own level. He cannot be placed on a level of reality outside of the world he creates on the island, nor is his relationship with Fate and Fortune, the outside forces which rule the universe, ever completely clear. Reality in this domain of the play dissolves and is lost in a confusion of dreams and shadows, illusion opening out within illusion like the infinite regression of a set of Chinese boxes. (pp. 180–1)

When Prospero brings his work as master-masquer to the melancholy sweet conclusion of 'Our revels now are ended' (IV.i), he speaks ostensibly to the on-stage audience of Ferdinand and Miranda. Addressed to the whole theatre, however, his lines spoken in apparent criticism of 'the baseless fabric of this vision' seem to confirm the spectator's necessary part in his creation. For it is untrue that Prospero's illusions 'leave not a rack behind'.

6

Non-illusory theatre

It came as a delight and a surprise when the Royal Shakespeare Company's players introduced themselves without ado at rise of curtain in the formalistic openings of Clifford Williams's *Comedy of Errors* (1962) and Peter Brook's *Dream* (1970). Role-playing in its own time, however, was symptomatic of a kind of theatre so familiar to its audiences that its frank unreality was unremarkable. When Edgar in *King Lear* announced flatly to his audience, 'Edgar I nothing am', doubtless the Elizabethans heard this with less confusion than we do today. For us it means that Edgar chooses to suppress his identity; for them, it meant that the young male lead would assume another persona – a public and objective rather than a private and subjective function. One thing is clear: his image as the wronged son of the Duke of Gloucester was secondary to the work he next performed as ironic chorus to mad Lear and blind Gloucester. And this role-playing was only to subserve the whole illogical mode of theatre which swept its audience on to the heath and into the phantasmagoria of *Lear's* massive tragedy.

Illusion is the province of all theatre: a spectator goes to the playhouse in the expectation that he will be free to indulge it. In an introduction to Pirandello's *Six Characters in Search of an Author*, Lionel Trilling wrote, 'The word *illusion* comes from the Latin word meaning "to mock" (*illudere*), which in turn comes from the word meaning "to play" (*ludere*), and a favourite activity of the theatre is to play with the idea of illusion itself, to mock the very thing it most tries to create – and the audience that accepts it.' The term 'illusion' is obviously an embarrassment for criticism, and has been for years. The theatre which pretends an illusion, whether of real life or of fantasy, is to be distinguished from that which simply makes the occasion for imaginative activity, some of which may be illusory. The basis of Ibsen's theatre is illusory, at its best making an audience believe in the images it creates on the stage, while the basis for

Sophocles's theatre is non-illusory, never expecting belief in what is seen. The former mode is circumscribed by what is plausible; the latter has infinite flexibility and its drama can circle the globe, pass from the present to the past or the future, and leap from this earth to the clouds. The neutral stage allows an inexhaustible succession of dramatic images.

The bulk of medieval and Renaissance drama falls between the two, at one moment able to depict the Crucifixion in shocking realism, at the next asserting in overt homiletic passages the *memento mori* of the medieval Church; able to convince an Elizabethan audience that a king can go mad in resisting God's order, yet also able to use the character to strike at the injustices of ordinary life:

What, art mad? A man may see how this world goes, with no eyes. Look with thine ears: see how yond justice rails upon yond simple thief. Hark in thine ear: change places, and handy-dandy, which is the justice, which is the thief? (*King Lear*, IV.vi)

It is hard to tell, however, whether the senses to which Lear appeals are not those of the mind.

In its beginnings, non-illusory theatre in England retained its close kinship in immediacy of experience with the ritual drama which had its origins in the symbolism of the Mass and the liturgies of the medieval Church. The mystery plays essentially anticipate an unquestioned communion between stage and audience, so that actor and spectator together, as it were, play Christ on the Cross. Anne Righter believes that such drama was 'poised precariously between ritual and art': 'An awesome immediacy pervades most of the Mysteries, an identification of the plays with their subject-matter for which the liturgical origins of this drama must have been partly responsible' (p. 18). She also believes that the same kind of identification persisted in the later morality plays, suggesting that the spectators in the streets were 'entrusted in each play with the central role of Mankind', and that 'while the performance lasted, audience and actors shared the same ritual world, a world more real than the one which existed outside its frame' (pp. 20–1).

Tyrone Guthrie would extend this concept of shared dramatic experience to include all non-illusory theatre:

I believe that the theatre makes its effect not by means of illusion, but by ritual.

People do not believe that what they see or hear on the stage is 'really' happening. Action on the stage is a stylized re-enactment of real action, which is then imagined by the audience. The re-enactment is not merely an imitation but a symbol of the real thing.

(*A Life in the Theatre*, p. 313)

He finds an analogy in the action of the priest in Holy Communion breaking bread and pouring wine:

He is at this moment an actor impersonating Christ in a very solemn drama. The congregation, or audience, is under no illusion that he really *is* Christ. It should, however, participate in the ritual with sufficient fervour to be rapt, literally 'taken out of itself', to the extent that it shares the emotion which the priest or actor is suggesting. It completes the circle of action and reaction; its function is not passive but active.

Of the same order of experience was the immediacy of the Elizabethan theatre, though perhaps less awesome. William Poel believed that the Globe stage made possible 'a special kind of realism', its wide projecting platform, undisguised in daylight, suggesting 'a map of anywhere'. 'The audience was in the play, not in front of it; the action of the play was not in Rome or Alexandria; it was here and now; it was Elizabethan, and immediate' (Robert Speaight, *William Poel and the Elizabethan Revival*, p. 78). Non-illusory theatre not only takes liberties with place and time, but is also of a kind that will put ghosts and witches, demons and fairies on the stage without a qualm. Absolute belief was unimportant to the success of the image, and investigations into Reginald Scot's *The Discovery of Witchcraft* (1584) or Thomas Nash's *The Terrors of the Night* (1592) are probably a waste of time. This is not to say, of course, that Shakespeare and other playwrights were unwise to make extensive use of the supernatural: on such a stage it was a highly efficient way of starting their audiences along chosen paths of imaginative apprehension. A ghost or a fairy embodies both a fine perception and a powerful conception.

Non-illusory theatre is the kind that positively encouraged the notoriously English practice of mixing, and sometimes synthesizing, dramatic genres and elements which seem to belong on different stages. Plays like Thomas Preston's *Cambises* (c. 1569), whose classical heroes rub shoulders with morality figures like Shame and Diligence at one moment, and with native clowns like Hob and Lob the next, are usually spoken of snidely as 'transitional' when the critic gropes towards a pseudo-historicism. They are at the centre of the non-illusory tradition, and account for that ranging quality in English drama by which Falstaff can appear in the same play with Prince Hal and a sane and sensible Kate Hardcastle be juxtaposed with a riotous Tony Lumpkin.

We think of the techniques of alienation as a product of the contemporary theatre, but they are as natural to non-illusory theatre as they are contrived in the modern theatre of illusion. A more correct term for methods of destroying illusion today is '*anti*-illusory', since expectation must be forcibly contradicted by devices of writing, acting or setting. In earlier times the rupture between acceptance and rejection of a statement or image from the stage was possible with the turn of a phrase or the glance of an eye. Peter Weiss's *Marat/Sade* (1964) seems to depict one aspect of the French Revolution. But this is brought into question several times over: it is being demonstrated by the insane inmates of the asylum at Charenton, who in turn are directed by the Marquis de Sade – it is his vision; but what we see is being shown to the asylum's governor and his family some thirty years later, an on-stage audience through whose civilized eyes we partly view the play's violence and rebellion; these in their turn are only players manipulated by a real director, Peter Brook maybe, and a real author, both our contemporaries. We watch those who watch, and those whom they and we are watching watch us. The play is a brilliant structure of Chinese boxes compelling the spectator to assess and re-assess his perceptions. Yet at any time before the nineteenth century a playwright could similarly exploit the resilience of dramatic belief in his audience by less mechanically controlling the reality of the stage.

The uncertain interplay between the actual and the imaginary, between the play and the drama, was characteristic of the Elizabethan theatre, perhaps of all performance in varying degrees. Richard Southern cities the Folio stage direction which opens *Hamlet's* graveyard scene (v.i), '*Enter two clowns*'. This apparently destroys the illusion of life at Elsinore, so carefully built up. But on the line, 'Here's a skull now', one of the clowns throws up from the stage an actual skull, apparently creating illusion – until we remember that the grave is only the stage trap, which destroys it again. 'Is it an illusion of a graveyard? Is it an unquestioned acknowledgement that one sees an actor performing a part? (*The Seven Ages of the Theatre*,

p. 254). And yet, the skull was there for the moment to transport the audience into a state of illusion.

Bernard Beckerman echoes the ambiguity by supposing a dramatic imitation of a high-wire act, with a Marcel Marceau miming a rope-dance on an imaginary line drawn on the stage. The differences between the acrobat and the mime would be, he thinks, 'in the act itself, and in its sympathetic reflection in the audience':

In the act itself the principal motions achieved by the acrobat would be reflected in the body of the mime. By concentrating on the salient features of tempo, stride, posture, and so forth, Marceau would create the essential visual structure of wire-walking, thus producing a virtual image, or illusion. Naturally, his attention would shift from the acrobatic skill to the mimetic skill, in short, from the actual need to maintain balance to the imitation of the acrobat maintaining balance. In the audience there would be a similar shift, from imminent danger to the illusion of imminent danger. The spectator would experience a double image. First, through the process of feed-back, he would mentally 'check' the mimed wire-walking against the actual feat, marvelling or not, as the case may be, at the acted version. Second, he would see the mimed presentation as an act in itself, obedient to its own nature and enjoyed for itself alone. This would not be an either/or situation, in which we would see first one then the other image, but it may be characterized as a both/and situation, in which the illusion and its referent are contained simultaneously in the spectator's imagination. In fact, the presence of both images creates the kind of contrasting gap that sparks mental tension. (*Dynamics of Drama*, p. 57)

The agent of the drama, in other words, is both the actor and the character.

Of all those who have grappled with this insoluble problem, no one really gets any further than Bully Bottom and Peter Quince. The mechanicals support Shakespeare's own amused sense of the paradox by their contrary solutions to the difficulty of supplying stage moonlight to order:

BOTTOM: Why then may you leave a casement of the great chamber window (where we play) open, and the Moon may shine in at the casement.

QUINCE: Ay, or else one must come in with a bush of thorns and a lanthorn, and say he comes to disfigure, or to present the person of Moonshine. (*A Midsummer Night's Dream*, III.i)

Shakespeare's jest here arises because he has already persuaded his own audience to accept a moonlit wood for half an hour, and there are still two more acts of moonlight to go.

The answer would seem to lie, not in whether illusion was or was not an essential ingredient of the Elizabethan drama, but in what way illusion in a non-illusory context could keep an audience alert to its perceptual contribution. Without being unmindful of the need for a degree of credibility in the characters and their situation as in any drama, the spectator could be relieved of his realistic inhibition. This interaction of illusion and non-illusory devices is parallel to the way the two faces of actor and character blend or conflict. Elizabethan drama has the privileged power to mix the ritualistic and the realistic modes.

The apparent locale or setting of many Elizabethan plays illuminates the duality of non-illusion. The audience is not for a moment deceived by the Italianate background to Ben Jonson's earlier comedies, the first version of *Every Man in His Humour* (1598), *Every Man out of His Humour* (1599) and *Volpone* (1605), into thinking that the machinations of the characters are not those of its contemporary Londoners. Their ways are similar to the characters of Jonson's later comedies, *Epicoene* (1609), *The Alchemist* (1610), and *Bartholomew Fair* (1614) which are unblinkingly set in London. It is interesting that when Jonson published his *Works* in 1616, *Every Man In His Humour* was reset in London with all the characters Londoners: but in performance it would have made not a jot of difference. The setting illusion was not, as it often is in modern realistic plays, a means of impressing a sense of reality upon the consciousness of the audience, but a means of focussing or expanding its perception. Italy allows a certain licence of invention; London brings the wider world back home. In Jonson's satirical world, illusory Italians behaved much like real Londoners. The stage was all but bare, and only costume could have marked a difference; speech was the same and attitudes were repeated from play to play.

Similarly, the Elizabethan audience presumably had no difficulty in recognizing that the Vienna of Shakespeare's *Measure for Measure* pictured the sordid side of the London they knew, although the names of the characters absurdly confuse their Latin and Anglo-Saxon sources: Lucio the rake bandies words with Elbow the constable, Pompey the pimp follows his trade with Mistress Overdone the bawd, Abhorson the executioner must behead Barnardine his prisoner. In all these plays, sensational things happen in a familiar environment, and Jonson and Shakespeare take outrageous advantage of the unreality of their stage to have the real impinge upon the unreal.

It is this uncertainty about what was taken for real that has so troubled students of Thomas Middleton's exuberant city comedies, *Your Five Gallants, Michaelmas Term, A Mad World, My Masters, A Trick to Catch the Old One* (all *c.* 1605) and, later, *A Chaste Maid in Cheapside* (*c.* 1611). Middleton is frankly irreverent in his fast-paced treatment of London life; he has no axe to grind, no lesson to preach. His vitality seems to come of his objective reportage, his refusal to write with satirical bias. This objectivity has been the reason why some have judged him severely; but it does not make him a realist. The London setting for his young reprobates and scoundrels, the whores and loose wives, should not lead us into thinking that he was holding up a realistic mirror to a vicious contemporary scene, any more than the idle young ladies and gentlemen of *The Importance of Being Earnest* (1895) reflect their contemporaries in real life. Nor should the abundance of cheating and wenching in Middleton's plays lead us to suppose that the author was himself an immoralist enjoying the den of iniquity. By denying his audience the broader picture found in the London plays of Heywood and Dekker and refusing to adopt the moralistic position of Ben Jonson, Middleton created a pure comedy, one almost complete and consistent in unity of action, tone and impression. Had his characters been named for Italians and placed somewhere in Italy, no doubt he would have been more readily excused as a writer of satire. As it was, he was simply writing in a vein of non-illusion.

Some sense of the mode of theatre in Elizabethan times invites fresh thinking about its form and intent. The real importance of those much maligned central scenes of farce in Marlowe's *Doctor Faustus* (*c.* 1588) emerges from a study of the stage/audience relationship. Its heterogeneity of tone has always troubled those who wish to see the play as a clearly didactic and orthodox morality: the fact is that the simple moral choice made by Faustus is denied and complicated by the sheer jubilation with which Marlowe invites his audience to indulge their wicked fantasies – mocking the Pope, conjuring Helen, and so on – at the expense of the damnation of the whole house. In non-illusory theatre, there is a place for the black comedy of *The Jew of Malta* (*c.* 1589), and the savage and ironic tone of its wit may account for its being the most popular play between 1592 and 1597 according to Henslow's receipts. The success of Barabas's villainous appeal to the audience probably also explains why he became the model for Shakespeare's Richard III, Iago and Edmund. In both plays Marlowe was reaching out to his audience in perverse ways by diabolically exercising the convention of his theatre.

Recent acquaintance with the non-illusory theatres of cruelty and the absurd might well encourage a re-examination of John Webster's dark symbolic fantasies, in which the realistic and penetrating portrayal of women like Vittoria Corombona in *The White Devil* (*c.* 1610) and the Duchess of Malfi about three or four years later is effectively juxtaposed with the monstrous shocks and horrors of grotesque Italianate imaginings. In this stagey world a Machiavellian villain like Flamineo can acquire a special attractiveness by his bold indifference to received opinion, just as Barabas did. Italy is again the springboard for an extraordinary dramatic adventure into the diabolical, probing the meaning of evil and death. The scenes of the torture of the Duchess in *The Duchess of Malfi*, IV.i–ii, in which the lady is forced to witness her husband and children dead in effigy, and then to keep her sanity in the presence of a chorus of the mad, are made to work by having the spectator see horror through her sympathetic eyes. Regarded as some kind of melodrama, these scenes are self-defeating; as a test of the frontiers of the Elizabethan theatre, they are of crucial importance.

The astonishing diversity of experiment in Elizabethan and Jacobean drama is understandable in a rapidly developing theatre of unfettered conventions. Whatever the genre, the style or the fashion, from domestic tragedy to satirical farce, the plays all pursue devices of non-illusion in common. The Elizabethan audience evidently possessed the facility of leaping between moments of realism and fantasy without question. In *Shakespeare's Last Plays* (1938), E. M. W. Tillyard coined the term 'planes of reality' to explain the freedom with which, in the same play, Shakespeare passed from one genre or style to another. In *Shakespeare and the Popular Dramatic Tradition* (1944), S. L. Bethell argued for the 'multiconsciousness' of the Elizabethan audience. Whether we look to the text or the auditorium, Elizabethan dramatic action and response must have been wonderfully in tune to encompass such a range of experience. Nothing less can account for the convolutions of Ben Jonson's later plays.

Jonson's skill in promoting his audience's involvement and leading it into his play-world by tricks of mirroring, devices of framing, choric commentary of every kind and ingenious plays-within-plays makes him a sort of Jean Genêt of his time. No play better exemplifies the mercurial consciousness the Elizabethan spectator was capable of sharing than *Bartholomew Fair* (1614). It is structured like the ripples from a stone in a pond. It begins appropriately with a deceptive Induction by which the audience is first to be drawn into the action of the play: a familiar figure, the Stage-Keeper, apologizes for the delay in starting. He was no more than a common cleaner, and his appearance on the stage would have been immediately disarming: the reality of the stage and the audience is to remain all one for as long as possible. Jonson uses him mischievously to warn the audience against the unreality of what it is about to see, putting it off its guard:

But for the whole play, will you ha' the truth on't? (I am looking, lest the poet hear me, or his man, Master Brome, behind the arras) it is like to be a very conceited scurvy one, in plain English.

Is this to elicit approval or contempt?

At the same time, the Stage-Keeper subversively offers several substitute suggestions of what he thinks the audience would prefer, some obscene, all cheap-jack – the play lacks a sword and buckler man, a juggler, 'a punk set under her head, with her stern upward', and so forth. In writing these lines, Jonson is cleverly anticipating a more subtle entertainment to come, persuading the audience to take sides against the speaker. The effect is to have the audience reject the normal fare associated with the Hope playhouse, which was built to accommodate bear-baiting and other low entertainment as well as plays, and was now providing a stage for *Bartholomew Fair* itself – the same kind of amusement for which Londoners actually went to the Fair. True, the play, like the Fair, will present a whole variety of common figures, a ballad-singer, a roarer, a bawd, a wrestler and many more of similar nature, but Jonson's spectators have already been induced to assume a superior attitude to what they are shortly to see.

The Stage-Keeper is replaced by the Book-Holder, another figure familiar to everyone who went to the play. With a mock-legal voice and flourish, his Scrivener reads Jonson's Articles of Agreement, whereby, if the audience contracts to remain in the theatre throughout the show, the author agrees to satisfy all the popular requests of the day. Again, the gap between the play and the audience is narrowed and the play's critics disarmed by being made to feel that it can continue only with their condescending permission – which, of course, is exactly true. Above all, this lengthy and ironic Induction in designed to make the audience conscious of its function as a contributor to the play. This process of induction persists in practice throughout the performance.

The saturnalia is not to begin yet, however. When act I begins, the audience seems to be in the house of John Littlewit watching a group of middle-class people preparing to go to the Fair, just as it had shortly before prepared to go to the play which was to present the Fair – a thoroughly Pirandellian situation. With act I we should be one step nearer the Fair, but the framing device by Littlewit is planned again to keep the audience at a satirical distance: he supplies yet another induction. When in act II the scene is that of the Fair itself, the audience again finds itself an onlooker at one remove, since it is immediately addressed by Justice Overdo, who announces that he is at the Fair disguised as the fool Mad Arthur, in order to spy on its 'enormities' and see that the law prevails. If he has come to the Fair to observe people like the Littlewits, he has therefore come to spy on all those assembled in the Hope as they take their pleasure as playgoers or visitors to the Fair.

In this way the audience is eventually treated to its first sight of the grotesques who inhabit Smithfield, Jonson's vivid collection of thieves and pickpockets, food vendors and whores. Even though they are all familiar, the spectator now looks at them askance, ready with fresh eyes for every satirical thrust, prepared to judge with laughter the several groups who make up the play, each in pursuit of the other. In particular, the most alienated characters are the Puritans Dame Purecraft and Zeal-of-the-Land Busy, a gluttonous Tartuffe, representing those who would close both the Fair and the Hope itself. In act V, Jonson trumps the whole pack with one final play-within-a-play, a puppet-show, in which the characters address the puppets as if they are alive, just as the spectators might do the characters, confusing reality and illusion:

BUSY: My main argument against you, is, that you are an abomination: for the male, among you, putteth on the apparel of the female, and the female of the male.

PUPPET: You lie, you lie, you lie abominably.

COKES: Good, by my troth, he has given him the lie thrice.

PUPPET: It is your old stage argument against the players, but it will not hold against the puppets; for we have neither male nor female amongst us. And that thou may'st see, if thou wilt, like a malicious purblind zeal as thou art.

The Puppet takes up his garment

EDGWORTH: By my faith, there he has answer'd you, friend; by plain demonstration.

Bartholomew Fair sets up a simultaneous series of distorting mirrors, so that when the play and the Fair are at their height, it is questionable whether the real audience is not as perplexed as the stage audience. It is Jonson's greatest dramatic joke, and probably the most difficult play in the language, only to be understood in terms of its own theatrical mode. It is as extreme an example as one can find of Elizabethan non-illusory theatre.

In the restless and experimental Elizabethan theatre at the turn of the sixteenth century, a new 'realistic' and narrative impulse was at odds with older ritualistic forms. The effect was to set at a distance the inner story, the narrative that was the ostensible pretext for the play. The developing drama employed a range of devices which continued to link stage and audience at the same time as they provided an excuse for the performance of an imaginative fiction. Allardyce Nicoll has recently drawn attention to the framing device common at the time, a convention that seems natural to a drama that was neither real nor unreal, and careless of the difference between the two. The *Taming of the Shrew* (*c.* 1593) provides the notable instance in Shakespeare.

The play tells its romantic tale of Kate and Petruchio as if to an on-stage audience which includes the Hostess of an inn, a drunken tinker named Christopher Sly and 'a lord'. These would have been such familiar figures and so recognizably 'real', that what they see of the play-within-the-play is automatically given the licence of credibility: if our representatives on the stage permit the delightful nonsense, why not we? Even inside the frame itself, the game of pretences is pursued, for when Sly wakes from his stupor to find himself on an elegant bed, he regards his former life as only a dream. Furthermore, the character of Petruchio whom Sly watches (when he is not asleep) himself assumes a disguise in order to deceive Kate. Nicoll makes the point:

The device is seen to be admirably concordant with the entire fabric of the romantic drama — deities and creatures of the folk imagination may thus envelope what purports to be the real, or the purportedly real may envelope the fantastic. . . . When we relate the device itself to the long-enduring disguise element so freely exploited in the interludes, we realize that both, taken in conjunction, combine to produce that constant interplay of appearance and reality which forms the inner core of this imaginative entity.   (*English Drama: a Modern Viewpoint*, p. 51)

As *The Taming of the Shrew* ends, Petruchio is himself again, Sly is returned asleep to the ditch whence he came ('the place where we did find him, / Just underneath the alehouse side below', if we accept the text of *The Taming of a Shrew*), and we walk out into our own dull world from the make-believe of the theatre.

The popular framing device was symptomatic of a range of conventions serving to expand and contract actuality and credibility. Throughout the period it was natural to have the spectators themselves represented on the stage by actors, as if they had emerged from the actual audience. The stage and auditorium were not adjacent rooms as in the nineteenth century, but the common playground. The familiar examples are Henry Medwall's *Fulgens and Lucrece* (printed 1497), in which the loosely identified characters 'A' and 'B' interrupt and interact with the main action of the play, and Beaumont's *The Knight of the Burning Pestle* (1609), in which George, Nell and Ralph, a grocer, his wife and his apprentice, mount the platform with the actors in order to start the burlesque. None of this would have seemed strange in a theatre where some spectators were already sitting on the stage. To mix actor with spectator seems characteristic of the early drama; it is not a far cry from the 'rehearsal' plays of the Restoration and Georgian period, in which the fictional author of the play-within-the-play was actually placed upon the stage with representatives of his critics and audience, who were then able to speak for the real audience as all watched the travesty together.

The Elizabethan induction is a happy extension of this arrangement for making actors of spectators. Opening characters were introduced to the audience of *Bartholomew Fair* and *The Taming of the Shrew* in order to set up the normative position from which the play proper could take flight. It was also, as we saw, an extravagant way of tricking the audience into accepting the improbable playworld. It is therefore of interest to find vestiges of the same device still working in the eighteenth century. In Gay's *The Beggar's Opera* (1728), the largely middle-class audience of the early Georgian theatre was led unsuspecting into the mixture of song and dance, pantomime and burlesque opera which scarcely concealed the political satire of Walpole's government. The first act frame-induction of the Player and the Beggar is all too brief before the play's acid social commentary begins, but it serves to permit a caricature of the times as disarming, and alarming, as Hogarth's.

Not unrelated to the more formal convention of an induction is the character-frame, by which a player assumes the role of presenter and agent for the show, its prime mover, while being himself its chief subject. The presenter in Marston's *The Malcontent* (1603) announces the double part he will play to secure justice for himself: he is to be both Altofronto, Duke of Genoa, and Malevole in a jesting disguise: we learn from the beginning that we are to enjoy his cynicism conspiratorially. In Tourneur's *The Revenger's Tragedy* (1607), Vindice addresses the audience at the beginning of the play at the same time as he addresses the skull of his mistress: like Richard III, he tells us his grotesque plans before he sets in train a series of horrors so sensational that only a direct and personal introduction could permit it: the audience not only takes the position of the play's central character, it is also induced to accept the savagery of the play's action. The device is echoed in all those choric soliloquies of heroes like Hamlet and villains like Iago which enable outrageous plotting to proceed by consent.

In the Georgian theatre again, a vestige of the earlier character-framing convention is found in the persisting prologue and epilogue which bracket a play, and are usually spoken by characters central to the action. (The use of Fainall for the impersonal prologue to Congreve's *The Way of the World*, and Millamant for its epilogue, is simply explained: these two were played by the leading actors Betterton and Anne Bracegirdle.) But while Horner speaks impersonally for all the actors in Wycherley's *The Country Wife*, the epilogue is spoken by his prey Lady Fidget on behalf of all the women who might become victims like herself. Archer, the fictional author of the stratagem in Farquhar's *The Beaux' Stratagem*, speaks its prologue, and probably its epilogue. A mourning prologue introduces Goldsmith's *She Stoops to Conquer* '*dressed in black, and holding a handkerchief to his eyes*':

> Excuse me, sirs, I pray — I can't yet speak —
> I'm crying now — and have been all the week!
> 'Tis not alone this mourning suit, good masters;
> I've that within — for which there are no plasters!
> Pray would you know the reason why I'm crying?
> The comic muse, long sick, is now a-dying!

After this knock at Hamlet, the play is appropriately followed by a laughing epilogue delivered by Tony Lumpkin. Sir Peter Teazle offers a challenging prologue to Sheridan's *The School for Scandal*, and this is followed by a suitably contrite, if still somewhat teasing, epilogue by his Lady.

The variety of conventions in the plays of these great ages of drama in England — chorus speeches, soliloquies and asides, both explicit and implicit — should remind us that direct address from stage to audience was the non-realistic norm of theatrical behaviour. They were the easy extension of other, less hardy, conventions like dumb-shows and inner plays. Non-illusory theatre, indeed, reverses the modern conception of the pretence that the dramatic experience should embody, and makes acting out of, rather than in, character the true expectation, and the pursuit of pretended action merely the exercise of special kind of perception.

Needless to say, by 'mixing actor with spectator' is not meant that kind of physical contact apparently originating with the Living Theatre of Julian Beck and Judith Malina in America in the 1960s. In the Latin play *Ulysses Redux* of William Gager, done at Oxford University in 1591, Penelope's suitors sat as handmaidens undetected among the women in the audience, and in the Jacobean court masque, actors commonly danced with spectators. But 'audience participation', that *sine qua non* of all successful performance, implies another order of experience than the merely physical. It is the direct outcome of a spectator's perceptual exertion called upon by the play. Thus anticipation is participation: as when we await the moment when Malvolio will see Maria's letter, or when the screen hiding Lady Teazle from her husband will be thrown down. And in non-illusory performance, dramatic perception can be more intense because it is self-aware: its tensions arising not just from the interaction between the characters of an illusion, but from the impact of the actuality of the stage upon the reality of the spectator. In

non-illusory drama perception can create a double response, one to the
fiction of the inner play, another to the sense of oneself in the role
of spectator — in a word, ambivalence.

To trace the principle behind non-illusory dramatic experience
and recreate the active ingredients of Elizabethan theatre raises
a host of keen questions. Is, for example, the Fool in *King Lear*
a character in any modern, illusory sense? The plot does not need
him, and he leaves the play when Lear is beyond further advice.
It has long puzzled commentators that the 'all-licens'd' Fool should
be able, not merely to criticize his master, but to speak as if he
were outside the action itself. His speech in LIV,

Thou wast a pretty fellow when than hadst no need to care for her
frowning, now thou art an O without a figure, I am better than thou
art now, I am a fool, thou art nothing. Yes forsooth I will hold my
tongue, so your face bids me, though you say nothing,

is in its last line addressed ambiguously both to Lear and to Goneril
as the King glares at his daughter and Goneril glares back. When
the jingle follows,

> Mum, mum,
> He that keeps nor crust, nor crum,
> Weary of all, shall want some,

the typically impersonal tag embraces the audience too. The stage
direction *'To Goneril'* often found preceding 'Yes forsooth I will
hold my tongue', originated with Pope and has been perpetuated
by most subsequent editors; in the context of non-illusory performance it seems impertinent.

The traditional picture of the Fool in the storm has him huddled
under Lear's giant legs, but in all his dialogue he never wholly shares
his master's suffering, as the tone of the following lines suggests:

O nuncle, court holy-water in a dry house is better than this rain-
water out o' door. Good nuncle, in, ask thy daughter's blessing; here's
a night pities neither wise men, nor fools. (III.ii)

It is characteristic of the Fool's line that we are expected to perceive
who is the wise man, who the fool. He concludes this scene with a
'prophecy' spoken in a sonnet of jingling couplets. The style and the
soliloquizing dissociate him spatially from Lear, and he ends his song

with an enigmatic line designed to dissociate him in time as well as space from the action on the heath:

This prophecy Merlin shall make, for I live before his time.

Even at the height of the agony and madness before the hovel, Shakespeare has the Fool jest at Lear's expense:

LEAR: Has his daughters brought him to this pass? Couldst thou save nothing? Wouldst thou give 'em all?

FOOL: Nay, he reserv'd a blanket, else we had been all sham'd.

(III.iv)

On the heath the Fool serves his turn in guiding us to a balanced, half-impersonal view of the grotesque situation: 'This cold night will turn us all to fools, and madmen.' When he finally departs the play on the characteristically topsy-turvy last line with which perhaps he curls up to sleep, 'And I'll go to bed at noon', he has divorced himself from both Lear and us. Lear's Fool was always more role-player and commentator than character, his licence more that of the eternal clown than that of the court fool. In his way he speaks to and for the audience, making himself the source of much of the direct ambivalence in the play.

This duality of the clown's role must better explain the freedom of Feste in *Twelfth Night* to pass unchallenged between the houses of Orsino and Olivia. It also permits the rare joke of having Pompey in *Measure for Measure* play the bawd in his formal character and the assistant executioner in his special, choric role. What Richard Brome called the clown's 'interlocutions with the audience', although an extreme instance of the convention, are characteristic, and their ambivalent relationship is symptomatic of the conscious impinging upon the unconscious mind, stimulating the active ingredient that belongs to all kinds of non-illusory theatre.

Hamlet in his death-throes seems to address not only the on-stage audience of Horatio and the Court, but everyone else in the theatre:

You that look pale, and tremble at this chance,
That are but mutes or audience to this act.

Muriel Bradbrook suggests that his speech from the throne 'suddenly widens out in concentric circles' to include us all. At such a moment, at the end of a play in which the audience has been in almost constant touch with the central character through his persisting series of soliloquies, it is proper that the leading player should take in the whole house as if with an unspoken epilogue. What is the appeal of Richard III's 'I am determined to prove a villain', or of De Flores in Middleton and Rowley's *The Changeling?* —

> Now I know
> She had rather wear my pelt tann'd in a pair
> Of dancing pumps, than I should thrust my fingers
> Into her sockets here, I know she hates me,
> Yet I cannot choose but love her:
> No matter, if but to vex her, I'll haunt her still;
> Though I get nothing else, I'll have my will. (I.i)

The excited perception is almost self-induced which comes of the careful disjunction between the repulsion felt towards a villain and the attraction of his frank confession. At such provocative moments the villain is not quite in character, but charms his audience as an actor in his role.

It is hard to accept Anne Righter's challenging proposition that the Tudor morality plays suffer from the tyranny of the audience because of 'meaningless audience address', and that at that time 'the traditional identification of the audience with a counterpart on the stage has begun to dissolve' (*Shakespeare and the Idea of the Play*, p. 32). If every appeal from the stage was a 'violation of dramatic illusion', it is welcome today, and can hardly have been felt as disruptive in an age when illusion was unnecessary to the play experience. 'Prologues, epilogues, and Chorus speeches acted as obvious bridges between the two realms of reality and illusion', she argues (p. 55); but what if there were no illusion to bridge? Indeed, she later accepts that 'Contact with the audience, no longer dependent upon the unwieldy means of extra-dramatic address, is sustained through recognition of the innumerable meeting-places of life and the play' (p. 77). One will find that 'it is hard to see how some of these passages [referring to playhouse business in the texts of the plays themselves] could ever have been anything but intrusive, leading the attention of the audience away from the play in hand' (p. 139) only if such attention is assumed to be exclusively paid to the world of illusion in the first place.

The duality in response to a leading player comes naturally to play after play in the years that follow the Elizabethan triumph of non-illusory theatre. The appeal of the pretended eunuch Horner

in Wycherley's *The Country Wife* (1675) is essentially one of ambivalent role-playing. In this he is the stimulating pattern for Dormimant
in Etherege's *The Man of Mode* (1676), who is summed up by Mrs
Loveit in terms which seem exactly to match the spectator's response
to him:

I know he is a devil, but he has something of the angel yet undefaced
in him, which makes him so charming and agreeable that I must love him,
be he never so wicked. (II.ii)

This is echoed by the elderly Lady Woodvill:

I hope you do not know him. He is the prince of all the devils in the
town – delights in nothing but in rapes and riots!... Oh, he has a
tongue, they say, would tempt the angels to a second fall. (III.iii)

Only the intelligent Harriet can take this ambivalence and turn it
for a more objective judgment:

He's agreeable and pleasant, I must own, but he does so much affect
being so, he displeases me. (III.iii)

The successful wits of later Restoration comedy owe their popularity, not to any moral or immoral position the audience chooses,
but to the simple challenge of a two-faced comedian, the felicitous
stroke of dramatic aesthetics: Valentine in Congreve's *Love for Love*
(1695), Loveless in Vanbrugh's *The Relapse* (1696), Archer in
Farquhar's *The Beaux' Stratagem* (1707), among others.

Wycherley's Horner is aesthetically attractive on several counts
simultaneously. He is the witty, amoral rake who follows the chase,
but he is also the moral reformer who selects his victims for their
hypocrisy, be they ignorant husbands or pretentious wives. If this is
not double-valued enough, we are still more amused to find that the
predator is preyed upon himself, for he meets his match in the frank
sensualist he discovers Margery Pinchwife to be. Unluckily for him,
Margery seems not to know the polite rules of the game he is playing.
The audience is invited to laugh at as well as with him: he is to be
enjoyed every way. We call him wicked, cry 'What a rogue!' with
the same mixture of condemnation and affection that might be
applied to a naughty boy. It is precisely this note of intimate affection that the actor inspires in his audience from the outset.

Horner's entrance into the play begins with an aside half in character, but this is only a continuation of the prologue he spoke a moment before as an actor:

> Poets, like cudgel'd bullies, never do
> At first or second blow submit to you;
> But will provoke you still, and ne'er have done,
> Till you are weary first with laying on.

After such direct address, he reappears with another player and an aside:

A quack is as fit for a pimp as a midwife for a bawd; they are still but in their way both helpers of nature.

Then he steps into the play:

HORNER: Well, my dear doctor, hast thou done what I desired?
QUACK: I have undone you forever with the women, and reported you throughout the whole town as bad as a eunuch, with as much trouble as if I had made you one in earnest.

Horner thus moves into his play by degrees. In introducing us to the other character on the stage, his opening remark begins the exposition of the notorious ruse he has devised to seduce the women and deceive the men. He speaks in so confident a tone about pimps and bawds that we have scarcely gathered breath to protest at his genial assumption that we know all about them ourselves, before we have been drawn into their company and plunged into a conspiracy with him. Yet it is not Horner's character but his unabashed smile and the detachment in his voice as an actor that disarms us. The audience is playing Wycherley's game before it knows it.

Many plays of our own time return to this manner of mixing dramatic illusion with extra-dramatic theatrical realities as a source of special, selfconscious perception. They are specifically associated with the work of Bertolt Brecht and the development of epic theatre since his death in 1956. Brecht's ballads, for example, repeatedly break convention: by directing them straight from the stage at the spectators, he automatically compels his actor to assume a more objective persona; visibly, his posture changes as if denying character, his voice projects as if beyond the play-world and he begins essentially to role-play. The epic stage tells a story in which the actors serve as both characters and narrators, not unlike the Chinese theatre in which the gesture of showing is at the heart of the style, and what Brecht calls 'historicization' – enacting moments from the story like someone reporting events in the past tense – is at the heart of the meaning. It is no wonder that Brecht returns to Sophocles, Marlowe, Shakespeare, Farquhar and Gay for his supply of readily adaptable materials, not to mention their content: each of these was working in an open, narrative convention of playwriting closer to Brecht's own needs than that of his immediate precursors in realism.

In the work of that attentive disciple of Brecht, John Arden, is found a further extension of the manner. Songs are inserted with such frequency that they no longer seem merely to break realistic illusion, but to be the norm of the convention. As in the music-hall tradition, they lend an ironic impersonality to the characters who sing them, but also, in spite of this, an immediacy to the whole performance. In the tangled structure of the 'dance of death' scene in the market place in *Serjeant Musgrave's Dance* (1959), act III, the Bargee's sarcastic use of the audience to supply the crowd of townspeople is an epic theatre extension of Shakespeare's use of the audience in the forum scene of *Julius Caesar*:

Here they are on a winter's morning, you've got six kids at home crying out for bread, you've got a sour cold wife and no fire and no breakfast: and you're too damn miserable even to fight – if there's owt else at all to take your mind off it – so here you are, you lucky people, in your own old market-place, a real live lovely circus, with real live golden sovereigns in somebody's pocket and real live taddy ale to be doled out to the bunch of you!

'*As there is no crowd,*' writes Arden, '*the speeches are delivered straight out to the audience, and the Bargee acts as a kind of fugleman to create the crowd-reactions.*' The scene, however, is capped by a surprise of Arden's own devising, since his audience is trapped by its ignorance of Musgrave's true nature and intentions.

Even in the anti-theatre of Samuel Beckett, the playwright reveals his consciousness of the game he is playing with the spectator by regular extra-dramatic reminders that the characters are aware of the theatre they are in. In this way the audience is made actively selfconscious of the theatrical experience from time to time and impelled to judge its own degree of involvement in Beckett's enterprise. In *Waiting for Godot*, Gogo faces the auditorium to say, 'Inspiring prospect', or Didi comments, 'It's worse than being at the theatre', and Gogo's greatest term of abuse is 'Critic!' One sequence includes this from Didi:

(*He takes Estragon by the arm and drags him towards front. Gesture towards auditorium.*) There! Not a soul in sight! Off you go. Quick! (*He pushes Estragon towards auditorium. Estragon recoils in horror.*) You won't? (*He contemplates the auditorium.*) Well, I can understand that.

In the death-wish play, *Endgame*, it is perhaps even more necessary that Hamm and Clov bring the audience to its senses occasionally with such ambiguous asides to the house as 'This is deadly', 'Why this farce, day after day?', 'We're not beginning to . . . to . . . mean something?', 'Do you not think this has gone on long enough?' and so on. Later, theatrical selfconciousness increases with explicit references to performance: 'Our revels now are ended', 'What is there to keep me here? . . . The dialogue', 'Did you never hear an aside before? . . . I'm warming up for my last soliloquy'. But none of this is as effective for non-illusory engagement as Beckett's general style of *Commedia* performance, mixed with circus and music-hall, in which the action is conducted as a whole.

By such extra-dramatic devices it is apparent that important dramatists of the twentieth century are trying to return to the condition of theatre which obtained effortlessly at the time of Shakespeare, when Fabian could conclude the taunting of Malvolio in *Twelfth Night*, III.iv with the naughty line,

If this were played upon a stage now, I could condemn it as an improbable fiction,

and rock the house with laughter as much at itself as at the players.

The aside belongs to the great family of non-illusory devices. Insignificant in reading, often ignored in literary criticism, it is always urgent in performance and central to the mechanism of a scene. The convention is greater than some throw-away line played inside the proscenium frame and practised for a quick laugh as in a modern farce. The aside on an open stage implies the complete embrace of the audience, for, strangely, an aside delivered to even one member of the audience catches the whole auditory in its net. It assumes an intimacy equivalent in strength to the soliloquy, and activates perception in performance in a way which outweighs the length and surface meaning of the lines.

Iago's menacing asides work like that. In *Othello*, II.i, he wholly destroys the pleasant image of grace and courtesy with which Cassio addresses Desdemona:

He takes her by the palm: ay, well said, whisper. With as little a web as this, will I ensnare as great a fly as Cassio.

As they mime to the lines upstage, Iago's words colour our vision so that we anticipate the possibility of mistaken appearances in the greater action to come. Iago is there again a moment later, physically interposing himself and blotting our picture of the idealized greeting between Desdemona and Othello:

Oh you are well tun'd now: but I'll set down the pegs that make this music, as honest as I am.

After this, nothing between the lovers will seem sweet again.

The same semi-choric quality in characterization is heard in the asides of Leontes in the early scenes of *The Winter's Tale* as he watches with us his wife and his friend:

> Too hot, too hot:
> To mingle friendship far, is mingling bloods.
> I have *tremor cordis* on me. (I.ii)

In Trevor Nunn's production of the play in 1969, the Royal Shakespeare Company appropriately 'froze' the stage into tableaux while such asides were spoken, giving them the prominence they deserved, suggesting Leontes's morbid imagination and solving the problem of the abruptness with which, in a more realistic presentation, his jealousy would seem to grow. The highly personal element in this kind of speech implies a split focus for the audience, and the mingling of the illusory with the non-illusory is powerfully ambivalent when Leontes's commentary on the action of Hermione and Polixenes is broken by the ironic remarks he throws to his son Mamillius.

> LEONTES: But to be paddling palms, and pinching fingers,
> As now they are, and making practis'd smiles
> As in a looking-glass; and then to sigh, as 'twere
> The mort o' th' deer; oh, that is entertainment
> My bosom likes not, nor my brows. Mamillius,
> Art thou my boy?
> MAMILLIUS: Ay, my good lord.

LEONTES: I' fecks:
    Why, that's my bawcock: what? hast smutch'd thy nose?
    They say it is a copy out of mine. Come captain,
    We must be neat; not neat, but cleanly captain:
    And yet the steer, the heifer, and the calf,
    Are all call'd neat. Still virginalling
    Upon his palm? How now you wanton calf,
    Art thou my calf?

Leontes divides his attention between his wife upstage and his son at his knee, so dividing ours between her charming image and the ugly domestic implication that his son is a bastard and his wife an adultress. When he later explodes with the soliloquy,

    Inch-thick, knee-deep; o'er head and ears a fork'd one.
    Go play, boy, play: thy mother plays, and I
    Play too; but so disgrac'd a part, whose issue
    Will hiss me to my grave: contempt and clamour
    Will be my knell. Go play, boy, play,

it is as if the actuality of the son's presence interrupts and stresses the self-indulgence of the father, inhibiting the freedom of the soliloquy convention itself.

On the Shakespearian stage asides and implicit asides occur with such frequency that often two plays seem to be in performance simultaneously, operating at two different removes from the audience and dialectically demanding two contradictory judgments to be reconciled. In extreme cases, such an aside as Cleopatra's

    I shall see
    Some squeaking Cleopatra boy my greatness
    I' th' posture of a whore

                      (*Antony and Cleopatra*, V.ii)

must seem today to be a kind of player's joke against his role, whereas one suspects that the Elizabethan audience found it merely a natural statement pointing clearly to the audience's proper function as judge and jury in the Globe Theatre itself. After all, from the beginning it had been accepting a boy as the glamorous Queen of the Nile, and for four acts had been repeatedly required to size up the woman and her reputation as the Roman crowd would have done.

The aside of Restoration comedy is developed as an outstanding perceptual agency, to the degree permitted by the excessively intimate playhouse and the unusual homogeneity of the audience. In Farquhar's *The Recruiting Officer* (1706), Silvia adopts the breeches-part of a young officer in order to follow Captain Plume, but finds herself having to sleep with Rose the country maid in order to prove her manhood. The joke redounds on all those involved, and is perfectly summarized in Silvia's aside to the house as she enters yawning through the proscenium door wearing a nightcap:

I have rested but indifferently, and I believe my bed-fellow was as little pleased. Poor Rose. Here she comes. (v.i)

The entrance is straight on to the apron, and the aside tells all at the outset, preparing the scene to follow. In this way, everyone, except Rose herself, is party to the situation.

Farquhar's technique of inclusion by aside is at its best a year later in *The Beaux' Stratagem*. In the scene of Aimwell's swoon, IV.i, asides-within-asides suggest the degrees of gulling present in the action. Aimwell is '*counterfeiting a swoon*' with a fine exhibition of groans and spasms in order to be brought into the presence of his beloved Dorinda. Thus the object is to deceive her mother Lady Bountiful. The Lady is duly deceived, for with her amateur cures she is overjoyed to have so worthy a patient – much to Aimwell's distress later when she burns feathers under his nose. He squeezes Dorinda's hand, who does not remain deceived for long, but Archer as his manservant stage-manages the situation like an expert. However, he is slyly observed by Mrs Sullen, Lady Bountiful's daughter-in-law. This is the pattern of dialogue which results:

DORINDA: Oh, my hand! my hand!

LADY BOUNTIFUL: What's the matter with the foolish girl? I have got his hand open you see with a great deal of ease.

ARCHER: Ay, but, madam, your daughter's hand is somewhat warmer than your ladyship's, and the heat of it draws the force of the spirits that way.

MRS SULLEN: I find, friend, you're very learned in these sorts of fits.

The amusing sexual ambiguity in Archer's uneasy discourse on thermodynamics is addressed to the audience over the head of Lady Bountiful in an implicit aside, and the innuendo in Mrs Sullen's retort to Archer gathers the audience still further into the total situation like another aside. The asides warn us of the degrees of guile and become instruments in the control and manipulation of our response.

In the eighteenth century the movement is towards greater verisimilitude in plotting, characterization, setting and performance; the apron retreats; the aside as a participatory device diminishes. However, the popular Restoration comedies were regularly revived in this period, and in the remarkable achievement of *She Stoops to Conquer* Goldsmith forced both his dramaturgy and his audience to reclaim the pleasures of a bygone age by the use of the aside. The Covent Garden stage in 1773 was still close enough to the audience, and the house sufficiently intimate, to achieve some success in this, but the instrument lacked the flexibility it enjoyed in the plays of those Restoration comedians Goldsmith most admired: in these dramatists the line between the actor's and the character's aside was a fine one. It is to Goldsmith's credit that he manages by verbal dexterity to ensure that the implicit aside operates well in two or three scenes. In act III Tony Lumpkin teases Mrs Hardcastle with the lie of the stolen jewels, and by Goldsmith's repeatedly placing the line 'I can bear witness to that' in Tony's mouth he prompts the wink to the audience which draws it into the joke. When later in the act Kate Hardcastle, playing the barmaid, teases Marlow with his pretentious talk about women ('O! then, sir, you are a favourite, I find, among the ladies?'), the more he pretends to his mastery of the fair sex, the more Kate can remind us of the truth by tone and glance.

Already it is clear that Goldsmith draws his asides from a situation he has contrived, and then points and embellishes the action with the further use of the device. The aside has here become a situational convention, the irony having been carefully built into the action. This use of the aside enables *She Stoops to Conquer* to be played successfully two centuries later inside the proscenium arch, whereas implicit asides may be lost altogether. Nevertheless, the situational aside continues the tradition of insisting that the audience see from two points of view simultaneously.

Two examples. In act II the house that 'looks for all the world like an inn' claims its victim: as a result of Tony's misleading information, Marlow believes himself to be a paying guest, and both he and his host find each other's behaviour puzzling. Only the audience has the pleasure of understanding the whole situation.

HARDCASTLE:　'Now', says the Duke of Marlborough to George Brooks, that stood next to him — you must have heard of George Brooks; 'I'll pawn my Dukedom', say he, 'but I take that garrison without spilling a drop of blood!' So –

MARLOW: What, my good friend, if you gave us a glass of punch in the meantime, it would help us to carry on the siege with vigour.

HARDCASTLE: Punch, sir! – (*Aside*) This is the most unaccountable kind of modesty I ever met with!

MARLOW: Yes, sir, punch! A glass of warm punch, after our journey, will be comfortable. This is Liberty Hall, you know.

HARDCASTLE: Here's cup, sir.

MARLOW (*aside*): So this fellow, in his Liberty Hall, will only let us have just what he pleases.

This technique thrusts the audience directly into the confusion, granting it the perspective of the foppish young man from town mistaking the manners of the country, and of the country gentleman mistaking the manners of the town. The situation is fraught with disaster in another dimension because Marlow has really come to ask for Hardcastle's daughter in marriage, and our sympathy with the absent Kate who charmed us in act I completes the comic equation. The asides also give the illusion that the pace of the scene is faster than it is: in effect, the audience is kept unnaturally busy following several dramatic threads at the same time, and the asides do not permit it to miss one shade of the multiple irony.

The scene of the sentimental interview between Marlow and Kate in act II, touched on in chapter 5, is a triumph of Goldsmith's use of the situational aside. The aside is used to maintain character, and even demonstrates the subject of the scene, social hypocrisy. Marlow finds Kate embarrassing, she finds him a bore. Their scene represents any stiff exchange between the sexes, here compounded by the conventional demands of honour in the man and modesty in the lady – very much the forms of sentimental comedy.

MARLOW: I was observing, madam – I protest, madam, I forget what I was going to observe.

MISS HARDCASTLE (*aside*): I vow and so do I. (*To him.*) – You were observing, sir, that in this age of hypocrisy – something about hypocrisy, sir.

MARLOW: Yes, madam. In this age of hypocrisy, there are few who upon strict enquiry do not – a – a – a –

MISS HARDCASTLE: I understand you perfectly, sir.

MARLOW (*aside*): Egad! and that's more than I do myself!

As Marlow fiddles with his lace and stutters through the pretences, and as Kate drily delivers her remarks on hypocrisy straight to the audience, it is almost as if their clichés have become asides themselves. For neither is looking at the other (Marlow cannot see Kate's face for her bonnet), but with a kind of comic schizophrenia both are counterfeiting what they assume they must. For all the stumbling, the contrapuntal tones of speech and aside again make the pace seem faster than it is: social form is preserved at one pace, slowly, while social criticism proceeds at another, quickly. The two levels of action run parallel, the sham on the stage, the reality shared with the audience. Marlow and Kate are burlesquing a Marlow and a Kate from another play, while the Marlow and Kate who speak in asides repeatedly remind us who they really are.

In Victorian domestic drama the aside is still in vigorous use, but by now it is entirely situational. It diminishes as a catalyst for audience participation as the drama becomes realistic. It does not exist for Shaw, more's the pity, and in the perfecting of the naturalistic method in Ibsen and Chekhov the aside is taboo, too destructive of illusion to be admitted. Hedda burning Lövborg's manuscript and whispering her thoughts the while, 'I'm burning your child, Thea!', or Hilda Wangel in her bliss uttering to the sky her naive refrain, 'Wonderfully thrilling!', remain completely in character and in the frame of the play. In Chekhov's *The Seagull*, act III, there is a curious incidence of an aside from Mme Arkadin after her quarrel with Trigorin: she marks her triumph with the surprising line, 'Now he's mine!' This is not a case of Chekhov's relapsing into the convention of former days, but a comic touch lightly applied to show that she is still the great actress enjoying her role. It is almost a Pirandellian effect by which she unexpectedly breaks through the fourth wall and transforms her audience into all the worshippers to whom she has played over the years: a momentary alienation which causes the aside to undercut the character without breaking illusion.

The story of the aside is told, but its partial return to the stage in the plays of recent seminal dramatists like Brecht, Beckett and Genêt suggests the beginning of a new chapter of history. If it makes a strong recovery after so short an absence, it should tell us that it is at the heart of participatory experience: not the frivolous appendage it is taken to be, but too valuable a device to be easily dispensed with.

Today, conventions like the soliloquy and the aside, and other forms of direct address to the audience which seem to shatter the frame of realism, are the chief signals of non-illusory theatre. There are many others more or less obvious to the eye and ear. The tableau or 'picture' of the nineteenth century, in which the whole stage froze at a chosen moment of suspense and meaning, each character striking the emotional and moral attitude his part represented, is lost, except occasionally at curtain-call. The picture at the end of *The Drunkard* calls for Edward Middleton, the reformed alcoholic, to be seen seated with his finger pointing to an open Bible, his wife Mary looking over his shoulder and his daughter Julia listening attentively at his knee. The triumphant point about faith and family is blatantly made. But this convention, too, is a natural development from a long tradition: the protagonist and antagonist of Greek tragedy, wearing *cothurni* and immobile on their *proskenion* ledge were in a permanent state of symbolic tableau.

Time and again in Elizabethan drama the stage action is suspended, often by choric speech from the stage, as the players depict the image of the situation. In *III Henry VI*, II.v, 'a son that has killed his father' and 'a father that has killed his son' symmetrically represent the horror of civil war as the King looks on and comments ruefully:

> Bad-hearted men, much overgone with care,
> Here sits a king more woeful than you are.

The stage littered with lovers in *A Midsummer Night's Dream*, III.ii enables Puck to survey his handiwork and make his observation about the simplicity of the mortals in his charge:

> Jack shall have Jill;
> Nought shall go ill;
> The man shall have his mare again, and all shall be well.

The curious direction which follows, '*They sleep all the act*', is tantamount to the Victorian requirement of a picture.

The impulse towards tableau is strong at the end of all the romantic comedies. In *As You Like It*, V.iv, the entrance of Hymen to the accompaniment of music transfixes the stage, until:

ROSALIND (*to the Duke*):   To you I give myself, for I am yours.

(*To Orlando*). To you I give myself, for I am yours.

DUKE SENIOR: If there be truth in sight, you are my daughter.

ORLANDO: If there be truth in sight, you are my Rosalind.

More of this follows. The verse patterning does not so much suggest that the recovery of Rosalind and the sorting of relationships have been made without movement, but that the composition of the stage has been stylized while recognition takes place. A few minutes later, Shakespeare has Jaques circling the platform to address each player in turn:

> You to your former honour I bequeath;
> Your patience, and your virtue, well deserves it.
> > (*to* DUKE SENIOR)
> You to a love, that your true faith doth merit:
> > (*to* ORLANDO)
> You to your land, and love, and great allies:
> > (*to* OLIVER)
> You to a long, and well-deserved bed:
> > (*to* SILVIUS)
> And you to wrangling, for thy loving voyage
> Is but two months victuall'd.
> > (*to* TOUCHSTONE)

During this ballet, each character is momentarily still as Jaques performs his choric function: in order to close the play, he has all but shed his character.

A comparable tableau which points towards a finality in *Twelfth Night* comes when Orsino tries to order his new 'rival' Cesario to follow him out of Olivia's presence. The lady, however, stops everyone short on her word 'husband':

> DUKE: Come, away.
> OLIVIA: Whither, my lord? Cesario, husband, stay.
> DUKE: Husband?
> OLIVIA: Ay husband. Can he that deny?
> DUKE: Her husband, sirrah?
> VIOLA: No my lord, not I.   (v.i)

The repetition checks all movement, and anger, incomprehension and fear are registered on the three faces. Like the prolonged embrace of Leontes and Hermione in *The Winter's Tale*, v.iii,

> POLIXENES: She embraces him.
> CAMILLO: She hangs about his neck,
> If she pertain to life, let her speak too,

the moment summarizes the action and allows time to the audience to evaluate its full impact at a crucial point; meanwhile, speech focuses exclusively what the eye has gathered generally.

The tableau designed for laughter is undying, and part of Feydeau's stock-in-trade. It is unmistakable in Sheridan's *The School for Scandal* when Joseph Surface's screen is thrown down in act IV. As the stage freezes, Charles Surface addresses each character in turn:

Sir Peter, this is one of the smartest French milliners I ever saw. Egad, you seem all to have been diverting yourselves here at hide and seek, and I don't see who is out of the secret. Shall I beg your ladyship to inform me? Not a word! — Brother, will you be pleased to explain this matter? What! Is morality dumb too? — Sir Peter, though I found you in the dark, perhaps you are not so now! All mute! Well, though I can make nothing of the affair, I suppose you perfectly understand one another; so I'll leave you to yourselves.

Upon Charles's exit, Sheridan has the stage direction, '*They stand for some time looking at each other*', and indeed the situation is outrageous enough for the parties involved to be eloquent in their silence. Sheridan hardly had need to spatter Charles's speech with his comments on their dumbfoundedness, 'Not a word! ... Is morality dumb too? ... All mute!', unless he sensed their value as implicit asides to the audience and was half accounting for the use of the unrealistic convention of the tableau.

The melodrama of the next century was unashamedly unreal and used the tableau to excess, but under pressure of the new realism the device is rarely found again. Hedda Gabler's suicide in act IV is a posed tableau behind the portières, but then she was simulating the theatrically romantic death of her dreams, and Ibsen manages to contrive it without disturbing the realistic manner of the play: her end is quite in character. In *Three Sisters*, act IV, Chekhov seems almost to revert to a tableau for Olga, Masha and Irina: visually a unit at the last, they listen to the music of the departing regiment and when they speak they echo each other's thinking; each has had her own dream, but now as they clutch each other they are at one in their sense of martyrdom. Chekhov seems to pose his family group again in act II of *The Cherry Orchard*, when the party gathered in the country dusk is held by the sound of the breaking string, their pose this time summing up their disunity and the innocent confusion of their attitudes at the time when their lives are up for auction like the estate: the sound seems to stop the play, to catch their spirit of unease and to bring time itself to a standstill. Chekhov is moving towards a new symbolism, and dares by this conjunction of the visual and the aural to take a leap forward into the mid twentieth century. If the tableau is apt at a moment of suspense, it is overwhelming at one of unresolved ambiguity.

Those scenes which work powerfully in open-stage, non-illusory theatre by having the stage seem to mirror the auditorium are loosely designated 'crowd' scenes. By its sheer proximity on a thrust stage, a crowd is likely to be as much a part of the audience as of the illusion. Shakespeare's different handling of the citizens in *Julius Caesar* and *Coriolanus* is illuminating in this. The contrast between the mob which reacts like a wild animal to Antony's subtle politics and the several groups which debate the character of Caius Martius is apparent on any stage, but after the forum scene of *Julius Caesar*, Shakespeare must distinguish crowd from audience by the brutal little scene that follows, in which an innocent Cinna is torn to pieces. The crowd in the forum scene of *Coriolanus*, II.iii is very different, approaching Coriolanus courteously, essentially as individuals, 'by ones, by twos, and by threes'. *Julius Caesar*'s on-stage audience does not speak for us, and Antony is seen to be a more dangerous politician than Brutus. The on-stage audience in *Coriolanus* speaks with so controlled a degree of logic that we tend to take its position in judging the immoderate behaviour of the man who seeks to be the people's consul. Shakespeare keeps his Roman citizens in this play in debate to the last:

2 CITIZEN: He mock'd us, when he begg'd our voices.
3 CITIZEN: Certainly, he flouted us down-right.
1 CITIZEN: No, 'tis his kind of speech, he did not mock us.

In verse, we observe, the crowd in *Coriolanus* keeps us in two minds about the tragic centre of our attention.

The nineteenth-century notion of 'supers' muttering 'rhubarb' through the action belongs to another kind of stage. In the modern theatre, a crowd on stage may complete the social background of the play; on the Elizabethan stage, a crowd is a character representing an attitude or opinion often in careful opposition to the central character and contributing to the total action. The court who watches

Claudius's contest with Hamlet during the play scene is the public opinion which compels him to stop the play. The Venetian Senate that judges the relative guilt of Iago and Othello reinforces the public horror behind the private agony. The Lords who witness Macbeth's distraction upon the entrance of Banquo's ghost indicate the chasm between the King's public role and his private collapse. Each of these scenes could have been managed without witnesses, but Shakespeare calls for a double audience to sharpen our perception of the farther boundaries of his play.

To return once more to the crowded scene in *Macbeth* in which Duncan's murder is discovered, II.iii. There are four parties on stage: the Investigators (Macduff, Lennox and Ross), the Suspicious (Banquo), the Guilty (Macbeth and Lady Macbeth) and the Innocent (Malcolm and Donalbain). Each group is dramatically related to the dead king and in the mêlée separated and related to the audience: we are to share each distinct reaction ourselves. Macduff evaluates the crime as the sin of regicide:

> let us meet,
> And question this most bloody piece of work,
> To know it further. Fears and scruples shake us.

Macduff and everyone on stage shout assent: Banquo's doubting role is a natural extension of Macduff's first declaration of horror.

Between the two stand the guilty and the innocent. Macbeth and his Lady control the main action, he with his hypocrisy 'studied', and she drawing all eyes by her trickery (no audience who heard her earlier duplicity can believe she faints in earnest). Carefully placed between the lines that draw attention to Lady Macbeth's fall are heard the voices of the innocent sons of the murdered king. They move aside to speak to each other and to us, and debate what they must do in their predicament. They are left alone on stage after the crowd has gone, and their decision to flee the new danger prompts the next development in the plot:

> Where we are, there's daggers in men's smiles;
> The near in blood, the nearer bloody.

Here then are four on-stage audiences, one watching another, while we, the true audience, take from each the burden of the whole scene.

There was never a stage so able to induce such varying sympathies by the range of aural and visual proximity at its command. That many of these sympathies still work in the modern theatre is due to the strength of Shakespeare's situations, but we may not forget that they are calculated for the simple flexibility of the 'unreal' theatre he had mastered.

However much we discuss Prince Hal's notorious rejection of Falstaff upon becoming king, the event is set up as a precise sequence of viewpoints, as it were a reproduction of changing public attitudes to the uneasy relationship between the new national leader and the old reprobate. *II Henry IV*, v.iii brings 'sweet Pistol' with the news of the old king's death, and Pistol, the justices Shallow and Silence, Bardolph and Davy are witnesses to Falstaff's elation:

I know the young king is sick for me. Let us take any man's horses; the laws of England are at my commandment. Happy are they which have been my friends, and woe unto my lord chief justice!

A sharp warning follows soon after in v.iv when Falstaff's women Mistress Quickly and Doll Tearsheet are dragged off by the beadles for whipping and prison:

O the Lord! that Sir John were come; he would make this a bloody day to somebody.

With v.v, the stage is full for the witnessing of what Falstaff takes to be his due:

FALSTAFF: Stand here by me, Master Robert Shallow; I will make the king do you grace. I will leer upon him, as a' comes by; and do but mark the countenance that he will give me.
PISTOL: God bless thy lungs, good knight.
FALSTAFF: Come here, Pistol; stand behind me. O! if I had had time to have made new liveries, I would have bestowed the thousand pound I borrowed of you. But 'tis no matter; this poor show doth better; this doth infer the zeal I had to see him.

Upon the King's processional entrance to the sound of the trumpets of his coronation and before the cheering citizens of London, Falstaff hails 'his sweet boy' with overweening confidence and enthusiasm; but swiftly comes the riposte: 'I know thee not old man.' One speech, Hal's last in the play, destroys the fat knight. The royal party passes on, and the change in tone from elation to dejection is heard in Falstaff's flat line,

Master Shallow, I owe you a thousand pound.

In this way the audience hears the rejection through the ears of the old man himself and those who love him. When the Lord Chief Justice orders Falstaff to the Fleet, the Elizabethan audience hears his sentence with the hind-sight of 200 years. The last words of Prince John indicate that weightier matters lie ahead:

> I will lay odds, that, ere this year expire,
> We bear our civil swords and native fire
> As far as France.

The rejection of Falstaff by the King is not only foretold and inevitable, it is shown publicly, with the crowd on stage as dry-eyed, mute assenting witnesses to the fact.

The Taming of the Shrew illustrated the popular use of a frame for the whole play. Illusion is a relative matter, a circle within a circle. The theatre audience watching an on-stage audience implicitly assumes the completion of the action by an inner play watched by its surrogate. What is loosely called a play-within-a-play can at one extreme be a rehearsal play like that of Pyramus and Thisbe in *A Midsummer Night's Dream* vastly distinguished from its context by its style of parody and burlesque, and at another extreme the intense and urgent subject of an eavesdropping incident like that in which Othello overhears Cassio talking with Iago of Bianca: in this, the Moor provides the on-stage audience and the true object of our criticism (*Othello*, IV.i).

A clear-cut play-within-a-play is a convenient plot device, but more importantly it is a stylistic measure of illusion and an ordering of attention. The Murder of Gonzago in *Hamlet*, III.ii both re-enacts Claudius's crime to force his hand and by its excessive theatricality stresses the 'reality' of Hamlet's grave concerns. Francis Berry in *The Shakespearean Inset: Word and Picture* thinks of this scene as a 'recessional picture' seen in 'long perspective' (p. 133). Yet in the lighter comedies something of the same force is felt.

The jape on Falstaff at Herne's oak in Windsor Park in *The Merry Wives of Windsor*, V.v resolves the choice of Anne Page's suitor and also ends the comedy on a high fantastic note of merriment. The Nine Worthies of *Love's Labour's Lost*, V.ii serve for a royal entertainment and simultaneously ridicule the learned pretentions of

Navarre. This is much like the burlesque at the end of *A Midsummer Night's Dream* which is a celebration of a marriage of love and at the same time travesties love's seriousness, except that the lovers who watch it fail to see the joke on them: this comedy had earlier already enjoyed the mockery of an inner play when Oberon and Puck had watched the silly quarrel of the lovers in III.ii:

OBERON: What hast thou done? Thou hast mistaken quite
  And laid the love-juice on some true-love's sight:
  Of they misprision, must perforce ensue
  Some true love turn'd, and not a false turn'd true.
PUCK: The fate o'er-rules, that one man holding' troth,
  A million fail, confounding oath on oath.

The on-stage spectators of the inner plays in these comedies seem a little more wise or 'real' because their plays are so fantastic.

The dramatic advantages of the inner play are more subtly integrated in the mature comedies. In *As You Like It*, the speech and manner of the pastoral lovers Silvius and Phebe are so carefully distinguished from those of Rosalind and Orlando that they make of their scenes, as old Corin says, 'a pageant truly play'd' (III.iv). They create an extraordinary inner play in which Rosalind is perforce caught, so that as its parodistic quality enlightens us, its irrationality educates her:

> Alas poor shepherd, searching of thy wound,
> I have by hard adventure found mine own.   (II.iv)

Upon listening to Silvius's complaint, Rosalind is drawn further into the circle:

> The sight of lovers feedeth those in love:
> Bring us to this sight, and you shall say
> I'll prove a busy actor in their play.   (III.iv)

Yet Rosalind is the true and 'realistic' glass through which we perceive the distortions of the deluded lovers. It is this disparity which forces her to prove a busy actor and us to get a proper perspective on her sincerity.

There is no play-within-a-play as such in *Twelfth Night*, but Feste's singing before, during and after the play supplies it with a frame: he stands apart from the play in order to cast a gentle shadow over the pains and perplexities of the lovers, his edge of melancholy touching the real world. When Viola puts on the clothes of a boy, all the major characters are inevitably and inescapably trapped in the deception until she declares herself. Their courses of action are so affected by her role-playing that the whole play seems to be 'an improbable fiction' in which 'nothing that is so is so', as Feste observes to Sebastian:

No, I do not know you, nor I am not sent to you by my lady, to bid you come speak with her; nor your name is not Master Cesario, nor this is not my nose neither. Nothing that is so is so. (IV.i)

There is a kind of mad elation in all those double negatives.

The artificial accent of the inner play is seen again in *The Winter's Tale*. Perdita is to be an essential player in the main action, but during those magic, lyrical moments of the sheep-shearing scene (IV.iv), she is first presented as an ideal image of youth and fertility, smothered in flowers, welcoming all to the harvest feast:

> Methinks I play as I have seen them do
> In Whitsun pastorals. Sure, this robe of mine
> Does change my disposition.

The lines warn us that there is another Perdita to come. Polixenes, the father of her lover Florizel, has watched the celebration from the periphery: when he stops it, reality returns. But the final movement of the play is coloured now by the ideal picture of the role she played in the inner play, and the theme of fulfilment is carried in the mind's eye as an image of Perdita 'the queen of curds and cream' to match the harmony of the fifth act.

The Elizabethan and Jacobean drama belongs to a revealing period of non-illusion, not because it is perfect and complete in its mode of theatrical ritual, but because it is imperfect and incomplete. It selfconsciously faces two ways, towards the real and the unreal; in the amalgam is created an unusually energizing set of perceptions. A large number of plays in this period incorporate inner plays, frame one action by another or devise a technique which seems to undermine its own foundation in belief. The English drama at this time was diverting itself in its new playground, exploring its unpredictable possibilities, trying every fashionable genre, every new trick. Bethell's Elizabethan 'multiconsciousness' could reconcile illusion with non-illusion; one suspects that this is the condition of mind of any spectator submitting himself to so explicit an act of the im-

agination as playgoing. In his *English Drama*, we will recall that
Allardyce Nicoll writes of 'that constant interplay of appearance and
reality which forms the inner core of this imaginative entity' (p. 51).

From the repeated use of allegorical devices, it seems that medieval
and Elizabethan audiences could think figuratively without trouble.
The spirit of the play-within-a-play lent itself readily to extended
allegorical statement. In Kyd's *The Spanish Tragedy*, we saw that
the Ghost of Don Andrea watches the action of the play with his
allegorical comforter Revenge at his side. In M. C. Bradbrook's
view,

> the play proper became a play-within-the-play on a gigantic scale ... The
> introduction of several figures into the induction made it quite a different
> thing from an isolated presenter. The point about all these characters was
> that they remained on the stage the whole time and commented on the
> action, and so the two planes of action were felt simultaneously.
>
> (*Themes and Conventions of Elizabethan Tragedy*, p. 45)

Anne Righter speaks of these presenters as 'simply the first in a
series of three illusions receding into depth': with the real audience
they watch the allegorical but ambiguous masque of Spanish fortunes
which Hieronimo prepares for the King of Spain to watch, although
their presence alone suggests that 'the audience in the court of Spain
is composed of actors in a larger, predestined drama'. In the fourth
act, Hieronimo's climactic play-within-the-play echoes what has
gone before and provides the occasion for his revenge. For a moment
the audience is deceived as to whether the action of the inner play is
not make-believe, but when it is over Hieronimo's return to the
norm of verse ('thus conclude I in our vulgar tongue') stresses the
fact that the stabbing of his enemies was done in earnest:

> Haply you think — but bootless are your thoughts —
> That this is fabulously counterfeit,
> And that we do as all tragedians do, —
> To die to-day, for fashioning our scene,
> The death of Ajax or some Roman peer,
> And in a minute starting up again,
> Revive to please to-morrow's audience.
> No, princes.   (IV.iii)

Truly a Pirandellian approach.

The mode of Marston's sophisticated farcical burlesque *Antonio and Mellida* (1600) is made possible by its Pirandellian frame. The Induction has the actors actually enter *'with parts in their hands, having cloaks cast over their apparel'*. They discuss how they are to perform:

ALBERTO: Whom do you personate?
PIERO: Piero, Duke of Venice.
ALBERTO: O, ho; then thus frame your exterior shape
　　　To haughty form of elate majesty.

In this way the audience is encouraged to take a distant view of anything the stage can offer, and the author to supply an unholy medley of elements. The actors indicate that they intend to play in the vein of caricature, 'in the old cut', and throughout the play a scathing interpretation is provided by an on-stage audience of one kind or another – by the fool Balurdo,

FELICHE: Stand! The ground trembleth.
PIERO: Ha! an earthquake!
BALURDO: O, I smell a sound,　　　　　　　　　　(I.i)

by the girls Mellida, Rossaline and Flavia *'above'* who discuss the characters below,

He is made like a tilting-staff, and looks
For all the world like an o'er-roasted pig;
A great tobacco-taker too, that's flat,
For his eyes look as if they had been hung
In the smoke of his nose,

and by Feliche, Marston's resident malcontent who gives a cynical commentary on the action as he enters *'following, wondering at them all'*:

Whop! Fut, how he tickles yon trout under the gills!
You shall see him take him by and by with groping flattery.

　　　　　　　　　　　　　　　　　　　　　　　(II.i)

The result is a boisterous romp which undercuts the notion of illusory theatre as fast as it satirizes sober romantic tragedy.

　　The audience is allowed even less respite in the more familiar comedy of Francis Beaumont, *The Knight of the Burning Pestle*, which more overtly burlesques heroic tragedy. Again the frame provided by the grocer and his wife, George and Nell, prepares the audience to enjoy the criticism of the play-within-the-play 'The London Merchant'. That George and Nell display such poor understanding and worse taste in their demands of the actors adds to the satire of the middle-class values they represent. However, the best of the joke is that they are clearly inferior in dramatic judgment to the audience they seem to belong to, because, unlike the Elizabethan playgoer, they seem incapable of separating the world of reality from the world of the stage. A recent editor of the play writes, 'Neither George nor Nell has artistic imagination; the 'reality' of a play is either the one extreme of pure illusion or the other extreme of pure fact, never the artistic mean' (*Regents Renaissance Drama Series*, p. xviii). He may have missed the point. Such an artistic mean did not exist for the Elizabethan playgoer in a context of presentational drama. Rather, the drama of this period seemed rarely to permit the audience to reach a point of imaginative equilibrium, for that would be to reject the theatre's power to grant an illusion at one moment and deny it the next.

Induction, frames, plays-within-plays, action half in and half out, on-stage audiences, disrupted plotting – at first sight the muddle is confusing. We may be looking for the wrong kind of unity, the unity of consistent action that belongs to modern realism. The mosaic of impressions and responses, with the kinds and degrees of intensity generated, is both the puzzle and its key. The Elizabethan drama is like a banquet in which the flavours are mixed to keep the appetite fresh while simultaneously satisfying it.

In the twentieth century, the wish to counter the persistent expectations of realism stimulated a variety of deliberately anti-illusory devices, and the play-within-a-play was found serviceable once again. As in Elizabethan times, it was accompanied by abrupt stylistic changes.

Pirandello framed *Six Characters in Search of an Author* (1921) with the trappings of real life, making the deception difficult to recognize by having apparently real actors come together for a rehearsal of, disarmingly, Pirandello's own last play; they come to the appropriate place, a theatre, at the same time as the audience comes to the same place to watch, it believes, an actual play by the same author. In the 1925 version, revised in the light of performance, this introductory business is greatly expanded, allowing more time to establish a convention of realism. This definitive version opens with the

hammering of a stage carpenter; the company takes longer to assemble, and a back-stage piano is played for a few of the actors to
dance as they wait; the Leading Lady is tardy, and makes a separate
entrance through the auditorium with a dog – a real one. All this
business is improvised naturally in order to lower our guard before the
disruptive anti-illusion of the Characters' entrance. With the Actors,
we tend to discount them until Pirandello judges it fit to convince us
by another play-within-the-play – the scene in the milliner's shop –
that the non-illusory Characters can offer a greater illusion of reality
than the Actors themselves.

Pirandello also expands the ending of his play. In 1921, he
brought down the curtain abruptly upon the contradictory cries of
'Pretence?' and 'Reality!', content merely to emphasize the uncertainty whether the Boy has shot himself in actuality or not. In
1925, the curtain is delayed so that startling effects can be created
to prolong the illusion. On the Director's order, an invisible hand
brings up the lights instantaneously, and as unnaturally plunges the
theatre into darkness. The Characters are momentarily silhouetted
by a green floodlight, then against a blue backcloth advance in
ghostly phalanx towards the audience, but uncannily without the two
children who were supposedly killed in the performance. The Director leaps off the stage in a fright, encouraging a similar response of
fear in the house. The Step-Daughter completes the cycle of illusion
by hurling herself up the aisle with a terrible laugh. She stops to look
back with another burst of laughter, then runs into the foyer beyond,
taking our complete attention. Her laugh is heard to the last, echoing
the confusion and discomfiture of the audience's sense of reality.
When it looks back, the curtain has closed off any further evidence of
the truth. Pirandello was reluctant to relinquish his hold and release
us from the constraints of his careful illusion.

Pirandello's later attempt to trap his audience by a play-within-
a-play in *Each in His Own Way* (1924) did not improve on this.
Jean Anouilh, however, is in some ways a more technically accomplished playwright than his acknowledged master Pirandello.
He has said, 'I have come from Pirandello, that's all. *Six Characters
in Search of an Author.* I haven't invented a thing since.' Anouilh
lures his audience into theatrical non-illusion by a greater variety of
subtle devices. He deceptively sets a play back in period to the 1910's,
the twilight between the romantic past and the reality of the present.
Like Pirandello, he often inserts a play into a theatrical and rehearsal

framework, as in *Le Rendez-vous de Senlis* (1938), *La Répétition* (1951), *Colombe* (1951), *Pauvre Bitos* (1956) and others since. He opposes mythical preconceptions with realistic presentation as in *Eurydice* (1941), *Antigone* (1942) and *L'Alouette* (1953). He flexes his styles to match the degree of unreality he seeks: in *Ardèle* (1949), *Colombe* and *La Valse des toréadors* (1952), he passes easily between Feydeau's farce and Strindberg's darkest realism, and in *La Répétition* he mixes modernity with Marivaux to confound the real with the unreal.

Tennessee Williams early progressed from an adulterated expressionism and built upon a base of realistic characterization with symbolism in his play structure and staging. He aimed at the release of the imagination belonging to anti-illusory expressionism without the dehumanizing quality of the German plays in this mode. After the inadequate jumble of styles in his early full-length plays *Battle of Angels* (1939), *You Touched Me* (1940) and the unpublished *Stairs to the Roof* (1941), he achieved the satisfying compromise of *The Glass Menagerie* (1942). In his preface to this play he wrote,

Expressionism and all other unconventional techniques in drama have only one valid aim, and that is a closer approach to truth. When a play employs unconventional techniques, it is not, or certainly shouldn't be, trying to escape its responsibility of dealing with reality, or interpreting experience, but is actually or should be attempting to find a closer approach, a more penetrating and vivid expression of things as they are.

The Glass Menagerie frames its play in Elizabethan fashion with a presenter/narrator in the person of Tom Wingfield, the son of the family, and he also functions as a character in the central action. By the use of screens, gauzes and a cut-away set built within the proscenium arch, the story of the play achieves an unusual objectivity of presentation that reminds one of Brecht and Pirandello together: look-at-it-this-way, says Tom; believe-it-or-not, says the author.

Brecht had been developing his own form of expressionism long before. When he produced his version of the *Antigone* in 1948 he seemed to practise a Pirandellian device in reverse. His actors sat on long benches in full view of the audience; when an actor's cue came, he would step into the acting area bounded by four posts hung with barbaric skulls of horses. In his foreword to the play, Brecht explained,

The reason why the actors sit openly on the stage and only adopt the attitudes proper to their parts once they enter the (very brilliantly lit) acting area is that the audience must not be able to think that it has been transported to the scene of the story, but must be invited to take part in the delivery of an ancient poem, irrespective how it has been restored.

(trans. J. Willett)

In *Six Characters*, Pirandello prepared the audience with the unromantic actuality of the stage in order to deceive it into accepting the unreal. In his *Antigone*, Brecht prepared the audience with the unromantic actuality of the stage in order not to deceive it about the reality of his play. This assertive rejection of the trappings of illusion is the source of his strength in Western drama today.

Brecht's *The Good Woman of Setzuan* (1941) and *The Caucasian Chalk Circle* (1945) both have inductions with the intention of having the play seem a parable and at the same time setting up a sharp contrast between the outer and the inner action. *The Good Woman of Setzuan* opens with a cynical discussion between the Gods about the wickedness of man: they must find one good human being if the world is to survive. They think they find one in the local prostitute, and the rest of the play is used to demonstrate how little they know about life on earth. *The Caucasian Chalk Circle* is framed by a very contemporary discussion (it is assumed to be near the end of World War II) about the right of two communes in Soviet Georgia to a piece of land. The old tale of the circle of chalk is thereupon presented, and the contest between the Governor's Wife and the maid Grusche for possession of the Governor's child teaches the lesson, 'What there is shall go to those who are good for it.' In both plays the story is naively simple, but the manner of telling strangely intricate. The historicizing device of the parable-within-the-play compels an audience to be conscious of its own responsibility as interpreter and judge.

In a parallel development, the element of conscious play-acting makes the drama of Jean Genêt equal in influence with Brecht's. *Les Bonnes* (1947) has two servants themselves act out the mistress-and-maid relationship in a recurring play-within-a-play with all the fierce exhibitionism characteristic of impostors. In this early play, Genêt is already using the drama like a 'reflection of a reflection', as he writes in his preface to the play; his critic J. H. McMahon believes that he uses the theatre 'to create a metaphor' (*The Imagination of Jean Genêt*,

p. 179). In *Les Bonnes*, the play-within-the-play is extravagantly passionate, yet because of the framework of theatrics it is perceived objectively. *Le Balcon* (1957) pursues its metaphor by externalizing the fantasies of the clients of a brothel, but these are all monstrously stage-managed by Mme Irma for her visitors' pleasure — and also for the audience's convenient distancing. As the scales are removed from the spectator's eyes, the sexual perverts project a portrait of society itself: marvellously, their fantasies are seen to be an image, albeit distorted, of political behaviour in the contemporary world.

Many plays in our time have followed the patterns of Pirandello, Brecht and Genêt. In the *Marat/Sade*, we saw how Peter Weiss invites his audience to suppose a series of mirrors. Marat's story of 1780 is interpreted by de Sade in 1808, but it is played by the insane and destitute, interpreted further by a Chorus and finally seen through the aristocratic eyes of the asylum's Governor and his family. The question remains, What then does the modern audience see? Friedrich Dürrenmatt with his pretended madmen of *The Physicists* (1962) echoes Pirandello's *Henry IV* (1922). The author seems to ask, 'If a madman says he is insane, is it true?' The jest is pursued relentlessly: says one, 'I'm no more mad than you are'; says another, 'Only as a madman am I free to think.' And these are the men who hold the future of mankind in their hands. The play is a Möbius ring which endlessly leads you back to your beginning.

The new plays are exploring the freedom of a theatre which need not create illusion in order to work and survive. Rather, it can manipulate that very quality of illusion which is its stock-in-trade. Just as *A Midsummer Night's Dream* and *The Winter's Tale* in their own time did not have to strain convention in order to illuminate life, soon it may no longer be necessary for a playwright to make anti-illusory flourishes before we begin to enjoy his medium. In non-illusory theatre, an audience sees, hears, thinks and feels, and knows it.

Criticism has recently borrowed the uneasy term 'Mannerist' from sixteenth-century Italian art history to describe the exploratory and transitional style of later Elizabethan drama. According to George R. Kernodle, it is characterized by plays like *Troilus and Cressida* and Marston's *Antonio and Mellida*. Mannerism describes a selfconscious style, an uncertainty of posture, which seems at this distance to be contorted and grotesque, falling into farcical satire which is sometimes ridiculous, sometimes frightening in its excess of violence and general cynicism. When conventions are changing rapidly, the theatre does not know whether it is real or unreal, in earnest or in sport.

Drama in the twentieth century is passing through a similar Mannerist phase, highly affected but gratifyingly experimental in its quest for a viable relationship between the stage and the audience. The gallow's humour and sick jokes of such as Ionesco and Dürren-matt, with their flamboyant, disjointed stage images, make up the contemporary Mannerist style. Mannerism is very much aware that it is playing a game of theatre, believing and not believing, but prepared to surrender illusion in order to indulge a self-mockery. Paradoxically, it seems to undercut the convention which makes communication possible.

7
Audience

Playhouse, script, actors, *mise en scène*, audience are inseparable parts of the theatre event. The concept of drama put forward in this book insists that the audience has an indispensable role to play. While Stanislavsky is right in saying that 'spectators come to the theatre to hear the subtext. They can read the text at home', he is speaking as a man of the nineteenth century. We do not go to the play merely to have the text interpreted and explained by the skills of the director and his actors. We do not go as in a learning situation, but to share in a partnership without which the players cannot work. In his *Réflexions sur l'art*, Valéry believed that 'a creator is one who makes other create': in art both the artist and the spectator actively cooperate, and the value of the work is dependent on this reciprocity.

If in the theatre there is no interaction between stage and audience, the play is dead, bad or non-existent: the audience, like the customer, is always right. Dramatic perception should be distinguished from the reading of a play as Susanne Langer distinguishes drama from literature:

Literature projects the image of life in the mode of virtual memory; language is its essential material; the sound and meaning of words, their familiar or unusual use and order, even their presentation on the printed page, create the illusion of life as a realm of events – completed, lived, as words formulate them – events that compose a Past. But drama presents the poetic illusion in a different light: not finished realities, or 'events', but immediate, visible responses of human beings, make its semblance of life. Its basic abstraction is the act, which springs from the past, but is directed toward the future, and is always great with things to come.

(*Feeling and Form*, p. 306)

Perception in drama is what occurs, not what might occur – it is a response of this order.

At its simplest reduction, the reciprocity of the theatre is the desire of the spectator to jump into the shoes of the actor on the stage, and of the actor to understand this. In his *A Defence of Poetry*, Shelley pointed to the implicit assumption behind poetry, that the reader can feel as another. Today criticism has adopted the term 'empathy' to describe an audience's innate ability to feel as, say, Hamlet feels. Strangely, audiences can also empathize with villains like Iago, so that any dramatist worth his salt can make capital out of our capacity to suffer different kinds of empathy, setting one range of feelings against another. We must understand Hamlet and Claudius, Antigone and Creon, Hjalmar and Gregers.

King Lear, I.iv demonstrates well Shakespeare's cunning balancing of an audience's sympathies. The King has entered to horns as from hunting, still a ruler with the appurtenances of power visible in the presence of his knights. We should distrust his swagger had we not heard Goneril plotting in the previous scene to treat old fools as babes. Immediately we encounter the new Kent in his disguise as a servant, placed in direct contrast with the fawning servant Oswald. Kent illustrates another order of service:

LEAR: Dost thou know me fellow?
KENT: No sir, but you have that in your countenance which I would fain call master.
LEAR: What's that?
KENT: Authority.

Loyalty is an important thread running through the play, and having set up a contrast beween the two servants, Shakespeare proceeds to adjust our response to the King by demonstrating their difference.

Oswald makes two cleverly illustrative entrances, the first almost in silence, ignoring the King. Lear addresses him with the same confident peremptoriness with which he calls for his dinner: 'You you sirrah, where's my daughter?' Coached by Goneril, Oswald disdains to answer, but stalks past the King: 'So please you — '. There is an astonished silence on the stage and the crowd is suddenly stock still as Oswald passes impertinently in a long exit through the assembled knights. Their rage evaluates the insult, and in another voice Lear breaks out with, 'What says the fellow there? Call the clotpoll back!' But Oswald has gone, having clearly exemplified how the wind sits. He repeats his performance a minute later and provokes Lear a second time; but he is now better prepared to retaliate, as we are to understand:

LEAR: O you sir, you, come hither sir, who am I sir?
STEWARD: My Lady's father.
LEAR: My Lady's father? My Lord's knave, you whoreson dog, you
slave, you cur.

For the audience there is a nice irony in 'My Lady's father', and
another for Lear. His repetitions are the measure of his anger.
This time he loses control and demeans himself in striking the
man. He vents his spleen on a servant, not seeing that Oswald is
merely Goneril's shadow. When Kent proves his loyalty and trips
Oswald, the company of knights is in a roar of laughter, and Lear is
foolishly pleased with himself.

The episode guides the audience's sympathies, adjusts its values.
We recognize Kent's devotion against Oswald's treachery. We feel
for the self-esteem of the King, now more humbled than elevated
by his display of violence; for the audience does not join in the
laughter, realizing that the incident reflects Lear's uncertain status.
The laughter is hollow in our ears because we are busy thought-
fully ordering our sympathies, weighing the tyrant against the man.
When Peter Brook improvised the scene for the Royal Shakespeare
Company's production in 1962, the knights ran riot, threw cups,
overturned tables, and Lear appeared to encourage the rumpus.
It was a wonderful piece of theatre, but it placed Goneril and
Oswald in the right and destroyed Shakespeare's careful balance.
Lear seemed to deserve his ordeal on the heath in act III.

In some degree empathy is prerequisite to any play which seeks
the participation of an audience. It is difficult to be sure of the form it
takes in extremes of non-illusory theatre where there is no expectation of realism in character or action, but even in highly ritualistic
or artificial drama there is undoubtedly a substitute process.

In *Christian Rite and Christian Drama in the Middle Ages*, O. B.
Hardison attempts an important re-examination of the beginnings of
the dramatic impulse in the medieval church. He argues for that
kind of participation which belongs to a congregation in a state
of unquestioning worship: 'The ninth-century Offertory, during
which the people bring candles, oblation loaves, and wine to the
deacon or celebrant, links them to the ceremony as participants rather
than as passive witnesses. The symbolism of the preparation of the
bread and wine also emphasizes the idea of participation' (p. 59).
Later, he asks the fundamental question: 'Did the congregation sense
its role-playing function continually, or only during those ceremonies

and prayers when it was assigned definite actions and speeches – the Introit procession, the reading of the Gospel, the Offertory, the Kiss of Peace, the Communion?' (p. 78). In her Clark Lectures, *Shakespeare the Craftsman*, M. C. Bradbrook pursued the idea that in such ritual the people found contact with the divine: 'The principle of medieval pageantry is a sacramental one, the principle of Transformation. In game or play creatures appearing to come from a world beyond the world erupt to meet the audience. By participating in the play, the audience enter into relation with that other world' (p. 6). With the change from ritual to representational drama, elements of illusion are mixed with non-illusion. The audience is increasingly called upon to piece out the play's imperfections with its thoughts, and argue for its feelings.

The spectator's uncertainty about his role continues happily throughout the Elizabethan period. Particularly in the comedies, the kinds of response are markedly disparate. In the scene in which Viola meets Olivia in *Twelfth Night*, I.v, it is not possible finally to say whether an Elizabethan audience's sympathies are more with Viola than Olivia. Both players are acting a part, both are in disguise, Olivia with her veil, Viola with her doublet and hose, equally non-illusory. It would be impossible finally to argue that Viola's willow cabin speech was more affecting than Olivia's moment of truth at the end of the scene:

> I do I know not what, and fear to find
> Mine eye too great a flatterer for my mind.

Throughout the comedy, the audience retains an objective superiority to the action, although its Olympian omniscience permits understanding where it tends to deny sympathy.

This same omniscience enables a scene of multiple errors like IV.i to operate imaginatively. An unsuspecting Sebastian time after time finds himself taken for Cesario; he speaks for our normality of non-involvement. While the innocent Andrew is overwhelmed to discover that the cowardly Cesario can now handle his weapon, and Olivia in her ignorance has a big shock in store, Sebastian naturally accepts her somewhat improper invitation. His reiterated questions to the audience, 'Are all the people mad?... Am I mad?' remind it that, if it has enjoyed the fun, it is only because it has not been deceived like those on the stage.

Upon the Duke's cry, 'Call your executioner, and off with Barnardine's head' in *Measure for Measure*, IV.iii, could the Elizabethan audience expect a fine and bloody show to follow? It is no doubt a mistake to think that the audience in a theatre without illusion indulged a simple vicarious pleasure like its modern counterpart watching the violence of a popular film. In a theatre with such a range of conventional devices, from boys playing girls to free-run clowns, the audience may not have been surprised that the executioner who appears is not the fearful Abhorson but his comic assistant, Pompey the clown; nor that he delivers the preposterous message that prison is like Mistress Overdone's brothel — 'for here be many of her old customers'. When he proceeds to name a dozen ready for the block, so clear an address to the audience may have been more disturbing than the fate of Claudio in the inner play.

The playwright of real life perforce devised other ways of touching the spectator without destroying belief in what was happening on the stage. Ibsen spent his best years perfecting an expository method designed to stagger his comfortable audiences in their seats. A combination of familiar behaviour, reproduced and irresistibly accumulated in fine detail, and an insidious thematic suggestion to excite a special order of involvement and interest, was Ibsen's substitute for participatory drama. We think of such cruces as

NORA: I saved Torvald's life, you see.
KROGSTAD: Your father seems to have signed this paper three days after his death.   (*A Doll's House*)

MRS ALVING: Ghosts — Those two in the conservatory — Ghosts — They've come to life again!   (*Ghosts*)

TESMAN: What are you looking at, Hedda?
HEDDA: I'm just looking at the leaves — they're so yellow — so withered.
                                           (*Hedda Gabler*)

REBECCA: They cling to their dead here at Rosmersholm.
MRS HELSETH: If you want my opinion, miss, it's the dead that cling to Rosmersholm.   (*Rosmersholm*)

In Ibsen, these are magnetic moments, painstakingly constructed.

To empathize is the natural human impulse, but in alienation lies the drama. An audience is most trapped by a character or situation if it is held in a state of uncertainty as to how to respond, and ambiguity in a central character especially extends an audience's affective perceptions. Richard III as an evil king would not have survived an act without the charm of his direct appeal; Richard II as a pathetic failure would equally have sunk his play had Shakespeare not also shown him ruthless. The relative innocence of Romeo is tempered by his friendship with a bawdy Mercutio, the artlessness of Juliet by the grossness of her closest companion the Nurse. In these plays there is challenging rhythm of contradictory response.

However, the important balance of alienation is possible only if an audience is permitted sympathy in the first place. *Timon of Athens* and *Coriolanus* are two plays in the Shakespeare canon so undercut by choric commentators in the earlier scenes that the central character must struggle to gain any rapport with the audience. Anti-illusory distancing in modern drama risks the same danger of imbalance. The poseurs Sergius and Raina in Shaw's *Arms and the Man* burlesque the convention of Victorian military romance by which the smartest uniform wins the prettiest girl, but in creating his style for the play, Shaw shakes our sense of his characters' reality. Sergius and Raina, after all, are the ones who must make the sensible choice of marrying the practical Louka and the solid hotel-owner Bluntschli. Actors have difficulty in securing a dimension of credibility while sustaining a level of high style: for any distancing device places a character in a fiction and has the power to change the audience's relation to the stage.

The ambiguity of fact and fiction, illusion and alienation, is never easy to resolve in performance. The production of Brecht's plays has taught that no amount of technical trickery will alienate a Mother Courage or a dumb Kattrin if the sympathetic emotion is strong enough: an audience adjusts quickly to a new convention, and within the frame of almost any fictitious style we can still feel an emotion. Alienation in Brecht's drama works best when it is structurally controlled, when the plotting itself is dialectical: *Galileo* achieves a perfect balance when the good scientist is morally compromised by his bad actions.

Any theory of dramatic response must take into account the stretch and strain of mind and feeling which keeps an audience receptive and perceptive. The element of anxiety which comes of uncertainty and ambivalence produces a most serviceable tension and is the likely source of most interplay between stage and audience. Shakespeare himself is not above the tactics of simple suspense. When Lear and

Cordelia are prisoners and their lives in danger, he holds his audience in suspense for as long as he dare (*King Lear*, v.iii).

Before learning the fate of the King and his daughter, an audience must first await the result of the duel between Edgar and Edmund, and stay the length of Edgar's 'brief tale'. After this delay, Shakespeare contrives a series of false alarms which increase the tension further still. With a leap forward in pace, first the Gentleman with the bloody knife makes his appeal:

GENTLEMAN: Help, help: O help.
EDGAR: What kind of help?
ALBANY: Speak, man.
EDGAR: What means this bloody knife?
GENTLEMAN: 'Tis hot, it smokes, it came even from the heart of – O she's dead.
ALBANY: Who dead? Speak, man.

But it is only Goneril who is dead, with Regan poisoned – though little the audience cares, aroused as it is. Next, the entrance of Kent looking for the King spurs our hope soon to learn the fate of those who most interest us, the point emphasized by Albany's cry,

> Great thing of us forgot,
> Speak, Edmund, where's the King? and where's Cordelia?

Even at this moment two bodies are solemnly carried in – but this is another false lead, and they prove to be those of the sisters. Now the stage comes alive with our anxiety:

> EDGAR: Quickly send,
> (Be brief in it) to th' Castle, for my writ
> Is on the life of Lear and on Cordelia:
> Nay, send in time.
> ALBANY: Run, run, O run.

The stage is suddenly all animation, until it is transfixed by the inhuman sound of Lear's howling as he enters with Cordelia dead in his arms.

This is situational tension at its simplest; as a technique it might be regarded as a little shabby in another play. It brings Shakespeare's most complex tragedy to its last crisis. The excitement is of course to be capped by the more profound tension of ambiguity in Lear's death. Thinking Cordelia alive, did he die of joy, or thinking her dead, did he die of grief? It is the ancient conundrum, but we are not to know. We can only respond by feeling both of his sensations perhaps simultaneously, a final ambivalence. For the scene deals, not in Lear's last suffering, but ours.

To categorize the great variety of tensions possible in the theatre would want another book. An example or two will suggest the range. In the last scene of *The Winter's Tale* the audience's role is unfathomable. The tragic suspense felt by Leontes as he sees the statue of the wife he spurned is partly felt by us, because for once in a comedy the playwright carefully conceals the truth about Hermione's survival; and yet the aura of prophecy and magic induced by Paulina allows a comedic optimism that goes beyond the anguish of the contrite husband.

The hybrid genres and mongrel moods which have plagued neoclassical criticism are today seen as natural to the theatre, for in each mixture lies the secret of engaging an audience. The tonal contradictions within *Measure for Measure* do not fit any theory of tragicomedy, but they work marvellously well in performance. Lucio, the devil's advocate, clips his words wickedly when reporting Claudio's sin to his sister Isabella in her convent. By so doing, he sharpens an audience's perception of the contradictory positions, and the intention is not merely to muddy its response.

> LUCIO: Gentle and fair: your brother kindly greets you;
> Not to be weary with you; he's in prison.
> ISABELLA: Woe me; for what?
> LUCIO: For that, which if myself might be his judge,
> He should receive his punishment, in thanks:
> He hath got his friend with child.   (I.iv)

To Isabella's chaste blushes, Lucio thereupon expatiates upon the natural wonder of procreation, although in the circumstances he somewhat sensually wraps his tongue round the words:

> As those who feed, grow full: as blossoming time
> That from the seedness, the bare fallow brings
> To teeming foison: even so her plenteous womb
> Expresseth his full tilth, and husbandry.

He is mocking her other-worldliness, a man among women, a rake in a godly house; but he speaks with disarming honesty, and puts the audience on its mettle. The acute opposition of their two attitudes to moral law, both deserving, compels the audience to choose a side when partisanship is embarrassing. The effect is not dissimilar to O'Casey's naughtiness in act II of *The Plough and the Stars*, where he forces his Irish audience to hear the holy words of Easter 1916 through the indifferent ears of Rosie Redmond the prostitute.

That Shakespeare's problem plays are mongrel in genre is quite academic for the popular audience. *Troilus and Cressida* refuses it a stereotyped response to heroics, *All's Well That Ends Well* to love and marriage, *Measure for Measure* to sin and justice. The test is whether the induced mood succeeds in stimulating the spectator to wakefulness.

The execution of Barnardine for murder in *Measure for Measure* is placed in provocative parallel with the sentence on Claudio for fornication. For different reasons, neither of them is 'absolute for death', the one insensitive, the other too sensitive. It is possible to rationalize this coolly in the study, but in the theatre an audience is made to feel that the increase in tension towards the moment of death is accompanied by an increase in irreverence and ambiguity. The cases of Barnardine and Claudio do not merge in reasonable comparison, but divide in mind splitting, stylistic contrast.

In IV.ii, the Provost calls both the condemned men together to announce their execution, but only Claudio – who has evidently not had a wink of sleep – appears:

PROVOST: Look, here's the warrant Claudio, for thy death,
　'Tis now dead midnight, and by eight tomorrow
　Thou must be made immortal. Where's Barnardine?
CLAUDIO: As fast lock'd up in sleep as guiltless labour
　When it lies starkly in the traveller's bones,
　He will not wake.

Shakespeare shows us the fearful Claudio, dragged out in the night to hear he has but eight hours to live, and thus increases suspense by setting the hour precisely, while the murderer sleeps on without a sense of guilt, 'fearless of what's past, present, or to come'. Shakespeare pursues the comedy of Barnardine relentlessly. Upon the Clown's amusing 'Master Barnardine, you must rise and be hang'd, Master Barnardine', he is heard cursing within; when he roars that he is too sleepy, the Clown's timid answer is the delicious line, 'Pray Master Barnardine, awake till you are executed, and sleep afterward'. All this to make a joke of contrition. By widening the reference of the action with such comedy, Shakespeare deliberately distances Claudio and his conscience.

When pimps and clowns execute the law, a play is doubtless taking gross liberties with the audience. When in *Antony and Cleopatra*, v.ii Cleopatra jests with a clown about her imminent death, fondles the repulsive asp and applies it like a baby to her breast, the ugly has been added to the comic. It is yet another source of ambivalence, and with Lessing we might argue, 'Who does not feel, at the same time, that the disgusting is in its proper place here? It makes the terrible horrible; and the horrible is not altogether displeasing even in nature, so long as our compassion is engaged' (*Laocoön*, trans. E. A. McCormick, ch. XXV). Even within the limitations of the naturalistic stage some incongruity of the *grässlich* is possible: as when Hedda learns that her protégé has unromantically shot himself, not in the chest, but sordidly in 'the bowels', or when Solness the master builder falls gracelessly from his final tower into a stone quarry and has 'his whole head crushed in'. Thus is the audience sobered, and by such strong perceptions Ibsen leaves it where good naturalistic drama should: in a position to make its own final judgment, aroused but cool.

Opposite feelings coexist in life as in the theatre, but in the latter they challenge the decorum of an audience because they are presented more vigorously and objectively. So it is with all dramatic mixtures, and even in sentimental comedy the jerk of contradiction can tax the sensibilities. In Congreve's *The Old Batchelor* (*sic*, 1693), Heartwell is the surly bachelor of the title. Echoing previous plain dealers like Molière's Alceste and Wycherley's Manly, he pretends to hate women while being secretly smitten by Silvia. In such a captivating revelation as this, Congreve spins out the inconsistency:

Why whither in the Devil's name am I going now? Hum — let me think — is not this Silvia's house, the cave of that enchantress, and which consequently I ought to shun as I would infection? To enter here, is to put on the envenom'd shirt, to run into the embraces of a fever, and in some raving fit, be led to plunge myself into that more consuming fire, a woman's arms. Ha! well recollected, I will recover my reason, and be gone . . . Well, why do you not move? Feet do your office — not one inch; no, foregad I'm caught — There stands my north, and thither my needle points — Now could I curse myself, yet cannot repent. O thou delicious, damn'd, dear, destructive woman! (III.ii)

No doubt Betterton played this for all it was worth, just as every actor who has undertaken Sir Peter Teazle exploits his teasing confession about his wife:

She dissipates my fortune, and contradicts all my humours; yet, the worst of it is, I doubt I love her, or I should never bear all this. However, I'll never be weak enough to own it.   (I.ii)

Sheridan's audience now not only knows Sir Peter's secret, it anticipates more than he can what advantage Lady Teazle will take of his weakness.

The tension of a double value, a doubt about a character's motives, a choice to be made, the difference between the expectation and the actuality, the disjunction between the content of a scene and its style – there are innumerable ways of arousing an audience. There is much, however, in the given condition of dramatic representation which engenders participatory response without one contrivance or trick of technique.

In his exhaustive study of motives in human thought and action, Kenneth Burke is particularly concerned with the characteristic modes of persuasion in the arts. His four master tropes, metaphor, metonymy, synecdoche and irony (*A Grammar of Motives*, p. 503) have the literal application of what he calls perspective, reduction, representation and dialectic. If we borrow them for the drama, it is because they are all active as soon as performance begins, the one shading into the other. Metaphor gives a perspective view in terms of something else: drama itself is such an image of life. Metonymy conveys some intangible state in terms of the tangible and immediate: thus a stage character reduces a general spiritual condition to a particular problem, whereby an audience is exercised to apply the particular to the general. This is not unlike synecdoche, which offers the part for the whole, just as on the stage a sensory representation demands its wider application and evaluation. Irony grants the spectator his superior insight, and the interaction of the different viewpoints of the play and the audience generates the dialectical activity all playgoing involves. These large concepts are part of the nature of theatre and are built into the structural design of a good play. We can accept them while awaiting their particular treatment by perceptual criticism in the future.

Whatever the nature of the medium, whatever the device, an audience must sense urgency and immediacy in the experience. Thornton Wilder's notion that the action of a play 'takes place in perpetual present time' is irrefutable: 'on the stage it is always now'. The point is worth making that this applies even to a period play, one that belongs to another place and time, another society and belief. The flexible mind of the audience provides the infinitely adjustable link between the dramatic past and present. In this, a play is like a ritualistic game.

Imaginative elasticity is possible because the game permits place and time to be spanned according to rules the audience decides. *Homo ludens* is never more conspicuous than in the playhouse. An audience adapts itself to the world of other experience and makes it its own, because theatre, like any game, is, in McLuhanese, 'an extension of social man' (*Understanding Media*, p. 208). For McLuhan, games are a form of communication contrived to allow 'simultaneous participation of many people in some significant pattern of their own corporate lives' (p. 216). Again, he declares that 'play . . . implies interplay. There must be give and take, or dialogue, as between two or more persons or groups' (p. 213). The playhouse and the stage, the form and style of the play, the conventions of acting – all are finally interrelated in order to set out a game pattern for participation. General rules are laid down, but there are no certain limits to the scope of the game, provided the playwright can sustain immediacy and persuade his audience to follow. It is through game conventions that place and time can be governed indefinitely.

A game is an imitation of life, and at times some sense of its sportfulness rises consciously to the surface. Such a moment occurs when Millamant and Mirabel play their proviso scene in Congreve's *The Way of the World*, IV.v. (A similar moment occurs when Harriet and Young Bellair pretend to be lovers in Etherege's *The Man of Mode*, III.i.) Their conditions for a certain freedom in marriage are irrelevant to the play's plot and they are more than a display of wit; the scene is essentially of the theatre. Since both the players and the audience know the outcome of the exchange, the movements and gestures on the stage are not between actor and actor, but between actor and audience, as first Millamant, then Mirabel, present and demonstrate the female and the male principle. As Millamant makes her demands, Mirabel conveys his reactions to the audience for counter-approval; then he makes his demands on behalf of all men while Millamant acts as his foil. The form of the dialogue has the audience divide neatly into two teams, male and female, as they cheer on their champions. As at a game, the spectators are partial judges, but the bargain is struck to the satisfaction of all parties, not least that of the audience.

Any illusion here is that of mirrors which reflect each other repeatedly, until the image is blurred. When Samuel Beckett collects quick laughter in *Waiting for Godot* and *Endgame* by breaking convention in music-hall fashion, as we saw (Hamm: 'This is deadly'; Nagg: 'I've never told that joke worse'), these are reminders that the play is merely a charade. They grant Beckett his licence to continue to beset the audience with his unpalatable images and the interjections simply recall the rules of the game we have already accepted. Perception in the theatre comes mostly from what you expect, or are led to expect.

Beckett creates his stage microcosm like any earlier writer of non-illusory drama. The kind of activity in Ben Jonson's little playhouse worlds is proposed initially by a Volpone, a Truewit or a Subtle. They invite complicity in their outrageous schemes and set the standard for monstrous caricatures. To leap the years, Sheridan in the same way projects a primary image, sets a moral tone, to enable his comedy to operate. This is the proper work of Lady Sneerwell's slow, smooth-tongued opening line, 'The paragraphs, you say, Mr Snake, were all inserted?', as she calmly attends to more surface appearances before her mirror.

Style lays down the rules of play, and quasi-symbolic action is the extension of them. Gordon Craig believed it to be at the heart of the game: 'Symbolism is the very essence of theatre.' It speaks to an audience with the kind of vivid economy that suits the high concentration of play-perception, and enables it to construct an image both specific and universal. The action can be direct and inescapable in symbolic statement, as when the game of chess in Middleton's *Women Beware Women* (*c.* 1620), II.ii is played throughout the seduction of Bianca by the Duke of Florence — a pawn overwhelmed by the black king. But even the great naturalists, Ibsen, Strindberg and Chekhov, felt the need of symbolic suggestion the better to articulate their meaning, lest their audiences were in danger of absorbing the particularity of their realism at the expense of the larger theme. Nevertheless, the playgoer will not tolerate loose ends. In the closing minutes of *Hedda Gabler* or *The Master Builder*, Ibsen gathers up by the bunch his symbols of vine-leaves and pistols, the wreath and the shawl, in order to assist his audience in the task of tying up the threads.

The drama was quick to pursue expressionistic forms of non-illusion, and Ibsen's last plays would have been more comfortable if they had been written for a theatre of twenty years later. It is possible to believe that an audience prefers its more traditional, obvious game-playing function. The continual revivals of Shakespeare in this century of photographic media are strong evidence of this. The blatantly ritual form by which a Richard III piously displayed himself with such explicit irony between his two bishops puts a theatre audience more at ease than all the submerged suggestion of symbolic action in Ibsen. An audience willingly allows Shakespeare to raise *Othello* from domestic *drame* to symbolic tragedy by his sequence of ritualistic devices: by cracks of thunder and idealized storm poetry, the pact with Iago and the magic handkerchief, Desdemona's connubial death-bed and the sacrificial climax. The Globe's audience was universal in its readiness to allow the transmutations of drama, and so Shakespeare brings statues to life and conjures up magic islands still.

Ritual is the name of the game, but on the stage it cannot be arranged for the asking. Custom is everything. A congregation would be alarmed, to say the least, to go to church at Christmas and hear the Easter service. In the last sixty years there have been enough plays based on Greek myths to constitute a theatrical phenomenon. This development, chiefly in the French and American theatre, is the product of two wishes: to place modern man in a new philosophical setting which may also be shown to be timeless, and to return theatre to its ritual function. Both attempts were bound to be abortive. The two plays in this category which were most engaging, Sartre's *Les Mouches* (1943) and Anouilh's *Antigone* (1944), succeeded because of the unique condition of the audience in occupied Paris. Played under the eyes of the German censor, these plays invited audiences to join in a conspiracy with Orestes and Antigone against the common enemies, Zeus, Creon and Hitler.

The difficulty in putting a myth on the stage two thousand years late is that audiences may not know, quite simply, what to expect of the story, thus denying a prerequisite of ritual, which is based on expected repetition. Even if the audience is well-read and knows its Sophocles, it is most unlikely to have a feeling knowledge of the story. If, soon after the rise of the curtain, the playwright cannot stir

in us some earthy sensation of our archetypal heritage, we join in
only an intellectual game, and good theatre is never that. The tensions which come from an audience's foreknowledge are those that
cut deepest, because it has brought a good part of the play with it
into the theatre: at rise of curtain the spectator is already a player.
Cocteau fails with *La Machine infernale* (1934) because in his ob-
session with the mechanical gear-shifting of the anti-realistic movement he forgets to engage those tensions.

Even if Cocteau's declared intention of making the play speak
the language of its own medium was better realized by his successors,
we must give him the credit for the right idea. 'Mythology has one
great advantage', wrote Schlegel, 'that which perpetually eludes
consciousness is here fixed and made visible', and Cocteau decided
for myth because it has two virtues: it is simple and it is concrete.
Unfortunately, by the time he had finished, it was neither. Myth also
supplies that skin-tight form in which any drama looks shapely, and
T. S. Eliot's classical mind was drawn to the known patterns of myth
when he made his dramatic excursions. However, in every case Eliot
so departed from his myth that an audience needed footnotes to
remind it of its presence. In the theatre, Hugh Dickinson has dryly
observed, nothing is so bootless as a footnote.

Myth supplies material to the theatre which is rich in passionate
feeling of the most element kind, strong in its simplicity, the kind that
can move us without our having first to stop and ask what it means.
The appeal of myth to the more realistic playwright who wishes to
place its audience into its niche in cosmic history is the general assumption that it is cyclical, that what happened must happen again.
The chance to liken the ancient and the modern is what attracted
O'Neill to Aeschylus when he wrote *Mourning Becomes Electra*
(1931). Cocteau's idea that time is a man-made notion which could
be shown to have real meaning by juxtaposing the old and the new
within the theatre event has appealed to all the modern playwrights of
ancient myth. The problem, however, is to make an audience realize
and experience this simultaneity of time, but without inhibiting its
response by the distracting anachronisms that are likely to develop
like measles. It is not enough to supply a new psychological cloak for
the action: Cocteau gave Oedipus an Oedipus complex and O'Neill
gave Electra an Electra complex, forgetting that in the theatre com-
plexes are always what other people have, never oneself. Psycho-

logical realism will remain domestic and parochial, at best a curiosity, until we all become efficient self-analysts.

Nietzsche in 1872 knew that myth was no substitute for faith, but a way of speaking, a 'metaphor for the inexpressible'. Gilbert Murray in 1912, in consonance with anthropological thinking at the turn of the century, explained Greek tragedy as the original drama of death and rebirth. Drama study since then has recognized that the best theatrical life in any age hinges on the needs of community living, answering society's secular need for ritual as the church once answered the religious. This kind of recognition is a long way from Broadway, the West End or the Paris boulevards, where any sense of community is conspicuously missing. For although the ritual of theatre turns on good playwriting, good playwriting begins with an intimate knowledge of the audience, when the playwright is himself a close spectator of life.

Creating drama is most obviously a social act. Susanne Langer insists that art is made for other people, not personal reverie (p. 392), and its social intent gives it its value. Measures of value, therefore, can only be truly made with reference to what a play says, not what it is trying to say. A profound idea only partly communicated is as nothing against a shallow one wholly communicated: content, form and medium cannot be judged apart. The virtue and energy of a play must be tested upon an audience, which implies the importance of exercising full dramatic perception. Perceptual criticism is finally performance criticism.

It is the mark of civilized man that he can organize his experience, both individual and collective, into meaningful pictures and patterns. The stage, of all artistic media, has the power to harness the ingredients of human imagination for community experience, guiding an audience towards moral or religious consciousness, inducing a compassionate or satirical attitude, educating it through discussion or dialectic, encouraging the celebration of its past or present, persuading it to the balance and composure of dramatic objectivity. All this may be done in the much-abused name of recreation and entertainment. Under whatever pretext, we have the pleasure of perceiving, compelled to exercise our eyes and ears, our wits and feelings, beyond the ordinary.

Beyond the ordinary: the value of a play lies in the elusive change produced in its audience. Recent thinking about received ideas in literature, that the Greeks believed in the omnipotence of their gods, that the Elizabethans held to the notion of a great chain of being, and that these concepts must be read back into their literature, has undergone a timely revision. An artist of any merit is not a reporter, and if an audience senses no difference between a received and a transmitted idea, a good playwright has been reduced to a bad journalist, and the imaginative effort of the audience has gone for nothing.

What Bedlamite had been viewed with the compassion shown Edgar by Lear, what comic Jew with the objectivity afforded Shylock? Before *Troilus and Cressida*, the name Helen of Troy summoned up all the glamour for the Elizabethans that it did for Marlowe's Faustus. The spectator's mythical expectation was doubtless an important contribution to any play in which she appeared. But Shakespeare deliberately refuses a sight of the ostensible cause of the ten-year Trojan War until the middle of the play. When Helen finally appears in III.i, she is presented as in a bawdy comedy of courtly manners, bandying words as Pandarus's equal, fondling and flirting with him, enjoying his obscene song: the stage image is one of any common Nell off the London streets. By denying the received idea, Shakespeare taints the Homeric idyll at a stroke. No doubt the spectators who paid their pennies to see *Antony and Cleopatra* would not have been satisfied had they not seen the adulterous queen of legend in something of her glory, tearing a passion to tatters and splitting the ears of the groundlings. But they got more than they bargained for in Shakespeare's devious heroine, and when at her death she rose to heights unknown of poetry, he showed them intimations of another immortality.

John Webster certainly had his eye to the main chance when he sought out the lurid details of the treacherous life and death of Vittoria Corombona's original as material for a play, but he was too good a playwright merely to satiate his audience with another seductive Italian courtesan, another she-devil incarnate. In both *The White Devil* (1612) and *The Duchess of Malfi* (1613) Webster stimulates his audience to a new response by thrusting before it creatures of unexpected depth and sensibility, characters far removed from the stereotypes of female evil associated with Italianate revenge tragedies. Through plays as powerful as these, an audience emerges from the playhouse richer in mind and spirit, challenged and changed.

This is not to say that a good play conceals a message which an audience has a duty to perceive. If a good play encapsulates a moral, the dialectic of the dramatic process ensures that its audience must undergo the total treatment of transmission, reception and perception before it is felt. Good drama does not meet the social need by pouring out medicine; it prescribes a change of air. Dramatic perception is like breathing fresh air, making unaccustomed use of eyes and ears, and stretching the mind.

Everything moves to this point: that the study of drama must be pursued in its own medium, the theatre, where an audience makes its perceptions and has its social experience. It is a growing voice which urges that criticism which ignores the theatrical experience is peripheral, even irresponsible. But no one belittles the magnitude of the task remaining.

Bibliographical references

Achard, M. Introduction to Feydeau, *Théâtre complet*, trans. M. D. Dirks in *Let's Get a Divorce! and other plays*, ed. E. R. Bentley, New York, 1958.

Artaud, A. *The Theatre and Its Double*, trans. M. C. Richards, New York, 1958.

Baker, H. *History of the London Stage*, London, 1904.

Barnet, S. 'Charles Lamb and the Tragic Malvolio', *Philological Quarterly*, XXXIII, 1954.

Bartholomeusz, D. *Macbeth and the Players*, Cambridge, 1969.

Beckerman, B. *Dynamics of Drama: Theory and Method of Analysis*, New York, 1970.

Bentley, E. R. *The Life of the Drama*, London, 1965.

'The Psychology of Farce', Introduction to *Let's Get a Divorce! and other plays*, ed. E. R. Bentley, New York, 1958.

Berry, F. *The Shakespearean Inset: Word and Picture*, London, 1965.

Bethell, S. L. *Shakespeare and the Popular Dramatic Tradition*, London, 1944.

Boas, F. S. *University Drama in the Tudor Age*, London, 1914.

Boas, G. 'The Influence of the Boy Actor on Shakespeare's Plays', *Contemporary Review*, 152, 1937.

Booth, M. *Hiss the Villain*, London, 1964.

Boulding, K. *The Image*, Ann Arbor, 1956.

Bradbrook, M. C. *Shakespeare the Craftsman*, London, 1969.

Themes and Conventions of Elizabethan Tragedy, Cambridge, 1935.

Bradley, A. C. *Shakespearean Tragedy*, London, 1906.

Brecht, B. *Brecht on Theatre*, trans. J. Willett, London, 1964.

Brook, P. *The Empty Space*, London, 1968.

Brown, J. R. *Shakespeare's Plays in Performance*, London, 1966.

'The Theatrical Element of Shakespeare Criticism' in *Reinterpretations of Elizabethan Drama*, ed. N. Rabkin, New York, 1969.

Burke, K. *A Grammar of Motives*, New York, 1945.

Charney, M. *How to Read Shakespeare*, New York, 1971.

Shakespeare's Roman Plays: The Function of Imagery in the Drama, Cambridge, Mass., 1961.

Cibber, C. *An Apology for the Life of Mr Colley Cibber*, ed. B. R. S. Fone, Ann Arbor, 1968.

Clinton-Baddeley, V. C. *The Burlesque Tradition in the English Theatre after 1660*, London, 1952.

Cohn, R. *Currents in Contemporary Drama,* Bloomington, 1969.

Collingwood, R. G. *The Principles of Art*, London, 1938.

Craig, E. G. *Henry Irving,* London, 1930.

On the Art of the Theatre, London, 1911.

Dickinson, H. *Myth on the Modern Stage*, Urbana, 1969.

Dobrée, B. *Restoration Comedy*, London, 1924.

Doran, M. *Endeavors of Art: A Study of Form in Elizabethan Drama*, Madison, 1954.

Duchartre, P. L. *The Italian Comedy*, trans. R. T. Weaver, London, 1929.

Eliot, T. S. *The Three Voices of Poetry*, Cambridge, 1953.

Erasmus, D. *The Praise of Folly* (1511), trans. H. H. Hudson, Princeton, 1941.

Fernald, J. *A Sense of Direction*, London, 1968.

Fletcher, A. *Allegory: Theory of a Symbolic Mode*, Ithaca, 1964.

Frye, N. *Anatomy of Criticism*, Princeton, 1957.

Gardiner, H. C. *Mysteries End: An Investigation of the Last Days of the Medieval Religious Stage*, New Haven, 1946.

Gombrich, E. H. *Art and Illusion*, New York, 1960.

Granville-Barker, H. *The Exemplary Theatre*, London, 1922.

On Dramatic Method, London, 1931.

Grebanier, B. *The Heart of Hamlet*, New York, 1960.

Grotowski, J. *Towards a Poor Theatre*, London, 1973.

Guthrie, T. *A Life in the Theatre*, London, 1959.

Hapgood, R. 'Speak Hands for Me: Gesture as Language in *Julius Caesar*', *Drama Survey*, vol. 5, no. 2, summer 1966.

Hardison, O. B. *Christian Rite and Christian Drama in the Middle Ages*, Baltimore, 1965.

Heilman, R. B. *The Iceman, the Arsonist, and the Troubled Agent: Tragedy and Melodrama on the Modern Stage*, Seattle, 1973.

Hollingshead, J. *My Lifetime*, London, 1895.

Hovland, C. I., Janis, I. L., Kelley, H. H. *Communication and Persuasion*, New Haven, 1953.

Huizinga, J. *Homo Ludens: A Study of the Play Element in Culture*, London, 1949.

Kernodle, G. R. *From Art to Theatre: Form and Convention in the Renaissance*, Chicago, 1944.

Knight, G. W. *The Wheel of Fire*, London, 1930.

Knights, L. C. *Explorations*, London, 1946.

Kott, J. *Shakespeare Our Contemporary*, trans. B. Taborski, London, 1964.

Langer, S. K. *Feeling and Form*, New York, 1953.

Laver, J. *Costume in the Theatre*, London, 1964.

Lea, K. M. *Italian Popular Comedy*, London, 1934.

Lessing, G. E. *Laocoön: An Essay on the Limits of Painting and Poetry* (1766), trans. E. A. McCormick, Indianapolis, 1962.

Mack, M. 'Engagement and Detachment in Shakespeare's Plays' in *Essays on Shakespeare and Elizabethan Drama in Honor of Hardin Craig*, ed. R. Hosley, Columbia, 1962.

    'The World of *Hamlet*', *Yale Review* XLI, New Haven, 1952.

McAfee, H. *Pepys on the Restoration Stage*, New Haven, 1916.

McGaw, C. J. 'Against the Illusionistic Approach to Directing', *Educational Theatre Journal*, I.1, March 1950.

McLuhan, M. *Understanding Media: the Extensions of Man*, New York, 1964.

McMahon, J. H. *The Imagination of Jean Genêt*, New Haven, 1963.

Meisel, M. *Shaw and the Nineteenth Century Theatre*, Princeton, 1963.

Meyerhold, V. E. *Meyerhold on Theatre*, trans. E. Braun, London, 1969.

Moore, S. *The Stanislavski System*, New York, 1965.

Morgann, M. *Shakespearian Criticism*, ed. D. A. Fineman, Oxford, 1972.

Murray, G. 'Excursus on the Ritual Forms Preserved in Greek Tragedy' in *Themis: A Study of the Social Origins of Greek Religion*, ed. J. E. Harrison, Cleveland, 1962.

Nassar, E. P. 'Shakespeare's Games with his Audience' in *The Rape of Cinderella: Essays in Literary Continuity*, Bloomington, 1970.

Nelson, R. J. *Play within the Play*, New Haven, 1958.

Nicoll, A. *English Drama: A Modern Viewpoint*, London, 1968.

    The World of Harlequin, Cambridge, 1963.

Nietzsche, F. W. *The Birth of Tragedy*, trans. F. Golffing, New York, 1956.

Oreglia, G. *The Commedia dell'Arte*, trans, L. F. Edwards, New York, 1968.

Pastore, N. *Selective History of Theories of Visual Perception: 1650–1950*, London, 1971.

Rabkin, N. *Shakespeare and the Common Understanding*, New York, 1967.

Reiss, T. J. *Toward Dramatic Illusion: Theatrical Technique and Meaning from Hardy to Horace*, New Haven, 1971.

Righter, A. *Shakespeare and the Idea of the Play*, London, 1962.

Rose, M. *The Wakefield Mystery Plays*, London, 1961.

Sanders, N. *The Dramatist and the Received Idea: Studies in the Plays of Marlowe and Shakespeare*, Cambridge, 1968.

Seltzer, D. 'The Actors and Staging', *A New Companion to Shakespeare Studies*, ed. K. Muir and S. Schoenbaum, Cambridge, 1971.

'Shakespeare's Texts and Modern Productions', in *Reinterpretations of Elizabethan Drama*, ed. N. Rabkin, New York, 1969.

Southern, R. *The Seven Ages of the Theatre*, New York, 1961.

Speaight, R. *William Poel and the Elizabethan Revival*, London, 1954.

Summers, M. *Restoration Theatre*, London, 1934.

Tillyard, E. M. W. *Shakespeare's Last Plays*, London, 1938.

Trilling, L. *The Experience of Literature*, New York, 1967.

Wells, S. *Literature and Drama*, London, 1970.

Wickham, G. *Shakespeare's Dramatic Heritage*, London, 1969.

Wilder, T. 'Some Thoughts on Playwriting' in *The Intent of the Artist*, ed. A. Centeno, Princeton, 1941.

Willeford, W. *The Fool and His Scepter*, Evanston, 1969.

Wittgenstein, L. *Philosophical Investigations*, ed. G. E. M. Anscombe, London, 1953.

Wollheim, R. *Art and Its Objects*, New York, 1968.

Yeats, W. B. *Essays and Introductions*, London, 1961.

Index

Index

Index

Index

Index

Index

Index

Index